The Clash of Trademarks
and Domain Names
on the Internet

I0082853

Also by Gerald M. Levine

DOMAIN NAME ARBITRATION
Trademarks, Domain Names and Cybersquatting:
A Practical Guild to the Uniform Domain Name Resolution Policy
(1st Ed. 2015; Second Edition Revised and Expanded 2019)

The Clash of Trademarks and DOMAIN NAMES on the Internet

Combatting Cybersquatting & Protecting Rights

by **Gerald M. Levine**

foreword by **Georges Nahitchevansky**

Volume 2: Indexes *and* **Tables of Cases**

lcp legal corner press

The Clash of Trademarks and Domain Names on the Internet,
Volume 2 © Gerald M. Levine 2024

Cover design and art direction by Stephanie Tevonian
Design implementation and technical support by Alex Grover
Publication assistance Melissa Rosati

ISBN (Paperback): 978-0-9915829-6-9

Purchasers of *The Clash of Trademarks and Domain Names on the Internet* are entitled to PDF copies of the books without charge upon submission of purchase receipt and request to below email

Legal Corner Press, LLC
New York, New York
Email: inquiries@legalcornerpress.com

TO

HUGH C. HANSEN
Present at the beginning

CONTENTS

INTRODUCTION

The book that has become *The Clash of Trademarks and Domain Names on the Internet* is entirely different from what I originally envisioned. The first draft was simply a selection of earlier published essays. But having assembled these, I saw that the collection lacked coherence as a book. So, I decided on an entirely different approach, one that focused more directly on the body of legal principles applied in adjudicating claims of cybersquatting. This was appropriate because 2024 is the twenty fifth year since ICANN's implementation of the UDRP, and as WIPO anticipated, there has developed a mature jurisprudence to suppress cybersquatting. As I point out in the text, WIPO even named its 2017 Overview, the Jurisprudential Overview.

One of the consequences in reconceptualizing *Clash*, though, was that the text grew to such an extent that it consumed the entire volume and left no room for the indexes and tables. This is because the printing protocol limits the number of pages to 840 so that what was originally intended for a one volume book has grown to two volumes of unequal length.

While it may have been more aesthetic to have two books of the same length, it seemed a clumsy solution to divide the Text. So I decided to leave the Text in one volume and the Indexes and Tables in the other. This division of Text in one and Indexes/Tables in the other is justified for an entirely pragmatic reason. I think that having a separate volume for the Indexes and Tables is more efficient in using Volume 1. If the Indexes are placed as they usually are at the back of the book then researching for specific material would require some considerable dexterity in examining the referenced pages, but if the volumes are sitting one above the other or side by side, researching the text will be more comfortable and easier.

I put the issue to colleagues in my weekly Chat group (see Preface in Volume 1) who had been receiving drafts of the book and they agreed with this approach. In any event, that was my thinking and I hope the division into two volumes for the reasons I have explained will be approved by my readers without reproach.

ABOUT THE INDEXES AND THE TABLE OF CASES

Where a book is written to be used rather than read there must be an adequate index to assist readers in finding what they are searching for. In the paper book medium, indexes can never be as functional as a Boolean search, and because of this a general index is ill equipped to be totally satisfactory. This is why I decided to offer a pdf of the text as a free addition to purchasing the two volumes. It is available on request from the publisher at inquiries@legalcornerpress.com

WIPO foresaw in its Final Report that a jurisprudence would emerge from reasoned decisions and it did and has. So large is the database of UDRP decisions

(over 100,000) that only those with the most powerful memories could possibly recall even a fraction of them. I have tried to capture a wide selection of panelists' voices to illustrate my argument for the rise and development of a domain name jurisprudence and also to illustrate that this jurisprudence is law created from the bottom up rather than as with statutory law from the top down, very much like the creation of English common law before its codification to statutes.

WIPO celebrates panelists' achievement in creating domain name law by naming its present volume of overviews the Jurisprudential Overview (2017). Decisions come down by the dozen every day and for those with a masochistic streak they can be readily accessed at Providers' websites or, even better, from <udrp.tools>.

The third and fourth items in this second volume are Tables of Cases of UDRP decisions and US, UK, and EU cases. They do not require much explanation. Because of the size of the database of UDRP decisions some of my choices for citation and discussion may be unfamiliar, but I wanted to illustrate my argument for a jurisprudence by a wide spectrum of voices for it is the Panels who have created the law and it is they who should be heard in all their fluency of reasoning and logic. The cases cited in the fourth Table were mostly cited by panelists, not so much in recent years but certainly in the earlier years when the jurisprudence was being formed. What is mostly cited now are UDRP cases and WIPO's current overview of the jurisprudence, the Jurisprudential Overview (2017).

Copies of UDRP decisions can be located at each of the Provider's websites: Domain Names can be researched on current and former provider websites:

> WIPO: http://arbiter.wipo.int/domains/search/index.html
> FORUM: http://www.adrforum.com/SearchDecisions
> CAC: https://udrp.adr.eu/adr/decisions/index.php
> CIIDRC: https://ciidrc.org
> ADNDRC: http://www.adndrc.org/mten/UDRP_Decisions.php

> Former Providers:
> eResolution: http://www.disputes.org/index.htm (also accessible on <udrp-search.com>).

You can also find WIPO, Forum, CAC, and CIIDRC cases at my preferred search tool, <udrp.tools> and Reverse Domain Name Hijacking cases at <rdnh.com>, generously available without having to pay annual fees.

The Clash of Trademarks and DOMAIN NAMES on the Internet

GENERAL INDEX

A

Abandoned (referring to domain name) xvi, xx, 25, 51, 122, 138, 145, 170, 199, 202, 222, 226, 374, 395, 399, 442, 474, 487, 489, 494-495, 550, 634, 638, 668, 703-705, 732, 756, 764
See also INADVERTENT, DROPPED, PUBLIC AUCTION

Abraham, Spencer (US Senator from Michigan who introduced the Bill that became the ACPA) 731

Abuse of the administrative proceeding xx, 369, 657-658, 660-664, 672-673, 676
See also RDNH, UDRP RULE 15(e)

Abusive registration (a tort distinctive from trademark infringement) xiii, xix, 6, 15, 27, 88, 90, 104, 136, 224, 305, 371, 398, 423, 443, 458, 461, 464, 466, 483, 508, 510, 518, 520, 541, 573, 603, 606, 619, 662, 693, 732
See also CONCEPTUAL OVERLAP, CONJUNCTIVE BAD FAITH, UDRP PARAGRAPH 4(a)(iii)

Accusation (of cybersquatting by mark owner) 215, 436-438, 549, 593, 598, 651, 663-664, 672, 676, 699, 750
See also CYBERSQUATTING, CYBERSQUATTING COMPLAINTS

Achievement of consensus ix, 75, 98, 112, 127, 793
See also CONSENSUS, JURISPRUDENTIAL OVERVIEW

ACPA xxi, xxvi, 6, 9, 12, 77, 91, 301, 730-731, 737
See also ATTORNEY'S FEES, INJUNCTION, INTENT TO PROFIT, LANHAM ACT, STATUTORY DAMAGES

Acquiescence 385-386, 594-595
See also NOMINATIVE FAIR USE

Acquired distinctiveness 19, 94, 132-134, 139, 211, 307, 315, 322-324, 330, 332-335, 338-341, 534, 561, 569, 583-585, 598, 741
See also INHERENT DISTINCTIVENESS, SECONDARY MEANING

Acquisition in bulk *See* HIGH-VOLUME REGISTRANTS

Acronyms (lexically common strings of letters) 64, 85, 166, 169-170, 227-229, 231, 400, 656, 688, 690, 693, 695

Across the Dot xiv, 203, 347, 367

Action pending in court of competent jurisdiction 143
See also UDRP RULE 18

Actionable claim xviii, 6, 44, 91, 123, 127, 164, 203, 219, 264, 294, 306, 312, 320, 336, 338, 347-348, 374-376, 437, 462, 476, 517, 540, 559, 562, 565-566, 593, 602, 619, 645, 648, 651, 658, 667, 669-670, 712, 742, 749, 758, 760, 764, 769, 774-775,

784-785, 790

See also NO ACTIONABLE CLAIM

Active website   xv, xxv, 43, 90-91, 99, 146, 165, 232, 388, 390, 398, 406, 459, 493, 541, 559, 728

See also PASSIVE HOLDING, TELSTRA TEST

Actual knowledge   xviii, 23, 26, 56, 61, 92, 107, 113-114, 124, 133, 142, 153-154, 156, 166, 172, 190, 195-196, 213-214, 219, 226, 229, 260, 320, 333, 366, 378, 398, 411, 422, 507, 534, 538, 553, 561, 569, 573, 575-577, 579, 608, 617, 621, 627-628, 631-633, 666, 689, 705

See also CONSTRUCTIVE NOTICE, DISTANCE (PARTIES FROM EACH OTHER), GOODWILL, REPUTATION

Actual notice   38, 133, 412, 476

Adding letters or words to dominant element   xiv, 131, 191, 194, 351-355, 365-367, 384, 429, 472, 586, 607, 609

See also CONFUSINGLY SIMILAR, PREFIXES AND SUFFIXES, SUBSTITUTION OF WORD OR LETTER, UDRP PARAGRAPH 4(a)(i)

Admissibility of evidence   xvii, 178, 537, 581, 638

See also WEIGHT TO BE APPLIED TO THE EVIDENCE

Adult content   286, 391, 469

Advantage   14-15, 43, 45, 109, 134, 142, 148, 153, 160, 166, 177, 182, 189-190, 204, 206-207, 221, 232, 245, 252, 266, 286, 302, 317, 325, 338, 368, 382, 397, 419, 458, 464, 477, 488, 490, 497, 515-516, 524, 529, 537, 564, 592-593, 606, 608-610, 625, 671, 678, 688-689, 691, 698, 701-702, 707, 714, 724, 738, 789

See also TAKE ADVANTAGE

Adversary system (as opposed to the inquisitorial system)   237, 536

Adverse   32, 45-47, 84, 97, 198, 259, 337, 397, 453, 460-461, 534, 541, 563, 654, 733, 745, 759, 773

Affiliation   103, 148, 152-153, 166, 231, 317, 320, 395, 417, 423-424, 431, 434, 441-442, 445-446, 450, 453, 477-478, 481, 496, 513, 516, 521, 524, 530-531, 547, 588, 614, 649, 704, 745, 771, 787

See also UDRP PARAGRAPH 4(b)(iv)

Affirmative Defenses) *See* UDRP PARAGRAPH 4(c)(i-iii)

Alexandria Division, D. Va.   46, 138, 620, 733, 742, 744, 768, 775-780, 786

See also FRAUDULENT TRANSFER, IN REM JURISDICTION

Allowable research *See* UDRP RULE 10

Alter ego   372

Annex   32, 38, 42, 68, 248-249, 279, 311, 342, 535, 560, 565, 567, 640, 673

Annulment of UDRP award   388, 421, 576, 729, 736, 741, 751, 768, 786

Anonymous offer (from complainant)   504

See also SOLICITING TO SELL WHO CONTACTS WHOM

Anonymously   288, 713
See also PROXY SERVICE

Anticybersquatting Consumer Protection Act   vii-viii, xxi-xxii, xxvi-xxix, 6-9, 12,
    16-20, 25, 36, 39, 44-49, 74, 80, 82-84, 92, 94, 99, 102, 112-113, 121, 135, 143,
    204-205, 213, 250, 263, 289, 304, 307, 335-336, 345, 347, 373, 386, 405, 408,
    421, 432-433, 452, 464, 483, 541, 544, 559, 562, 576, 601, 603, 608, 619, 624,
    626, 690, 692, 694, 712, 729-734, 736-739, 741-742, 744, 747-754, 756-759, 761,
    763-781, 783-788
See also ACPA

Any rules and principles of law deemed necessary *See* UDRP RULE 15(a)

Appeal of commonly used descriptive and dictionary terms   163, 182, 419, 506
See also DESCRIPTIVE TERMS, DICTIONARY TERMS, HIERARCHY OF
DOMAIN NAMES,

Appearance *See* REPRESENTED BY COUNSEL, PRO SE

Appearance (where beneficial owner is substituted for proxy)   33
See also PROXY SERVICE

Appearance to answer the complaint   vii, xii, xx, 26, 29, 36-38, 42, 64, 175, 198,
    254-255, 284, 327, 344, 382, 420, 438, 444, 456, 496, 510, 512, 521, 580, 645,
    682, 684-685, 739-740

Appellate   8, 79, 83, 112, 135, 177, 219, 404, 737, 746-747, 763, 785

Applicable disputes   16, 34, 51

Application filed (trade and service mark pending certification)   164, 408

Application for trade or service mark   312, 339, 583, 675
See also TRADE AND SERVICE MARK APPLICATION AND ISSUANCE OF
MARK CERTIFICATION

Applying for trade and service mark   312, 339, 583, 650, 735

Appointment of Panel   259

Appropriating another's goodwill   103

Arbitrage   xx, 13, 206-207, 216, 501, 688-691, 694, 698, 731, 775
See also SPECULATION

Arbitral Panel *See* APPOINTMENT, RECUSAL

Arbitral process of the UDRP   vii, xxx, 26-27, 37, 39

Arbitrary   x, 13, 133, 140, 147, 157, 166, 168-169, 181, 211, 215, 228, 231, 322,
    396, 486, 492, 494, 642, 653, 712-714

Arbitration   27, 35-36, 39, 48, 68, 234, 240, 255, 533

Architecture (of the UDRP)   xiii-xiv, xvi, 18, 27-28, 40, 302, 377, 452, 734
See also STANDING, RIGHTS AND LEGITIMATE INTERESTS,
CONJUNCTIVE BAD FAITH

Archive.org   29-31, 241, 390, 544
See also WAYBACK MACHINE

Associated website   260, 386, 409, 478, 495-496
See also CURATION OF WEBSITE, RESOLVING WEBSITE
Associated with mark owner   ix, xiii, xxxii, 22, 24, 51, 64, 82, 85, 130-131, 134, 143, 154-155, 157-159, 167, 170-171, 185, 190, 194, 200, 207, 209, 214, 219, 221, 227, 229, 231, 238-239, 277, 285-286, 327-329, 354-355, 360, 363-364, 368, 374, 407, 419-420, 422-423, 425, 440, 443-444, 460, 462, 468, 470, 474, 480-481, 485, 488-491, 493-496, 511, 517, 524, 529, 533, 545, 564, 578, 580, 600, 602, 604, 613-614, 629, 632-633, 661, 678, 695-696, 702, 719, 728, 732, 768
See also UNIQUELY ASSOCIATED
Associational   85, 130, 212, 325, 507, 542, 568, 717
Athlete (common law rights) *See* CULTURE CREATORS
Athletes (common law rights)   75, 376, 491
Attempt to deprive *See* RDNH, UDRP RULE 15(e)
Attorney fees   xiv, xxii, xxv-xxvi, xxxii, 19, 46-47, 49, 104, 109, 124, 205, 372-373, 376, 540, 643, 654, 666, 734, 741, 749-751, 765-766, 769, 776, 782-787, 789, 793
See also COUNSEL, LAWYERS
Attorneys   xiv, xxii, xxv-xxvi, xxxii, 19, 46-47, 49, 104, 109, 124, 205, 372-373, 376, 540, 643, 654, 666, 734, 741, 749-751, 765-766, 769, 776, 782-787, 789, 793
See also CORPORATE OFFICERS, LAW FIRM
Attracting internet traffic   286, 326, 440, 469, 477, 480
See also UDRP PARAGRAPH 4(b)(iv)
Auction   13, 25, 51, 58, 60, 65-66, 124, 155-156, 162, 195, 213, 216, 218-219, 221, 296, 387, 414, 436, 446, 490, 492-493, 495, 533, 544, 563, 598, 610, 634, 639, 689, 701-707
See also ABANDONED, DROPPED, PUBLIC AUCTION
Aural and phonetic similarities *See* IDENTICAL OR CONFUSINGLY SIMILAR, UDRP PARAGRAPH 4(a)(i)
Aural and phonetic similarity   357
See also CONFUSING SIMILARITY, SIMILAR AND CONFUSING
Australia   49, 91, 244, 269, 271, 277-278, 291, 430, 480, 494, 509, 571, 617-618, 671, 675
Authority   xxix, xxxii, 4, 9-11, 34-35, 47, 63, 67-68, 70, 75, 77-79, 81, 83, 87, 95, 98, 116, 166, 203, 235, 239, 250, 256, 263, 272, 287, 301, 313, 320, 325, 331, 347, 363, 365, 369, 393, 415, 421, 437, 445, 457, 483, 547, 554, 599, 601-603, 607, 617, 638-639, 732, 738, 745, 749, 763, 768, 775, 785-786, 789-790, 793
Authorized use   36, 188, 307, 332, 365, 386, 390, 453, 466, 475, 516, 534-536, 551, 668
See also ACQUIESCENCE, NOT AUTHORIZED
Authors   13, 67, 75, 299, 327, 371, 375-376, 492
See also CULTURE CREATORS, PERSONALITIES

Award Contested by Complainant *See* UDRP PARAGRAPH 4(k)

Awareness *See* ACTUAL KNOWLEDGE, IMPLAUSIBLE DENIAL

Awareness (respondent's awareness of complainant and its mark)   23-24, 62, 124, 144, 149, 154, 167, 217, 231, 258, 328, 396, 464, 545, 573, 586, 625, 652, 664, 666, 672, 674

B

Bad faith   xvi, xxii, xxvii, 31, 40, 89-90, 92, 110-111, 125, 148, 175, 304-305, 318, 346, 372, 421, 458-459, 462, 464, 479, 521, 529, 582, 590, 688, 721, 769, 788, 790
See also CONJUNCTIVE BAD FAITH, UDRP PARAGRAPHS 4(a)(iii) and 4(b)

Bad faith attempt to deprive registrant of domain name   xi, xx, 7, 62, 133, 148, 176-177, 216, 264, 266, 438, 471, 574, 579, 586, 593, 597, 606-607, 619, 639, 657-658, 681, 686, 717, 756, 789
See also RDNH

Balance of probabilities   xviii, 97, 145, 257, 262, 361, 493, 507, 540, 550-551, 573, 622, 628, 631, 687, 729
See also STANDARD OF PROOF

Baseless (referring to filing a complaint)   637, 664, 669, 750
See also RDNH

Before any notice of claim   412, 454, 585, 591
See also UDRP PARAGRAPH 4(a)(i)

Beneficial owner *See* IDENTITY OF RESPONDENT, PROXY SERVICE

Benefit and resolution of doubt   xii, 118, 261-262, 405, 669

Berryhill, John   209, 657

Better right theory (debunked)   x, 176, 178-179, 578, 623, 649, 669, 690, 789

Beyond the scope of the Policy   8-9, 21, 56, 71, 130, 165, 217, 250-253, 289-294, 297, 434, 437, 524, 556, 668, 732, 761
See also PANEL'S ROLE; SCOPE OF THE POLICY

Binary (conjunctive requirement)   117-119, 121-122, 441
See also UNITARY (DISJUNCTIVE)

Blindness   xvi, xix, 25, 59, 61-62, 96, 484-486, 622-624, 626, 630-633, 729
See also WILLFUL BLINDNESS

Board member   253-254, 292, 352, 448

Body of precedent   67, 80
See also PRECEDENT

Bona Fide Offering of Goods or Services   xv, 13, 40, 75, 85, 104, 109, 116, 137, 151, 157, 176, 186, 194, 211, 233, 289, 304, 307, 309, 365, 378, 381-387, 390-391, 393-394, 396, 400, 410-415, 417, 454, 471, 478, 490, 492, 523, 525-526, 546, 549, 564, 570-572, 586-587, 590-591, 593, 596, 607, 615, 639, 653, 676, 688, 697, 703,

714, 718, 725, 734, 774, 780
See also NOT MAKING A BONA FIDE USE, UDRP PARAGRAPH 4(c)(i)
Brand names   16, 60, 630, 693, 731
See also WELL-KNOWN AND FAMOUS MARKS
Brandable   708
Breach of agreement   52, 80, 91, 118, 185, 251, 289, 294-295, 298, 336, 389, 492, 496, 555, 621, 726
Brokers (soliciting complainants)   498, 501, 507-508
Brokers (soliciting to purchase)   174, 594
Burden of production   xiv, xviii, 22, 40, 42, 75-76, 143, 147, 152-153, 291, 294, 309, 319, 333, 346, 379, 381-387, 399-400, 411, 415, 451, 470, 524, 540-541, 543, 549, 570, 577, 579
See also SHIFT OF BURDEN
Burden of proof   xviii, 41-43, 153, 175, 206, 254-256, 262, 376-377, 379-382, 387, 400, 429, 454, 476, 484, 492, 542-543, 545, 549, 552, 554, 565, 579, 625, 632, 741
See also UDRP PARAGRAPH 4(a)
Burden of proof (or persuasion)   xiv, xvii-xviii, 22, 40-43, 97, 145, 147, 153, 175, 188, 206, 241, 247, 254-257, 262, 307, 309, 320, 328, 361, 376-377, 379-385, 387, 392, 399-400, 415, 429, 454, 476, 484, 492-493, 507, 534-536, 540, 542-543, 545, 549-552, 554-555, 565-567, 570, 573, 579, 586, 622, 625, 627-628, 631-632, 635, 687, 702, 721, 729, 741, 766, 790
See also CONCRETE EVIDENCE, DOCUMENTARY EVIDENCE
Burden shifts   40, 43, 140, 173, 309, 380, 383, 387-388, 476, 546, 566, 570, 579, 628
Business Assets   xxi, 7, 604, 606, 717, 719
Business Disputes   290-292, 556, 738, 761
Business identifiers   15, 712
Business Models   84, 222, 689, 712
See also MODELS
Business Names   xv, 74, 116, 185, 425, 678
See also TRADE NAME
Business partners   xiii, 253, 290
By deliberately using   496
Bypassing 4(a)(i) (unnecessary to assess complainant's rights where it cannot prove bad faith)   337, 346-347, 382
See also UDRP PARAGRAPH 4(a)(i)

C

Calder v. Jones   762-763

Canada   22, 36, 77, 92, 136, 174, 210, 229, 255, 257, 271, 353, 388, 392, 406, 425, 459, 482, 522, 572-573, 585-586, 655, 659, 695, 743, 772

Cancellation   xxx-xxxi, 3, 6, 11, 14, 18, 32, 36, 38-39, 47, 50-51, 132, 160, 163, 216, 218, 224, 294, 299, 303, 313, 348, 356-357, 457, 535, 550, 589, 733, 763, 765-766
See also REMEDY

Cancellation of Complainant's Trademark on grounds of genericness   299
See also TRADEMARK TRIAL AND APPEAL BOARD

Candor   215, 598, 669
See also DUTY OF CANDOR

Capitalize   150, 184, 223, 231, 262, 402, 419, 466, 489, 522, 618, 710, 714, 761
See also TARGETING, TRAFFICS IN

Cease-and-desist notice   xviii, 22, 136, 145, 275, 293, 404, 411, 462, 517, 585-588, 595, 654, 659, 673-674

Celebrities   xxv, xxvii, 327, 371, 375-376, 386, 492
See also PERSONALITIES

Certification of pleadings   xix, 38, 42, 256, 273, 537, 540, 636-640, 643, 662, 669, 681, 736
See also DISMISSED FOR ABSENT OR FALSE CERTIFICATION; UDRP RULE 3(xiii) (COMPLAINT), UDRP RULE 5(viii) (RESPONDENT)

Chain of (Title)   xiii, xv, 316, 321, 401-403, 406
See also CORPORATE FAMILY

Challenging UDRP award *See* DE NOVO, SETTLEMENTS, UDRP PARAGRAPH 4(k)

Challenging UDRP awards   xxii, xxvi, 45, 48, 91, 123, 593, 730, 732, 739, 746, 748, 750, 764-765

Circumstances of the case   104, 120, 175, 215, 260, 341, 344, 572, 640, 664
See also BAD FAITH

Civil Law   21, 83, 102, 124, 195, 329

Civil law mark owners proving common law rights   329

Classic Plan   679
See also PLAN "B", RDNH

Classification   147, 201, 214, 412, 534, 591, 722-723, 725
See also ARBITRARY, DESCRIPTIVE, FANCIFUL, SUGGESTIVE

Clear and convincing *See* STANDARD OF PROOF, UNIFORM RAPID SUSPENSION SYSTEM (URS)

Click through revenue   480

Clinton, William J. President of the United States   4

Close cases (or close issues)   17, 53, 62, 72, 89, 198, 499, 552-553, 707, 789

Cohen, Nat   18, 657, 669, 753, 789

Coined word *See* FANCIFUL

Coined word (one of a kind)   x, 4, 130-131, 144, 149, 154-156, 165, 172, 176, 181, 184, 187-188, 193, 195, 203, 208, 215, 218, 220, 261, 399, 484, 486-487, 494, 505-506, 564, 568, 580, 633, 653, 678, 691, 718

Colloquial term   146, 190, 197

Combining words or names   85, 155, 188, 190, 261, 353, 356

See also CONFUSINGLY SIMILAR, UDRP PARAGRAPH 4(a)(i)

Commencing Proceeding   vii, xxv, 26, 29, 44, 47, 289, 336, 412, 452, 496, 559, 575, 659, 674, 755, 776

See also BAD FAITH

Commerce, US Department of   5

Commercial activity   184, 316, 410-411, 694, 718

Commercial gain   7, 379, 428, 516

See also HYPERLINKING, LINKING TARNISHMENT, PASSIVE USE

Commercial use   13, 88, 99, 107, 131, 171, 320, 379, 384-385, 406, 413, 432, 436, 487, 494, 501, 519, 634, 706, 731, 748

Committee on the Judiciary (US Senate)   16, 53, 731

See also SENATE REPORT

Commodification *See* WHO OWNS WHAT?

Commodification of language   xi, 13, 100, 202, 208, 221, 692-693, 709, 713, 717

Common Law Rights *See* ACQUIRED DISTINCTIVENESS, SECONDARY MEANING, STANDING

Common law rights   viii, xiii, 21, 49, 73, 75-76, 82, 88, 95, 97-98, 132, 137, 149, 195, 200, 225, 227, 241, 271, 306-307, 310, 312-316, 321-325, 327-335, 338-339, 341, 372, 374-376, 407-409, 438, 440, 466, 506, 537, 540, 546, 554, 562, 576, 579, 583, 598-600, 619, 622, 641, 647, 652-655, 671, 705, 715, 722, 775-779, 781, 790

Common lexicon   x-xi, 6, 25, 54-56, 58-59, 70, 89, 100, 116, 125, 131, 142, 163, 168, 181-182, 184, 187, 192, 197, 203-204, 207, 210, 212, 214-215, 218-219, 482, 487-488, 543, 551, 562, 564, 579, 585-586, 593, 599, 604-606, 609, 644, 661, 691, 693, 700, 705-706, 708, 717, 719

See also MONOPOLIZING LEXICAL CHOICES, WORDS CANNOT BE OWNED (OR MONOPOLIZED)

Common Terms   51, 55, 133, 139, 162, 180, 184-185, 193, 210, 212, 220, 240, 322, 375, 468, 489, 502, 578-579, 695, 698, 716

See also ALSO ACRONYMS, DESCRIPTIVE WORDS, DICTIONARY WORDS

Commonly Controlled Persons (Transfer Between)   xv, 321, 401

Commonly known by   xv, 149, 165, 182, 200, 309, 342, 378, 381-383, 392, 425-427, 454, 508, 572, 596, 600, 627, 719

See also UDRP PARAGRAPH 4(c)(ii)

Communications xviii, 207, 580-581, 710

Comparing (Domain Name and Mark) xiv, 306, 345, 347-348, 357, 363-364, 429, 512

See also IDENTICAL OR CONFUSINGLY SIMILAR

Competing services 146, 153, 186, 224, 242, 304, 344, 396-397, 417, 470, 478, 480, 514, 517, 735, 738, 772

See also NON-COMPETING

Competitive 98, 156, 230, 418, 471, 515, 564, 605, 761

Competitor xvii, xxv, 14, 85, 125, 129, 141, 170, 222, 327, 419, 421, 441, 452, 465, 472, 474, 478, 482-483, 496-497, 499, 511-515, 521, 539, 543-544, 563-564, 580, 615, 627, 641, 667, 690, 710, 715, 735, 747, 755

See also PARAGRAPH 4(b)(iii)

Complex issues 8, 251, 298, 667

See also SCOPE OF THE POLICY

Concealing identity and other information 91

See also GDPR, PROXY SERVICE

Conceivability (conceivability test) 52-53, 76, 90, 94, 131, 149, 160, 171, 191, 197, 207, 215, 220, 232, 338, 399, 404, 440, 446, 459, 461, 476, 484-485, 518, 530, 534, 539, 543, 572, 622, 660, 670, 672, 700, 709-710

See also TELSTRA TEST

Conceptual overlap (between trademark infringement and abusive registration) 6, 8-9, 21

See also ABUSIVE REGISTRATION, TRADE AND SERVICE MARK INFRINGEMENT

Concrete evidence 124, 158, 172, 183, 349, 379, 381, 407, 598, 605, 624, 630, 636, 717, 791

Concurrent Use xiii, 298-299, 667, 748

Confidentiality of written communications *See* SETTLEMENT DISCUSSIONS

Confusingly Similar xiv, 59, 89, 136, 139, 159, 192, 302, 306, 311, 341, 343, 346-349, 351, 353, 355, 357-360, 362-365, 367-369, 457, 520, 530, 538, 570, 593, 607, 656, 705, 768

See also IDENTICAL OR CONFUSINGLY SIMILAR, LIKELIHOOD OF CONFUSION, SIMILAR BUT NOT CONFUSING, TYPOSQUATTING

Confusingly similar 306

Confusion (causing) 186, 194, 424

Congress *See* HOUSE OF REPRESENTATIVES, SENATE

Congress (US) xxi, 6, 16, 28, 53, 92, 105, 452, 690, 731, 735, 737, 747-748, 752-754, 758, 769, 783

Conjunctive Bad Faith   xxvii, 18, 52, 108, 117-121, 205, 296, 303-304, 309, 347, 441, 453, 460, 462, 468, 478, 559, 693, 730, 769
See also UDRP PARAGRAPH 4(b)
Connotative (Connotation)   xxvi, 15, 94, 101, 132-133, 135, 151, 156, 191, 374, 491, 641, 685, 702, 710-711, 788
See also DENOTATIVE
Consensus view   viii-ix, xviii, 37, 67-70, 73-74, 78-81, 84, 87-88, 95-96, 98, 108, 111-113, 116-117, 120, 166, 179-180, 195-196, 211, 241, 245, 282, 303, 314, 320, 355-356, 371, 380, 390, 392, 398-399, 410-411, 418, 428, 485, 489-490, 517, 531, 542, 551, 574-575, 588, 590, 622, 653, 685, 696, 700, 709, 714, 727, 767
See also ACHIEVEMENT OF CONSENSUS
Consent to transfer   xii, xvi, 39, 45-46, 67, 115, 263, 265-268, 294, 307, 317, 323, 332, 356-357, 372, 386, 444, 449, 500, 502, 550, 691, 739-740, 743-744, 752
Consequences of default   xii, 36, 254-256, 390, 438
Consistency (ensuring that it be so)   ix, xv, xix, xxviii, 12-13, 16, 18-19, 23, 30, 37-38, 52, 57, 65, 67-71, 73-74, 78-81, 84-85, 87, 95-98, 105-106, 110, 112, 118-120, 141, 143, 148, 152, 164, 168, 189, 195, 197, 208, 215, 219, 247, 258-259, 270, 277, 281, 283, 299, 322-324, 327, 342, 360-361, 371, 373, 375, 379-380, 386, 389-390, 400, 402, 405, 407, 411, 414, 418-419, 427, 431-432, 438, 440, 442, 457, 459, 466, 472, 479, 488, 496, 499, 503, 528, 534, 540-541, 547-548, 568, 571, 575, 577, 581, 587-588, 591, 598-599, 602, 618, 627, 644-646, 658, 681, 688, 694, 700-702, 706-708, 714, 716, 718-719, 728, 732, 734, 736, 761, 766, 769, 786
See also PREDICTABILITY
Consolidated   xii, 116, 159, 204, 210, 273-275, 277-281, 381, 560, 693-694, 720
Consolidation (complainants)   xii, 278-279
Consolidation (domain names)   x, 67, 168, 197, 274, 276, 278, 280-282, 710
Consolidation (respondents)   xii, 123, 273-278, 280-281
Constitutional   21, 69, 101, 104-105, 783
Construction of Policy terms   viii, xii, xxi, 20, 25, 30, 48, 52, 67, 70-74, 83-84, 87, 96-98, 102, 112, 117-118, 120, 122, 124, 137, 172, 215, 224, 236, 238, 250, 253, 270, 292, 360, 392, 405, 455, 459-460, 466, 514, 519, 553, 586, 624, 663-664, 674, 685, 696, 701, 720, 730, 737, 742, 744, 751-752, 754, 757-758, 767, 782
See also DISAGREEMENTS; DISAGREEMENTS
Constructive knowledge or notice (not applied in UDRP)   xviii, 24, 56, 61, 140, 167, 219, 390, 412, 475, 514, 573-576, 625, 646, 660
Constructive knowledge(not applied in UDRP) *See* ACTUAL KNOWLEDGE, IMPLAUSIBLE DENIAL
Constructive notice (knowledge of mark owner)   xviii, 56, 167, 390, 412, 573-576, 625, 646
See also ACTUAL KNOWLEDGE

Consumer recognition 63, 129, 135, 143, 147, 150, 180, 628, 630, 653, 710, 724
See also REPUTATION IN THE MARKET

Consumers (misled and harmed in some way) 7, 16, 19, 156, 379, 428, 451, 516, 521, 525, 561, 616, 732, 734, 768

Contact details 91, 233, 276, 283, 427, 461, 616

Contacting *See* SOLICITING TO SELL, WHO CONTACTS WHOM

Content of respondent's Website (as factor in determining bad faith use) 86, 100-101, 103, 107, 142, 145, 222, 225, 256, 290, 309, 363, 418, 425, 428, 433, 441, 444, 448, 459, 482, 517, 557, 573, 768

Contested cases 102, 346, 411, 770

Contingency (of a party's rights) 14, 50, 101, 134, 202, 264, 383, 579, 751, 756

Contract Rights vii, xix, xxvii, 24, 26, 29, 31-32, 35-36, 38, 45, 50, 132, 134, 160-161, 177-178, 191, 221-222, 225, 251, 253, 286, 289, 292-295, 297-298, 300, 303-304, 319, 391, 457, 481, 498, 528, 588, 625-626, 655, 657, 693, 752, 756
See also PROPERTY RIGHTS

Contractual Basis for UDRP xix, 24, 32, 35-36, 38, 50, 161, 222, 289, 292-293, 295, 297, 303, 391, 457, 498, 625-626, 657, 756

Contractual obligations vii, xix-xx, 19, 25, 27, 32, 34-35, 38, 50, 52-53, 61, 63, 88, 122, 211, 244, 254, 261, 289-290, 304, 356, 454, 457, 493, 504, 579, 587, 625-626, 631, 643, 658, 681-682, 685-686, 689, 698-699, 728, 732, 756

Copyright 152, 252, 289, 463, 524, 531, 605, 793

Corporate family 318-319, 321, 403

Corporate name 90-91, 138, 384

Corporate officers xiv, 205, 372, 764
See also KNOWN TO EACH OTHER

Corporate officers and attorneys xiv, 205, 370, 372

Counsel (appearing by) 242, 247, 327, 567, 596, 645-647, 651, 654, 662, 664-665, 681, 685
See also Professional Representative

Counterfeit goods xix, 99, 244, 269, 604-605, 617-618, 731, 761

Counting differences (number of omissions, transpositions, and substitutions to determine confusing similarity *See* CONFUSING SIMILARITY, TYPOSQUATTING

Counting differences between mark and domain name *See* LOOKING AHEAD TO BAD FAITH EVIDENCE

Country code xxv, 11, 20, 22, 44, 49, 56, 59, 104, 167, 211, 233, 261, 270, 304, 367, 369, 426, 501, 541, 550, 690, 694, 697, 714, 746, 761

COURT OF COMPETENT JURISDICTION 12, 28-29, 35, 38-39, 47, 69, 91, 112, 251-252, 289, 298, 324, 367, 402, 437, 788

Court of competent jurisdiction (belong in) 8, 186, 194, 253, 295, 306, 648

Creation date (original registration date)   xxii, 31-33, 127, 174, 259, 404, 455, 651, 655, 730, 745, 751, 755, 757, 787

Credibility (credible)   298, 518, 542, 553, 662

Credible evidence   332, 410, 414, 558

See also EVIDENCE

Criminal Activity   430, 436-437, 439, 491, 526, 528, 611, 616, 664, 672

Criticism (must be genuine to be effective as a defense)   93, 101, 104, 107-109, 125, 183, 268, 300, 429, 431, 434-435, 439, 444, 527

See also UDRP PARAGRAPH 4(c)(iii)

Cryptocurrency   143, 152, 610

Cultural resource   x, xvi, 7, 13, 75-76, 88, 100, 130, 141, 154, 161, 183, 188, 197, 202, 204, 208, 214, 305, 327, 336, 375-376, 473, 491, 585, 606, 690-692, 713, 716-718

Culture creators   75-76, 97

See also ATHLETES, ARTISTS, AUTHORS, ENTERTAINERS, GOLFERS, PERFORMERS, PERSONALITIES, SPORTS, STAGE AND FILM STARS,

Curation of Website *See* CURATING CONTENT OF WEBSITE (Issues Index)

CURATION, HYPERLINKS   133, 145, 229, 344

Cybersquatting   9, 37, 250, 253, 552-553

Cybersquatting complaints   9, 17, 34, 37, 41, 194, 206, 250, 253-254, 256, 390, 464, 552-553, 585, 618

See also DEFAULT (IN RESPONDING TO COMPLAINT), INTENTIONAL, RESPONDING TO COMPLAINT, UDRP RULE 5

D

Damages   xxii, 19, 45-48, 457, 523, 734, 748-751, 766, 769-770, 773, 776, 782-785, 787

See also ACPA

Database   xxx, 25, 51, 53, 60-61, 66, 68, 95, 156, 168, 219-220, 238, 241, 261, 286, 374, 541, 578, 626-627, 630, 693, 711, 788

De minimus links *See* PPC LINKS

De minimus links (rejecting targeting)   421

De Novo Action   viii, 12, 25, 28, 36, 39, 45-48, 106, 252, 298, 405, 626, 742, 745, 747-749

De Novo Action/iW *See* UDRP PARAGRAPH 4(k)

Dead ends   ix, 37, 82, 87, 97-98, 112-114, 345, 571, 659

See also RETROACTIVE BAD FAITH

Dealership Agreements   xiii, 92, 293-294, 447, 463, 497, 523, 670

Deceive   216, 422, 438, 447, 449, 516, 520, 525, 529, 573, 611, 710

Deception   xvii, 20, 86, 359, 423, 430, 516, 522, 525

Deceptive   xvii, 20, 42, 86, 198, 312, 359, 423, 430, 446, 516, 522, 525, 529, 611

Decisional law   xv, 21, 49, 68, 82, 88, 98-99, 101-102, 105, 110, 122, 132, 138, 162, 182, 258, 270, 272-273, 322, 404, 428, 432, 434, 441-442, 446-447, 484, 508, 547, 583, 589, 696, 772

Decisions   xxx, 17, 40, 67-69, 72, 85, 87, 95-98, 623, 693, 788-790
See also PUBLICATION, REGISTRARS, UDRP RULE 16

Decisive factor   160, 223, 344, 518, 555, 587, 608, 737

Declaration (a statement on personal knowledge of the facts declared)   39, 42, 49, 60, 81, 318, 538, 545, 548, 558, 578, 679, 747, 749, 768, 784, 791

Defamation   9, 104, 254, 435, 437

Default (in responding to UDRP complaint)   xii, 22, 36, 46, 51, 218, 240, 254-256, 335, 378, 387, 438, 456, 459-460, 480, 517, 519, 585, 638, 653, 685, 740, 780
See also CONSEQUENCES OF, NONAPPEARANCE

Default (in responding UDRP to complaint)   255, 460, 542, 621, 636

Deference (as it relates to authoritative decisions   79

Deference (no deference in courts of competent jurisdiction, referring to UDRP decisions)   48, 739

Deference (no deference in courts of competent jurisdiction) *See* CHALLENGING UDRP AWARDS

Deference to US State trademark registrations   28, 48, 79, 109, 314-315, 389, 404-405, 739

Deficiency of proof (leading to dismissal of complaint)   xviii, 21-22, 43, 215, 243, 256, 310, 330, 333, 341, 387, 533, 535-537, 566-567, 597-600, 625, 637, 643-644, 647-648, 655, 661, 663, 760, 772-773, 791

Deficient pleadings   xviii, 21-22, 43, 164, 215, 243-244, 256, 310, 330, 333, 341, 387, 533, 535-537, 566-567, 597-600, 625, 636-637, 643-644, 647-648, 655, 661, 663, 760, 772-773, 791
See also INSUFFICIENT EVIDENCE

Defining rights   viii, xii, xix, 12, 76-77, 92, 131, 178, 283, 292, 468, 518, 630, 661, 694, 700, 712

Delay in commencing proceedings   xviii, 268, 280, 460, 549, 589-590, 592-593, 595, 652
See also BEFORE ANY NOTICE OF CLAIM, LACHES

Demonstrable preparations   xv, 136, 232, 254, 309, 378, 383-384, 387, 393, 396, 398, 411-416, 446, 549, 572, 577, 641
See also UDRP PARAGRAPH 4(c)(i)

Demonstrating (that is, having proof) of allegations   120, 318, 323, 330, 378, 380, 382, 450, 533, 587, 623, 702, 721, 777

Denial of Bad Faith   11, 23, 26, 133, 143, 149, 172, 207, 212, 255, 294, 321, 324, 388, 420-421, 467, 482, 500, 502, 542-543, 553, 564, 570, 573, 576, 631-633, 741, 766

Denial of knowledge   143, 149, 172, 207, 212, 467, 502, 542, 553, 573, 633
See also AWARENESS, IMPLAUSIBLE DENIAL; IMPLAUSIBLE DENIAL

Denotative   181, 219, 374, 710
See also CONNOTATIVE

Deprive registrant of its domain name   xi, xx, xxxii, 7, 62, 93, 133, 148, 176-177, 216, 264, 266, 438, 447, 471, 574, 579, 586, 593, 597, 606-607, 619, 639, 657-658, 681, 686, 690, 717, 789

Depriving a respondent of its domain name   xi, xx, 7, 62, 133, 148, 176-177, 216, 264, 266, 438, 471, 574, 579, 586, 593, 597, 606-607, 619, 639, 657-658, 681, 686, 717, 789

Descriptive terms (or phrases)   x, 13, 55, 57, 59, 63-64, 66, 85-86, 94-95, 133-135, 138-140, 145, 147, 157, 159-160, 162-163, 167, 169, 182, 186, 191, 194, 197, 203, 213, 215, 219, 223, 225, 252, 262, 315, 322, 325, 327, 339, 341, 343, 349-350, 352, 362, 364, 366, 368, 373, 385, 389, 394, 398, 419, 450, 467-468, 470-471, 489, 492, 502, 506, 538, 548, 567-568, 572, 574, 578, 580, 584-585, 592, 597-599, 627-628, 650, 670, 705, 712, 715
See also MERELY DESCRIPTIVE

Descriptive terms (weak mark)   x, 57, 59, 63, 66, 85-86, 92, 95, 133-134, 138-139, 145, 147, 156-157, 159-163, 167-169, 179-180, 182, 186, 191, 193-194, 197, 213-215, 219, 223, 225, 252, 262, 310, 312, 315, 322, 325-326, 343, 349, 352, 359, 362, 366, 368, 384, 389, 398, 419, 450, 467, 502, 506, 512, 515, 538, 547-548, 567, 569, 574, 578, 580, 583-584, 592-593, 597, 628, 642, 650, 653-654, 670, 695, 710, 712, 714-715, 721

Descriptive words (weak mark)   55, 57, 64, 92, 135, 139, 145, 157, 159, 163, 191, 219, 223, 262, 312, 322, 341, 343, 349, 359, 373, 394, 398, 419, 478, 492, 506, 512, 568, 597, 628, 653, 670, 715, 721

Design elements   341, 343, 362
See also FIGURATIVE MARK

Design elements (relating to a figurative mark)   341, 343, 362
See also FIGURATIVE

Design-plus-word trademarks   xiv, 163, 341, 343, 351-354, 362, 364, 366, 506, 606

Design-plus-word trademarks   xiv, 341, 344
See also FIGURATIVE MARK

Devise trademark   342
devise trademark *See* DESIGN-PLUS-WORD TRADEMARKS

Dictionary word marks   163, 176, 193, 389, 419, 467, 506

Dictionary words *See* COMMON LEXICON. LEXICAL RESOURCES

Different national jurisdictions   vii, 3, 14, 22-23, 47, 64, 96, 98, 183, 233

Diligence   viii, xix, xxviii, 25-26, 54-60, 62-65, 404, 492-493, 555, 579, 625, 627, 629, 631, 633, 638, 674, 711, 723, 777
See also DUE DILIGENCE

Disagreements (as to meaning of the Policy terms)   75-76, 80, 114, 292
See also CONSTRUCTION

Disclaimer (not effective of association or affiliation)   xv, 422

Disclaimer (of association or affiliation)   xv, 422, 424, 588

Disclaimer to marks (by way of a USPTO office action)   344

Discredit   48, 117, 122, 127, 218, 321

Discretion   xii, 28, 33, 236-237, 242-247, 249, 256, 259, 262, 265, 273-274, 280, 283-284, 287, 289-290, 298, 363, 457, 482, 542, 640, 646, 658, 660-661, 681, 748, 787

Disjunctive bad faith   xxi, 18, 112, 117, 119, 205, 304, 390, 392, 452, 693, 730, 748, 761, 769-770
See also ACPA, CONJUNCTIVE BAD FAITH

Dismissal at complainant's request denied   266

Dismissed with prejudice (at complainant's request) *See* WITHDRAW COMPLAINT

Dismissed without prejudice   xviii, 44, 51, 264-265, 277, 303, 356, 554, 556, 558, 560, 562, 581-582
See also REFILE COMPLAINT

Dismissing complaint   xxx, 21, 23, 40, 98, 214, 232, 263, 293, 332, 347, 360, 431-432, 435, 447, 467, 537, 544, 712, 740, 751, 759

Dismissing complaint (before decision)   xxx, 214

dismissing complaint (before decision) *See* DISMISSED WITH PREJUDICE

Dismissing the complaint (before decision)   264-266, 554, 661, 741, 765

Disrupting the business of a competitor   141, 222, 430, 439, 452, 511, 526, 528, 627, 699
See also ABUSIVE REGISTRATION, UDRP PARAGRAPH 4(b)(iii)

Distance (Geographic determining actual knowledge)   23, 320-321, 436, 465

Distinct from (referring to the nature of respondent's business)   83, 86, 141, 167, 219, 449, 514, 564, 677

Distinctive (before domain name registration)   135, 307

Distinctive before domain name registration   135, 335-336, 345, 732, 734, 751-752, 756, 761, 763, 766, 772-773

Distinctive from (referring to the nature of respondent's business) *See* ASSOCIATED EXCLUSIVELY WITH, UNIQUELY ASSOCIATED

Distinctiveness *See* GOODWILL, MARKET PRESENCE, REPUTATION IN THE MARKET

Distinctiveness (in the marketplace)   ix, xxviii, 7, 19, 24, 26, 55-56, 58-59, 63-64, 82, 94, 99, 124, 128, 130, 132-136, 139, 141-142, 144, 147, 149-150, 157-158, 162-163, 165, 168-169, 175, 180, 182, 187, 192, 197, 203, 207-208, 210-211, 213, 220, 238, 285, 305, 307, 310, 313, 315, 321-325, 327-328, 330, 332-335, 338-342, 348, 354, 367, 373, 384, 419, 459, 468-469, 473-474, 476, 480, 484, 486-488, 490, 534, 543, 561, 569, 583-585, 592, 598, 625, 629-633, 650, 692, 701-702, 710, 723, 741, 757, 759, 781

Distributor   xiii, 170, 204, 293-294, 345, 413, 433, 447, 481, 523, 536, 604, 612-613, 615, 624-625, 641, 645

See also RESELLER

Divert to respondent's website   7, 153, 186, 194, 270, 349, 367, 379, 417, 428, 430, 457, 470, 478, 481, 512-513, 515-517, 525, 553, 561, 587, 603, 615, 731, 734, 765, 768, 772

Divesting registrants of their domain names   225, 403-404, 460, 465-466, 753

Documentary evidence (necessary to establish an allegation)   21-22, 27, 37-38, 41-42, 138, 181, 236, 238, 241-243, 246, 248, 250-251, 254, 268, 270, 275, 309, 311, 320-321, 325, 330, 341, 360, 414-415, 452-453, 497, 518, 533, 535, 538, 540-541, 549, 553, 565-566, 571, 582, 587, 598, 620, 624, 637, 640, 662, 669, 690, 728, 767, 791

Domain Investing (Elliott Silver)   701

Domain name predating mark   40, 43, 88, 133, 174, 176, 311, 313-314, 330, 398, 455, 459, 464, 466, 476, 493, 577, 584, 647, 662, 677, 756, 761

Domain Name Wire (Andrew Allemann   701

Domesticating principles from US decisional law (see also US LAW)   21, 68-69, 82, 99, 270, 272, 415, 445, 603, 788-789

Dominant term in a compound trade or service mark   xiv, 69, 163, 341, 343, 351-354, 362, 364, 366, 417, 472, 478, 506, 606

See also ADDITIONS, CONFUSING SIMILARITY, DESCRIPTIVE WORDS (WEAK MARKS)

Doppelgangers (distinguished from domain name investors)   xix, 12, 14, 90, 164, 207, 627, 689, 710

Dorer v. Arel   13, 168, 206, 690-691

dozens of other 'BB' marks   57

Drawing inferences   xii, 26, 31, 89, 175, 209, 251, 257-260, 381, 456, 478, 542, 546, 574, 595, 632, 708

See also UDRP RULE 14(b)

Dropped Domain Names   xvi, xx-xxi, 13-14, 24, 50-51, 58, 60-61, 66, 155, 195, 201, 207, 213, 221, 226, 376, 470, 487-490, 492-493, 533, 579, 618, 672, 702-707
See also ABANDONED, LAPSE, LOSS, PUBLIC AUCTION, RECLAIMING DROPPED DOMAIN NAMES

Due diligence searching for registered trademarks   viii, 24-25, 54-56, 59, 63-64, 154, 628, 674
See also SEARCH OBLIGATIONS, UDRP PARAGRAPH 2

Duty (concerning the representations of Paragraph 2 *See* CONTRACTUAL OBLIGATION

Duty (concerning the representations of Paragraph 2)   viii, 16, 26, 50, 53, 56-57, 60, 63, 66, 110, 118, 127, 251, 264, 281, 289, 295, 404, 412, 420, 536, 552, 632, 659, 669, 684, 718

Duty of Candor (concerning omissions from the pleading supportint RDNH)   669

E

Earlier registered (that is, respondent was first to register a noninfringing domain name)   161, 163, 195, 197, 292, 321, 331, 334, 680, 712
See also FIRST COME FIRST SERVED

Elements *See* UDRP PARAGRAPHS 4(a)(i), 4(a)(ii), 4(a)(iii)

Elements (referring to the three requirements of the Policy)   xiii, 40-41, 71, 84, 89, 96, 166, 168, 178, 187, 256, 258, 263, 267-268, 272, 279, 288, 302-303, 306, 310, 314, 330, 341-344, 346-348, 352, 355-356, 362, 364, 366-367, 369, 412, 452, 454, 456-457, 465, 473, 495, 497, 516-517, 534, 538, 546, 557, 565-566, 589, 595, 640, 663, 665, 670, 676, 707, 747, 755, 766-767, 774, 783

Email (legitimate interest)   200, 386, 388, 407
See also FRAUDULENT EMAILS (IMPERSONATING MARK OWNER)

Employer/Employee Disputes   296

Enforcement   xxviii-xxix, 8, 10, 20, 29, 35, 46, 69, 132-133, 281, 343, 397-398, 628, 740, 778, 793

Enhanced Investigative Responsibilities (of high acquiring domainers)   24-25, 59, 165, 173, 237, 239, 491, 534, 541, 576, 581, 586, 623, 641, 664, 672, 777

Entertainment   31, 78, 82, 90, 109, 152, 167, 193, 219, 235, 292, 338, 345, 371, 373, 376, 387, 391, 434, 443, 470-471, 478, 491, 501, 504, 514, 555, 563, 598, 601, 609, 637, 702

Entrepreneur   xx, 12-13, 179-180, 221-222, 690, 692, 695, 700, 773

Equitable *See* LACHES, STATUTE OF LIMITATIONS

Equitable remedies   xx, 589, 668

Errors of law (transferring domain name on weak records)   56, 196, 696

Establish rights   ix, 4, 12, 74, 114, 128, 131, 661, 692, 694, 700, 709, 790

Establishing a right *See* STANDING, UDRP PARAGRAPH 4(a)(i)

Establishing rights *See* METES AND BOUNDS

European Union   29, 31, 132, 273, 315, 653

EVIDENCE   124, 158, 172, 183, 349, 379, 381, 407, 598, 605, 624, 630, 636, 717, 791

Evidence (in support of contentions)   43, 286, 328, 330, 332, 425, 569, 613, 655

Evidence (sufficiency of lack of it)   38, 42, 138, 330, 414, 535, 540

Evidence (sufficiency of or lack of it)   xiv, 18, 31, 43, 55, 63, 90, 99, 126, 144, 150-151, 178, 190-193, 195, 201, 205, 222, 227-228, 244, 247, 269-270, 277-278, 290, 296, 307, 309, 312-313, 319, 329, 332, 339-340, 349, 351, 355, 365-366, 373, 375-376, 382, 385, 387, 407-408, 413-415, 420-421, 425, 427, 434, 441-442, 456, 460, 477, 486, 494, 497, 501, 516, 533, 536, 541, 546, 548, 552, 560, 567, 575-576, 579, 583-584, 593, 607, 609, 619, 632, 647, 655, 686, 688, 698, 703-704, 749, 762, 767, 777, 788

Evidence (sufficiency or lack of it)   149, 568, 627

Evidence (to prove one's contentions)   43, 164, 212, 222, 240, 330, 333, 387, 469, 475, 598-599, 640, 661

See also CONCRETE EVIDENCE

Evidence in the form (describing the different kinds)   60, 577, 613, 791

EVIDENCE IN THE RECORD   63, 173, 372, 505, 580

Evidence in the record (or lack of it)   63, 173, 269, 310, 372, 505, 580

See also CREDIBLE EVIDENCE

Evidentiary burden   27, 199, 535, 599, 654

See also STANDARD OF PROOF

Evidentiary demands   xvii-xix, xxv, 18, 42-43, 227, 258, 310, 452, 491, 496, 520, 533, 562, 575, 635, 644, 659, 665, 755

Evidentiary omissions   639

See also CERTIFICATION OF PLEADINGS

Ex parte injunction   744, 777

Exaggerating reputation   xx, 578, 635, 677

Exceptional   118, 185, 242-243, 246, 248-249, 255, 372-373, 401, 407-408, 445, 580, 621, 628, 660, 684, 723, 740, 749-750, 752, 766, 770, 781, 783-787

Excessive   501, 503, 535, 581, 623, 680, 716, 719, 721, 723-724, 726, 729

See also PRICING

Exclusive control (referring to complainant's right)   306, 347, 377

Exclusive rights   vii-viii, xiii, xvi, 6, 12-13, 20, 28, 39, 47, 58, 60, 64, 77, 103, 128-129, 133-134, 139-140, 148, 154-155, 157, 162, 171, 180, 183-185, 188-190, 193-194, 196, 200, 202, 207, 214, 217-218, 228-229, 238, 256, 265, 303, 305, 310, 319, 322, 326, 328, 333, 344-345, 359-361, 363, 377, 383, 395, 443, 449, 451, 456-457, 472, 485, 488, 496, 551, 556, 563-564, 568, 579, 584, 599, 630, 642, 654,

678, 682, 686, 696, 715, 719, 738, 740, 747, 756, 764, 768, 772, 774, 778
See also STATUTORY RIGHTS

Excusable circumstances   xvii, 501, 506

Execution of award *See* ENFORCING AWARDS

Executive summary WIPO Final Report   5, 15

Exhibits   68, 241, 320, 558, 571
See also EVIDENCE

Expired Domain Name Deletion Policy (ERRP)   14

Exploitation (of mark value)   12, 96, 108, 142, 146, 160, 164, 187, 206, 452, 458, 467-468, 501, 608, 629, 691, 709
See also CONJUNCTIVE BAD FAITH, UDRP PARAGRAPH 4(b)

Exploiting the value of marks   12, 142, 160, 164, 206, 458, 467, 629

Extortion   14, 144, 522-523, 603-604, 616, 765
See also PRICING

Extreme speech (relating to criticism)   436-437

F

Factors (the tests against which sufficiency of evidence is measured)   84, 109, 143, 160, 209, 218-219, 253, 490, 505, 521, 664, 736, 738-739, 768, 791
See also CIRCUMSTANCES, NONEXCLUSIVE, STATUTORY FACTORS (GOOD FAITH AND BAD FAITH)

Factual research *See* ARCHIVE.ORG, UDRP RULE 10, WAYBACK MACHINE

Factual research (by Panel)   30, 238-240, 243

Fail to prove claim or defense   viii, xviii-xix, 22, 24, 38, 43, 51-52, 55, 62-65, 137, 149, 217, 219, 227, 240, 245, 247, 255-257, 259-260, 286, 295, 307, 310, 323, 326, 328, 331, 334, 337, 346, 373, 377-378, 380, 385, 387, 390, 414, 423, 453, 456, 459-460, 480, 482, 490, 517, 533, 537, 542, 544, 565-568, 572, 585, 587, 598-600, 621-622, 626, 628-631, 635-636, 638, 640, 643, 646-647, 649, 653, 655, 662, 674, 677, 679, 682, 686-687, 790-791
See also EVIDENTIARY BURDEN

Failed to disclose (said of complainant)   92, 346, 495, 599, 634, 670, 672

Fair use   xii, 13, 106-107, 141, 234, 242-243, 252, 254-255, 311, 379, 381-383, 385, 394, 417, 419, 424, 428, 432, 435, 457, 463, 478, 492, 504, 519, 525, 532, 604, 693, 719, 734, 780, 784
See also NOMINATIVE, UNFAIR USE

False contact information   91, 286-287, 427, 735
See also CONTACT INFORMATION, GDPR

Falsely asserting or suggesting   xx, 93, 103, 166, 447, 451, 669, 671, 676-677

Fame   23-24, 43, 48, 135, 141, 151, 164-165, 311, 388, 564, 570, 714

Fame (and non fame)   59, 348

Fame (of a mark)   23-24, 43, 48, 108, 131, 135, 141, 143-144, 151, 164-165, 182, 212, 227, 311, 370, 375, 388, 461, 469, 492, 564, 570, 572, 608, 678, 714, 790
See also GOODWILL, REPUTATION
Familiarity with the Policy   xix, 635, 644-646, 648, 654, 665, 682, 791
Family   x, 155, 158-159, 182, 195, 198, 200, 266, 287, 296, 299, 319, 321, 364, 388, 403, 405-407, 426, 444, 460, 486, 548, 566, 600, 606, 625, 646, 696, 707
Family of Marks   x, 158-159, 606
Famous and Well Known   ix, 7, 9, 14, 55, 99, 129-130, 135, 150, 207, 219, 224, 366, 484, 496, 509-510, 518, 573, 588, 617, 700-701
Famous mark   xviii, xxvii, 40, 71, 86, 94, 129, 135, 157, 183, 192-193, 206, 211, 219, 311, 313, 328, 338, 352, 460, 472, 479, 502, 534, 550-551, 567, 585, 604, 622, 627, 631, 676, 706, 725, 733, 735-736, 738, 767, 774, 781, 790
Fan (Websites)   427, 439, 594
Fanciful   57, 64, 116, 140, 147, 154, 161, 170-171, 176, 181, 188, 193, 211, 230, 393, 409, 469, 487, 564, 606, 609, 714
See also COINED WORD, INHERENTLY DISTINCTIVE
Fast flux DNS   613
Faux (Registrant)   429
Federal Arbitration Act   737
Federal Rules of Civil Procedure   636, 669
See also CERTIFICATION OF PLEADING
Federal Rules of Evidence   581
Fiduciary duty   251, 289, 295
Figurative Mark   48, 55, 57, 74, 77, 87, 148, 156, 163, 166, 169, 197, 199, 204, 277, 341-342, 362, 530-531, 709
See also DESIGN ELEMENTS
Final Report   5-7, 10-11, 15-17, 20, 27-28, 34-35, 51, 54-55, 69, 78, 82, 84, 88, 92, 100, 104, 112, 161, 163, 250, 284, 300, 303, 336, 370, 392, 427, 432, 435, 462, 484, 550, 588, 593, 603, 625, 657, 692, 701, 711-712, 731
See also WIPO
First Amendment (U.S.)   7, 17, 27, 33, 103, 111, 280-282, 433, 436-438, 441, 517
See also UNITED STATES
First come, first served   xi, xv, 139, 146, 161, 167, 176-177, 179, 181, 185, 189, 207, 210, 218, 222-227, 233, 368, 372, 385, 393, 398, 400, 476, 487, 500, 577, 621, 714
First use in commerce   xiii, xx, 91, 135, 188, 208, 223-224, 314, 327-328, 330-331, 340, 393, 466, 506, 520, 557, 564, 583, 652, 676, 700, 714
See also COMMON LAW, REPUTATION
First use of mark in commerce   xiii, xx, 91, 135, 188, 208, 223, 314, 327-328, 330-331, 340, 393, 466, 520, 557, 564, 583, 652, 676, 700, 714

Foreign (Non-US Registrant)   138, 744

Forfeiture   viii, xxx, 8, 11, 18, 47, 53, 56, 114, 121, 127, 182, 284, 296, 457, 466, 490, 589, 604, 626, 691-692, 697, 703, 705, 720, 733
  See also BAD FAITH, TRANSFER

Forum Supplementary Rules   236, 316

Fraudulent activities   363, 525

Fraudulent activity   363, 370, 525

Fraudulent documents   251

Fraudulent documents (alleged)   251
  See also COURT OF COMPETENT JURISDICTION

Fraudulent emails (impersonating mark owner)   522, 526-528, 611-613, 615

Fraudulent intent   471

Fraudulent purposes   422

Fraudulent schemes   xvii, 14, 496, 525, 618

Fraudulent Transfer   xvii, xix, xxii, 14, 192, 241, 248, 251, 292, 363, 370, 422, 471, 481, 496, 522, 525-528, 597, 611-612, 614-616, 618-619, 733, 761, 775-777, 779-780, 786
  See also ALEXANDRIA DIVISION, D. VA, IN REM JURISDICTION

Fraudulent website   611

Free speech   xxvi, 21, 100-103, 107-109, 204, 304, 427, 430-431, 433, 436, 438, 442, 495, 761
  See also CRITICISM, UDRP PARAGRAPH 4(c)(iii)

Frivolous allegations and arguments   388, 407, 549, 570, 668, 686, 790

Functional necessity (referring to top level domain)   367, 369

Functioning as *See* STOCK TICKER, TRADE NAMES

Functioning as trademark   xi, xiv, 187, 212, 227, 329, 339, 370, 654

G

GDPR   vii, 29-31, 38, 175, 241, 260, 264, 275, 283, 377
  See also GENERAL DATA PROTECTION REGULATION

General Data Protection Regulation (GDPR)   29, 31

General powers of Panels   30, 236, 288, 304
  See also UDRP RULE 10

Generic and clever   xi, 12, 55, 58-60, 63, 85, 132, 134, 145, 157, 159, 162, 168, 177, 182, 188-189, 200, 206, 216, 219, 223, 262, 276, 310, 322, 335, 341, 343, 354, 394, 398, 478, 489, 496, 568, 598, 628, 690, 696, 701, 713

Generic combination of words   189, 623
  See also DICTIONARY WORD, FANCIFUL

Generic Terms   xi, 60, 85, 132, 134, 145, 162, 177, 216, 219, 223, 310, 354, 489, 496, 598, 696, 701, 713
See also DICTIONARY WORDS, LEXICAL RESOURCES
Generic Top Level Domains   5, 168, 183, 185, 269, 352, 354, 367, 468, 517
See also COUNTRY CODE, LEGACY, NEW TLDS
Genericness of words   xi, 210, 216, 296, 299, 311, 490
Geographic location   xxxi, 59, 116, 129, 139, 178, 193, 195, 214, 218, 271, 276, 307, 314, 321, 333-334, 342, 350, 353, 375, 396, 469, 502-503, 512-513, 547, 556, 563-564, 566, 584, 707, 755, 774
See also DISTANCE, LOCATIONS
Global   4, 10, 15, 49, 53, 60, 66, 114, 126, 132, 151, 168-171, 194, 224, 231, 248, 251, 261, 274, 310, 313, 338, 344-346, 375, 407, 410, 413, 473, 475-476, 507-508, 510, 521, 523, 526, 546, 556, 574, 601-602, 647, 688, 697, 711
Goal of the UDRP   17, 67, 71, 112, 250
GoDaddy   14, 44, 174, 241, 421, 481, 483, 493, 605, 626, 706, 742, 751, 760, 763, 774, 777
Good faith (acting in)   61, 117, 163, 250, 300, 304, 411, 419, 454-455, 461, 464, 506
See also RIGHTS OR LEGITIMATE INTERESTS
Good Faith (not acting in)   175, 260, 287, 453, 480, 485, 500, 631, 756
Goodwill (the degree to which a complainant has it and what it means) *See* REPUTATION
Google search   25, 66, 189, 199, 209
See also DUE DILIGENCE, SEARCH OBLIGATIONS
GoPets Ltd. v. Hise   xxii, 404-406, 751-758, 787
Graphical Elements   xix, 11, 17, 139, 195, 218, 271, 276, 307, 314, 334, 348-349, 353, 469, 547, 564, 584, 607-608, 716
See also DESIGN MARKS
Great Britain   199, 228
See also UNITED KINGDOM
Gripe (Sites)   102, 104, 433, 436-437
See also SUCKS

H

Hacking   292, 350, 439, 444, 616, 618-620, 776
Harassment   103, 288, 467, 505, 636, 657, 664, 666, 669-670, 672-673
Heritable rights   xv, 403
See also INHERIT (NO BREAK IN THE CHOIC OF OWNERSHIP)
Hierarchy (of domain names, of distinctiveness, of evidence, of trade and service marks)   105, 114, 129, 133, 139, 147, 149, 168, 177, 187, 197, 211, 271, 332, 384,

415, 419, 534, 545, 551, 583, 608, 650, 691, 700, 715-716, 736, 756
  See also SENIOR USER
High bidder   155-156, 195, 216, 221, 482, 487-488, 490, 492, 533, 705
  See also DROPPED DOMAIN NAME, PUBLIC AUCTION
High-Volume Registrants   viii, 60, 62-63, 157, 494
Historical data (no longer freely available *See* GDPR, WAYBACK MACHINE
Historical data (no longer freely available)   vii, 29-32, 175, 238, 647
Horizontal and vertical pattern of conduct   508, 510
Horizontal pattern of conduct   508, 510
  See also VERTICAL PATTERN OF CONDUCT
House of Representatives   16, 19, 53, 452
Hyperlink(ing) (Infringing)   146, 196, 284, 417, 419, 461, 470, 478, 480-481, 483,
  543, 617
Hyperlink(ing) (Not infringing)   195, 389, 411, 419, 421, 481-483, 548, 587, 602,
  702
Hyphens *See* TYPOSQUATTING
Hyphens (attempt to distinguish domain name from mark)   191-192, 369, 442,
  607-608

I

ICANN   vii-viii, 4-5, 7-8, 11, 16-18, 26-27, 29-30, 34-37, 42, 44, 50-51, 67, 69, 73,
  77, 84, 90, 100, 105, 136, 204, 238, 246, 250, 281, 284, 298, 303-304, 306, 313,
  325, 350, 369, 392, 433, 435, 452, 462, 484, 498, 523, 525, 550, 553, 555, 580,
  593, 606, 626, 641, 649, 670, 690, 693, 697, 701, 727, 770
ICANN Panel not empowered to question issuance of a mark   313
  See also US STATE REGISTRATIONS
ICANN Second Staff Report   37, 69, 120, 250, 435, 701
Identical or confusingly similar *See* COMPARING (DOMAIN NAME AND MARK)
Identity of respondent   244, 281, 362
  See also GDPR, PROXY SERVICE
Identity theft   248-249, 611
Illegitimate purpose (said of respondent)   117
Impersonating   xvi, 85, 93, 316, 432, 434, 437, 495, 520, 525, 528-531, 589, 604,
  617
Impersonation   ix, xxviii, 78, 88, 101, 107, 109-111, 387, 431, 434, 448, 495
  See also PRETENSE, QWERTY KEYBOARD
Impersonation (as it relates to pretextual)   14, 88, 96, 109
Impersonation is not fair   xv, 101, 433, 437
Impersonation test   ix, xxviii, 78, 107, 109-111, 387, 431, 434, 448, 495-496

Implausible Denial *See* DENIAL OF KNOWLEDGE, INCONCEIVABILITY TEST, OPPORTUNISTIC REGISTRATION, PLAUSIBLE DENIAL, TELSTRA

Implied affiliation (with mark owner)   138, 496
See also UDRP PARAGRAPH 4(b)(iv)

In mind (having trademark "in mind" when registering domain name)   xvi, 44, 54, 59, 85-86, 89, 92, 94, 111, 140, 143, 154, 156, 162, 165, 168, 177, 198-200, 216, 223, 344, 389, 396, 435, 455, 458, 466-469, 472-473, 475-476, 497, 501-502, 505, 539, 544, 558, 564, 573, 576, 605-606, 629-631, 640-641, 668, 678, 687, 695, 702, 720
See also ACTUAL KNOWLEDGE, CAPITALIZE, TAKING ADVANTAG, TARGETING

In rem jurisdiction   xxi, xxvi-xxvii, 18-20, 36, 39, 41, 46, 138, 263, 303, 519, 544, 619, 730, 733, 742-747, 762, 765, 775-777, 779-780, 786

IN REM, PERSONAL JURISDICTION, SUBJECT MATTER   vii-viii, xxi-xxii, xxv, xxvii, 3-4, 9, 12, 14, 16-24, 26-29, 35, 38-39, 44-51, 59, 64, 66, 68-69, 71, 73, 83, 91, 98-99, 101, 104-105, 107, 110-112, 123, 128, 133, 138, 141, 144, 150-151, 163, 168, 179, 216, 233, 235, 237, 250-252, 261, 270-272, 281, 289-291, 295, 298, 302-303, 311-313, 324, 329, 332, 336, 367, 390, 402, 405, 430, 437, 482, 538, 544, 554, 567, 574, 583, 600, 614, 619, 640, 648, 695, 723-725, 730, 733, 737, 739-746, 761-766, 769, 772, 774-777, 779, 783, 786, 788, 790, 793

Inactive or Passive Use   90, 99, 119, 477
See also PASSIVE USE

Inadvertent failure to renew registration   xvi, 24, 58, 217, 219, 489-490, 500
See also DROPPED, LOSING AND RECLAIMING DROPPED DOMAIN NAMES; RECLAIMING DROPPED DOMAIN NAME, DROPPED DOMAIN NAME,

Incomplete (referring to evidence)   xxvii, 73, 237, 258, 293, 566, 653, 683, 687
See also CREDIBILITY, RELIABILITY

Inconceivability principle   76, 160, 399, 459, 485, 534, 543, 670, 672
See also TELSTRA

Incorporating two brands   xiv, 355
See also REGISTRATIONS INCORPORATING TWO BRANDS

Individuals (question of common law rights)   88

Individuals (question of common law)   xxv, 4, 64, 88, 204, 249, 257, 323, 371, 409, 427, 433, 438, 440, 464, 498, 529, 664, 713, 751

Inference *See* NEGATIVE INFERENCE

Inference (deducing from the record)   xii, xix, 21, 23-24, 26, 30-31, 38, 41, 59, 62, 70, 77, 89, 120, 124, 133, 162-163, 175, 189, 198, 207, 209, 232, 234, 244, 251, 255-263, 276, 323, 335, 381, 390, 409, 412, 453, 456, 460-462, 464, 468-469, 473,

478, 502, 509, 520, 528, 533-534, 541-543, 545-546, 552, 554, 569, 571, 574-575, 587, 595-596, 614, 620-625, 629-632, 640, 652-654, 671, 699, 708, 713-714, 745, 755, 790

Information and belief allegations   xviii, 41, 565-566, 596, 665
See also PLEADINGS

Infringement *See* NO INFRINGEMENT, TRADE AND SERVICE MARK INFRINGEMENT

Infringement of a statutory right   185, 621

Infringement of statutory right   viii, 6, 32, 53, 55, 83, 91, 136, 138-139, 142-143, 167, 185, 209, 219, 344-345, 455, 470, 480, 603, 626, 642, 696, 709
See also CAPITALIZE, VALUE (SOURCE OF)

Infringing activity   xix, 4, 34, 370, 430, 491, 560, 603, 605, 611, 664, 672
See also NONINFRINGING ACTIVITY

Inherently distinctive *See* ACQUIRED DISTINCTIVENESS

Inherently distinctive (as opposed to acquired distinctiveness)   147, 468-469, 585

Inherit (no break in the chain of ownership)   56, 84, 162, 185, 401, 404, 753

Initial interest confusion   xvi, xxviii, 100-102, 111, 367, 422, 442-444, 496
See also IMPERSONATION, LIKELIHOOD OF CONFUSION

Initials   427, 471
See also ACRONYMS

Injunction   39, 733, 747, 749, 773, 777, 782-783
See also LANHAM ACT

Injunctive relief   7, 734, 742, 744, 749-750, 769
See also EX PARTE INJUNCTION (Issues Index); INJUNCTION (General Index); INJUNCTION (Issues Index)

Injunctive relief (restoring domain name to registrant *See* SECTION 1114(2)(D)(4) and (5)

Innocent   53, 149, 304, 411, 458, 463, 466, 501, 529, 575, 594, 616, 770, 776-777

Innocent purchaser   776-777

Inquisitorial role (as opposed to the UDRP's adversary system)   237, 536

Insider knowledge *See* ANTICIPATORY INFRINGEMENT

Insider knowledge (personal knowledge of an anticipated brand or presence in the market)   142, 145-146, 408-409, 501, 503, 709

Insufficient evidence   115, 117, 126, 144, 189, 222, 333, 387, 390, 414, 421, 509, 526, 574, 576, 585, 749
See also DEFICIENT PLEADINGS

Insufficient evidence'   421

Integrity (of the proceedings)   681, 684

Intellectual Property Rights   15, 17, 20, 35, 50-51, 54-55, 88, 112, 298, 603, 692, 711, 734, 780

Intent to profit   xxi, 15, 89, 92, 108, 116, 120, 132, 137, 148, 166, 197, 207, 211, 222, 228, 250, 258, 312, 323, 331, 340, 362, 372, 386, 407, 410, 420-421, 435-436, 452, 467, 469, 471-472, 475, 507, 528, 573, 583, 595, 603, 608, 627, 630, 678, 694, 697, 699, 708, 716, 727, 732-734, 736, 738-739, 741, 747-748, 751, 754, 757, 759, 761, 764, 766, 770, 772, 774, 779, 784

See also ACPA

Intent to use application *See* PENDING APPLICATION

Intent to use mark (basis 1(b))   132, 137, 312, 331, 340, 407, 410, 583, 741, 774

Intentional (unlawful) registration   xxxi, 24, 154, 457, 573, 594, 675

See also CYBERSQUATTING COMPLAINT, PARAGRAPH 2, RDNH

Intentionally attempting to attract visitors to respondent's website   xvi-xvii, xxxi, 15, 17, 24, 52, 54, 56, 65, 73-74, 88-89, 99, 101, 103, 108, 115, 120, 122, 125, 128, 147, 150, 153-154, 157, 173, 177, 185, 190, 205, 210, 214, 216, 222, 232, 246, 268, 290, 304-305, 309, 311, 340, 360, 364, 386, 392-393, 396, 404, 408, 410, 413-414, 419, 421, 423, 426, 429, 433-434, 442, 453, 456-458, 462, 465-466, 468, 480-481, 496-498, 501, 505, 509, 511, 515-516, 518-520, 523, 526, 532, 538-539, 549, 553, 571-573, 575, 594, 598, 603, 606, 608-610, 618, 627, 629-630, 632, 639, 675, 678, 688, 700-701, 705, 707, 711, 724-725, 735, 768

Interfering with the Proceedings   206, 356, 433, 470, 515, 604, 692

See also RDNH, UDRP RULE 15(e)

International Ad Hoc Committee (IAHC)   5

International Trademark Association   27, 304

Internationally known or famous   311, 482, 653

Internet archive   xi, 237-238, 241-242, 545

See also SCREENSHOT, WAYBACK MACHINE

Internet Assigned Numbers Authority (IANA)   9, 374, 430, 567, 647

See also INTERNET ASSIGNED NUMBERS AUTHORITY

Internet Commerce Association (ICA)   69, 98, 153, 657, 755, 789, 793

Internet Corporation for Assigned Names and Numbers   5

See also ICANN

Internet location (redirecting to other websites)   417, 425, 478

See also HYPERLINKING

Interpretation   20, 30, 48, 52, 70, 73-74, 83-84, 87, 97-98, 102, 117-118, 120, 124, 137, 172, 236, 238, 250, 253, 292, 360, 405, 455, 460, 466, 514, 519, 553, 586, 624, 663-664, 674, 685, 696, 720, 730, 737, 742, 744, 754, 757-758, 782

Invented words and coined terms   70, 152, 205, 220, 394, 476, 543, 608, 626, 642, 734

See also FANCIFUL

Inventory   xx, 13, 200, 400, 500, 506, 689-690, 700, 703, 709, 723, 725

Investor-victims   777, 779-780

J

Jackson, Ron   152, 523, 616, 688, 701

JURISPRUDENCE   ix, 67, 71, 83, 87, 96-98, 112, 697

Jurisprudence (developed over the past many years)   ix, xxvii-xxviii, xxx-xxxii, 12, 21, 36-37, 43, 67-68, 70-73, 77-79, 82-83, 87, 95-98, 105, 112, 116-117, 129, 138, 169, 182, 256, 405, 431, 466, 554, 560, 593, 635, 644-645, 648, 650, 662-663, 665, 681, 685, 694, 697, 717, 730, 732, 745, 761, 775, 788-791

Jurisprudential Overview   8, 34, 60-61, 68, 72, 81, 85, 89, 96, 103, 107-108, 111, 121-123, 143, 242, 255, 272, 278, 302, 320, 363-364, 398-400, 406, 434, 485, 529, 626, 658, 688-689, 789-790

Just Bulbs   559, 562, 770-771

Justifying Forfeiture   xii, xviii, 7, 75, 80, 88, 94, 100, 106, 118-119, 176, 178, 189, 201, 224, 234, 236, 240, 244-245, 248, 258-259, 263, 267, 272, 286, 297, 304, 313, 348, 391-392, 416, 422-423, 427, 438, 476, 484, 495-496, 507, 517-518, 522-523, 542, 550, 556, 559, 563, 574, 606, 638, 666, 675, 687, 691, 712, 726, 728-729, 772

See also FORFEITURE

K

Keyboard   xix, 192, 348-349, 607-608, 613, 646

See also QWERTY KEYBOARD

Knowing and material misrepresentation   749, 784, 787

See also SECTION 1114(2)(d)(4)

Knowledge (none of mark owner)   24, 86, 115, 183, 187, 388, 484, 570

Knowledge (of mark owner)   xviii-xix, 23-24, 26, 31, 44, 52, 55-56, 59, 61-62, 86, 92, 107, 113-115, 122, 124, 133, 137, 142, 144, 152-154, 156, 166, 170, 172, 175, 183, 187, 190, 195-196, 213-214, 219, 226, 228-229, 232, 255-257, 260-261, 296, 320-321, 327, 332-333, 336, 354, 366, 378-381, 383, 388, 393, 398, 408, 410-412, 421-423, 426, 465, 467, 471, 482, 484, 487, 494, 500, 507, 525-526, 528, 534, 538, 540, 542, 545, 548, 550-551, 553, 561, 569-570, 573, 575-577, 579, 595, 608, 617, 621-622, 625-628, 631-633, 636, 644, 650, 653-654, 658, 666-667, 670, 676-677, 687, 689, 699, 701, 705, 709, 722, 728, 737, 764, 790

knowledge (of mark owner) *See* ACTUAL KNOWLEDGE, ANTICIPATORY INFRINGEMENT, CONSTRUCTIVE KNOWLEDGE, IMPLAUSIBLE DENIAL, INSIDER KNOWLEDGE, SHOULD HAVE KNOWN

Known to each other (as opposed to strangers)   xii, 36, 70, 129, 139, 150, 161, 165-166, 207, 246, 253, 288, 290, 336, 378-379, 404, 408, 545, 570, 659, 719, 732
See also BOARD MEMBER, EMPLOYEE, PARTNER, STRANGERS TO EACH OTHER, VENDOR

L

Laches   xviii, 395, 411, 535, 588-596, 652
See also LAPSE OF TIME
Lacks credibility (of knowledge and website)   465, 629
See also CREDIBILITY (TESTING OF)
Lacks rights or legitimate interest   398
Language as a public resource   viii, x-xii, xxvi, xxviii, 3, 14, 27, 41, 46, 54-55, 64-65, 67, 72-76, 96, 98, 100-101, 117-119, 124, 135, 139, 151, 160, 162-163, 168-171, 175, 178-184, 199, 202-203, 209, 213, 215-216, 242, 268-270, 302, 306, 322, 362, 374, 391, 417, 423, 436, 438-439, 447, 459, 492, 514, 573, 582, 607-608, 621, 625, 633, 643, 645-646, 683, 692, 717-718, 749, 752, 758, 765, 769
See also MONOPOLIZING COMMON LEXICAL MATERIAL
Language of the proceedings   268-269
See also UDRP RULE 11(a) (LANGUAGE OF THE PROCEEDINGS)
Lanham Act   6, 9, 12, 17-19, 48, 84, 99, 129, 312, 314, 323, 371, 419, 436, 501, 575, 584-585, 734-735, 737, 746, 748-749, 769, 776, 783
  Section 1114(2)(D)   12, 46, 742, 747-749, 758, 774, 782
  Section 1117(a)   749, 782-784, 787
  Section 1117(d)   769, 782
  Section 1125(a)   19, 84, 129, 733
  Section 1125(a)(2)   84, 129
  Section 1125(d)   6, 9, 12, 19-20, 84, 335, 732-734, 741, 744-745, 748, 751-753, 755, 762, 765-767, 770, 774, 777-779, 782-783
Lapse of time (to support dismissing complaint)   132, 588, 596
See also LACHES
Lapsed Registration   xvi, xx-xxi, xxxi, 13-14, 24-25, 50-51, 58, 60-61, 66, 108, 122, 132, 137-138, 145, 155, 170, 178, 195, 199, 201-202, 207, 213, 218, 221-222, 226, 230, 313, 325, 328, 374, 376, 395, 399, 442, 470-471, 474, 487-495, 500, 533, 550, 579, 588, 596, 610, 618, 634, 638, 655, 668, 672, 702-707, 732, 756, 764
Latin and Latin tags   203, 493, 571, 702
Lawful purpose   52-53, 107, 162, 183, 202-204, 216, 302, 394, 406, 454, 457, 522, 546, 606, 626, 628, 690, 761
See also INFRINGING ACTIVITY, NON-INFRINGEMENT ACTIVITY, UDRP PARAGRAPH 2

Lawful use   xiv, 182, 388, 428, 446, 448, 578, 659, 693, 736
See also NON-INFRINGEMENT ACTIVITY, UDRP PARAGRAPH 2
Lawyers in law firm   228
Learning from the case law   96, 134, 157, 173, 183, 534, 658, 665
Leave to replead   562, 760
Legacy Domain Names   367, 713
See also NEW TLDS
Legal Mechanisms   vii, 3, 9, 788
See also ACPA, UDRP
Legitimacy   xxviii, 107, 161, 292, 306, 384, 388, 397, 406, 422, 429, 437, 587, 721, 761
Legitimate Interests   xv, 13, 149, 165, 176, 182, 200, 309, 378, 381-383, 390, 392-393, 410-411, 413-414, 425-427, 454, 508, 572, 577, 586, 588, 590, 596, 600, 627, 719
Legitimate purpose (without intent to infringe third party rights)   117, 224-225, 407, 476, 524, 694
See also UDRP PARAGRAPH 4(a)(ii)
Legitimate registration   28, 228
See also RIGHTS OR LEGITIMATE INTERESTS
Legitimate trademark dispute   299
See also PENDING COURT ACTION
Legitimate use (other than active website)   388, 406-407
Letter and Word Ordering and Reordering   xix, 85, 88, 142, 191-192, 203, 205, 218, 233, 274, 348-349, 352, 355, 357-358, 368-369, 426, 432, 442, 508, 527-528, 537, 588, 607-610, 616, 639, 643, 646, 778
Letters   x-xi, xvi, xix, 13, 64, 90, 94, 145, 147-148, 150, 153-154, 157-160, 166, 168-169, 172, 176-177, 181, 184, 186-188, 191-192, 194, 204, 208, 210, 212-215, 217, 221, 227-231, 233, 258, 310, 342, 347-349, 357-360, 367-368, 388, 410, 455-457, 470, 472, 486, 494, 504-505, 553, 588, 608, 610, 623-624, 653-654, 690, 693, 700, 708, 713-714, 717, 721, 757, 767
Leverage (use of in negotiations improper)   296, 517, 521, 674, 738-739, 769-770
Levy, Steve   18
Lexical choices   x, 55, 64, 131, 133-134, 139, 145, 147, 152, 154-155, 157, 160, 167-168, 176-177, 179, 182, 186, 197, 202-203, 206, 215, 221, 262, 302, 326, 362, 371, 417-418, 458, 545, 564, 621, 690-692, 696, 698, 710
See also COMMON LEXICAL MATERIAL
Lexical permutations   176, 218, 233
Lexical resources   13, 693
See also CULTURAL RESOURCE, GENERIC

Lexicon   x-xi, 6, 25, 54-56, 58-59, 70, 89, 100, 116, 125, 163, 182, 184, 187, 189, 192, 204, 207, 210, 212, 214, 218-219, 221-222, 305, 482, 487-488, 551, 562, 564, 579, 585-586, 599, 604-606, 609, 661, 679, 691, 693, 700, 705-706, 708, 713, 717, 719

Liability (models of)   xvii, xxi-xxii, 10, 18-19, 36, 39, 52, 74, 80, 83, 117, 123, 127, 130, 162, 252, 255, 291, 405, 418, 453, 455, 460, 481, 484, 499, 516, 519, 535, 537, 547, 554, 573, 623, 627, 630, 654, 659, 669, 709, 730-732, 748, 751, 757, 759, 761, 763-764, 766, 769, 772, 776-777, 786
See also CONJUNCTIVE BAD FAITH, DISJUNCTIVE BAD FAITH

Liability (Providers and Panelists, none)   36
See also UDRP RULE 20

Liability (registries and registrars, Lanham Act, none)   35, 763

Licensee   xiii, 4, 114, 138, 285, 291, 294, 316-317, 319-321, 385, 389, 391, 422, 446, 493, 527, 568, 613, 623, 694, 732, 750, 764, 767
See also STANDING

Likelihood of Confusion (UDRP 4(b)(iv))   xvii, xxvii, 43, 56-57, 59, 82, 86, 95, 136, 141, 145, 152, 154, 165, 182, 186, 189, 209, 212, 222, 286, 304, 309-310, 344, 348, 359, 366, 417, 428, 431, 434, 443, 453, 456-457, 471, 478, 488, 496, 513-514, 516, 518-521, 530, 561, 563-564, 573, 584, 600, 626, 631, 676, 705-706, 708, 723, 743, 768, 771

Limitations   xviii, xxvi, 42, 101, 105, 132, 177, 250, 588, 590, 640, 695
See also STATUTE OF LIMITATIONS

Limited factual research   30, 239, 243
See also UDRP RULE 10

Lindsay, David "International Domain Name Law: ICANN and the UDRP   4, 563

Linguistic community   13, 100, 114, 208, 210, 585, 695, 717, 723

Links   xv-xvi, 13-14, 31, 42, 65, 122, 141, 144-146, 153, 156, 171, 186, 196, 209, 241, 284, 349, 351-352, 367, 394, 397, 405, 418-421, 424, 430, 461-462, 465, 470, 474, 478-483, 492, 517, 528, 532, 564, 580, 586, 588, 595, 615, 667, 702-704
See also CURATE

Litigation   9-10, 12, 14, 28-29, 32, 35-37, 41, 47, 51, 85, 91, 106, 127, 255, 259, 289, 299-301, 436, 533, 535, 550, 554, 565, 581, 583, 725, 744-745, 784-785, 793

Local law   ix, 22, 72, 98, 100, 104, 106-107, 110, 123, 270-272
See also NATIONAL LAW

Location (as a factor in determining knowledge)   20, 23, 26, 56, 110, 135, 143, 476, 544

Lock domain name   8, 39, 45, 74, 222

Locking up the lexicon   xi, 221
See also COMMODIFICATION

Looking ahead to bad faith evidence to determine whether to grant standing on confusing similarity grounds   xiv, 89, 349, 362-364, 388
Losing and Reclaiming Domain Names   618
See also LAPSE OF REGISTRATION

M

Making a legitimate noncommercial or fair use of the domain name   379, 432
See also UDRP PARAGRAPH 4(c)(iii)
Making Changes to the Website   80, 297, 380, 421, 517, 789
Malicious   xix, 215, 522, 598, 603, 611, 613-614, 616, 670, 761, 773, 786
Malware   481, 525-526, 604, 606, 613-615
Mandatory   16, 41, 51, 77, 685, 740, 747
Marital *See* INHERIT
Mark in some jurisdiction   20, 312
Mark postdates domain name   40, 89, 133, 305, 310-311, 313, 320, 337, 345, 459, 462, 466, 476, 505, 536, 538, 559, 577, 579, 583-584, 652, 673, 741, 754, 773
See also MARK PREDATES DOMAIN NAME
Mark predates domain name   137, 210, 311, 320, 332, 339, 464, 493, 506, 577
Market presence (having a)   ix, xvi, 22, 140, 142, 181, 200, 203, 332, 404, 407, 464, 484, 491, 580, 630, 744
See also GOODWILL, REPUTATION
Market transaction (to purchase disputed domain name)   504, 661, 720
See also RDNH
Market value   154, 185, 211, 453, 466, 504, 542, 698, 717, 723, 725
See also THE MARKETPLACE
Marketplace (as the locus of value)   7, 24, 56, 76, 124, 128, 132-133, 139, 147, 150, 180, 182, 187, 203, 208, 307, 476, 486-487, 588, 630-631, 633, 677, 710
Materially misrepresents   599, 638
See also REACTIVATION OF DOMAIN NAME
Media coverage   33, 142, 146, 156-157, 285, 325, 373, 490, 546, 580, 645, 671
Merely descriptive ir deceptively misdiscriptive   139, 157, 312, 341, 478
Metes and bounds of rights   ix, 4, 12, 74, 114, 128, 131, 661, 692, 694, 700, 709, 790
Mimicking Strong Marks   470, 527-528, 724
Minor alterations (typosquatting as compared with major alterations that would reject confusing similarity)   358
See also CONFUSINGLY SIMILAR, NEITHER SIMILAR NOR CONFUSING, SIMILAR BUT NOT CONFUSING, TYPOSQUATTING,
Misconduct   88, 251, 439, 464, 555, 586, 755
mislead the Panel   637, 639, 643, 676, 686

Misleading Internet users   130, 152, 450, 495, 524, 563

Misleading statements of fact   ix, 7, 101, 110, 116, 130, 152, 164, 303-304, 325, 355, 362, 364, 379, 385, 420-421, 425, 428, 431, 434, 448, 450, 461, 465, 480-481, 484, 495, 516, 524, 528-530, 550, 563, 597, 599, 604, 618, 637, 639, 643, 676-678, 683, 686-687, 735, 780
See also RDNH

Misspelling   xi, 86, 187, 198, 205, 209, 218, 233, 358, 361, 463, 537, 608-610, 690, 768

Misstatements and specious argument   215, 598

Misstates the law (or evidence)   125
See also EVIDENCE, RDNH

Models (business)   12, 84, 499, 523, 710, 721

Models (of liability)   xxi, 4, 18, 74, 112, 304, 730, 761, 769

Monetizing   xxx, 12, 221, 399, 627, 703, 710, 718, 775, 778-780
See also RESELLING DOMAIN NAMES

Monopolizing common lexical material   x, 179, 182, 184-185
See also COMMODIFICATION

Monopoly on lexical choices   x, 95, 131, 160, 162, 177, 179-182, 184, 186, 193-194, 202-203, 215, 219, 224, 229, 233, 353, 361, 384, 447, 467, 506, 556, 568, 693
See also OWNERSHIP OF LANGUAGE

More likely than not   40, 65, 124, 134, 170, 219, 232, 240, 296, 305, 352, 543-544, 551-552, 573, 594, 622, 624, 631, 641, 702, 729, 766

More of an interest (referring to mark owner's claim)   377

Motion practice   39, 779
See also PLEADINGS, SUMMARY JUDGMENT

Motivation (the reason for the acquisition of domain name)   23, 52, 99, 118, 127, 152, 185, 257, 292, 302, 309, 399, 438-439, 518, 539, 544, 581, 620-623, 627, 663, 708, 787

Multiple complainants   xii, xviii, 10, 20, 73, 116, 123, 125, 140, 145, 148, 151, 169, 183, 194, 196-197, 204-205, 210, 212, 224, 228, 261, 273-275, 277-279, 313, 316, 364, 424, 505, 508-510, 536, 563-564, 568, 577-578, 656, 698, 717, 735, 737

Multiple Disputes   xii, xviii, 10, 20, 73, 116, 123, 125, 140, 145, 148, 151, 169, 183, 194, 196-197, 204-205, 210, 212, 224, 228, 261, 273-275, 277-279, 313, 316, 364, 424, 505, 508-510, 536, 563-564, 568, 577-578, 656, 698, 717, 735, 737
See also CONSOLIDATION

Multiple Domain Names   xii, xviii, 10, 20, 73, 116, 123, 125, 140, 145, 148, 151, 169, 183, 194, 196-197, 204-205, 210, 212, 224, 228, 261, 273-275, 277-279, 313, 316, 364, 424, 505, 508-510, 536, 563-564, 568, 577-578, 656, 698, 717, 735, 737
See also ALIASES

Multiple Registrants   xii, xviii, 10, 20, 73, 116, 123, 125, 140, 145, 148, 151, 169, 183, 194, 196-197, 204-205, 210, 212, 224, 228, 261, 273-275, 277-279, 313, 316, 364, 424, 505, 508-510, 536, 563-564, 568, 577-578, 656, 698, 717, 735, 737
See also CONSOLIDATION

Multiple Unrelated Complainants   xii, xviii, 10, 20, 73, 116, 123, 125, 140, 145, 148, 151, 169, 183, 194, 196-197, 204-205, 210, 212, 224, 228, 261, 273-275, 277-279, 313, 316, 364, 424, 505, 508-510, 536, 563-564, 568, 577-578, 656, 698, 717, 735, 737
See also CONSOLIDATION

Multiply used by others (as of a particular term)   xviii, 145, 148, 182-183, 212, 218, 455, 551, 564, 577, 698, 708, 788
See also ASSOCIATED WITH MARK OWNER, WIDE SPREAD USE OF THE TERM

Muscovitch, Zak   18, 560, 657, 669

MUTUAL JURISDICTION   46, 740

Mutual Jurisdiction   46, 740

Mutual jurisdiction   viii, 28, 35, 44-47, 49-50, 98, 101, 104-105, 107, 110-111, 123, 138, 300, 405, 739-741, 744-745, 761, 765, 769, 783, 786

N

Nahitchevansky, Georges   iv, xxiii, xxix-xxx, 18, 793

Narratives (presenting a case by having a good story)   14, 38, 68-69, 165-166, 206, 254, 323, 328, 386, 463, 490, 502, 507, 532, 545, 547-549, 562, 571, 576, 598

Narratives (their role in persuasive argument)   165, 168, 387, 533, 563

Narrow class of cases (referring to subject matter jurisdiction)   xii, 9, 17, 37, 250-251, 253, 552-553

Nascent   522

National Academy of Sciences   5

National jurisdictions (applying UDRP law)   vii-viii, 3-4, 14, 22-23, 47-48, 168, 233, 311

National Laws *See* LOCAL LAW

National Laws (application of)   21, 69, 101, 105-106, 111, 270, 272, 561

National Telecommunications and Information Administration (NTIA)   4-5, 82, 482, 711

Negative (difficult to prove)   380

Negative inference   209, 255, 257-258, 260-261, 409, 468, 533, 541, 543, 545, 571, 623, 625

Negotiating a sale   258
See also WHO CONTACTS WHOM

Negotiations   99, 258, 396, 477, 498-499, 504, 506, 557, 563, 581-582, 623-624, 651, 659, 674, 679-680, 683, 701, 714, 717, 719, 727-728
See also PRIVILEGE
Neither similar nor confusing   348, 357
Network Solutions Inc.   xxv-xxvi, 7-9, 173, 437, 732, 745, 767
Neu, Howard   657
Neutral decision maker   16, 27
New Acts by Respondent *See* REFILING COMPLAINT
New TLDs   185, 606
Nexus *See* REGISTRATIONS INCORPORATING TWO BRANDS
Nexus to mark owner sufficient to state a right   316, 318, 357, 372
Niche Market   21, 23, 25-26, 75, 130, 135, 143-144, 150, 154-155, 158, 166, 169, 177, 183-185, 188, 206-208, 216, 226, 231, 472-474, 479, 551, 564, 576, 592, 622, 630, 654, 711, 716, 723, 768
Niche market   23, 25, 75, 130, 135, 143-144, 150, 154-155, 166, 169, 183-185, 188, 206-208, 216, 226, 231, 472, 474, 479, 564, 576, 630, 716, 768
Nicknames (False names, Stage Names)   76, 329, 426
Ninth Circuit   xxii, 45, 93, 97, 112-113, 138, 307, 404-405, 455, 730, 740, 745, 751-757, 759-760, 762-763, 766, 782, 785-787
See also THIRD AND NINTH CIRCUIT SPLIT
No actionable claim   44, 91, 264, 320, 336, 347, 376, 476, 602, 658, 712, 784, 790
See also ACTIONABLE CLAIM
No deference (as it relates to UDRP decisions)   48, 314, 739
No deference (as it relates to US State Registrations)   314-315
no evidence, and no basis for inferring   394
No infringement   389
No longer current *See* RIGHTS AND LEGITIMATE INTERESTS
No longer current (respondent's use of)   7, 14, 30, 36, 50, 138, 176, 398, 428, 431, 570, 689, 758, 760
No presumption of bad faith   314, 472, 535, 575
No Reputation of the complainant or mark   149, 568
No Reputation of the complainant or mark)   321
No trademark rights   201, 370, 372, 418
Nominative Fair Use   xvi, xxviii, 7, 93, 143, 366, 445-451, 496, 509, 511, 592, 739
Nominative Fair Use (without merit)   739
Non exclusive factors or circumstances (referring to the Policy and circumstances of proof)   496
See also FACTORS

Non use (passive holding)   26, 71-72, 99, 108, 132, 176, 390, 455, 458-459, 465,
  548, 570-571, 764
Non-competing   133, 145, 229, 344, 664, 674
Non-Renewal of Registrar Registration Agreement   14, 707
  See also DROPPED, INADVERTENT LAPSE OF REGISTRATION
Non-targeting of complainant or its mark   123
  See also CAPITALIZE, TARGETING
Noncommercial   xv, 13, 27, 85, 100, 104, 107, 109-111, 379, 381-383, 417,
  427-428, 430, 432, 434-436, 441, 444, 478, 492, 525, 548, 734, 748, 775
  See also UDRP PARAGRAPH 4(c)(iii)
Nonexclusive remedy   vii, 20, 28
Noninfringing activity   12-13, 67, 100, 164, 178, 181, 184-185, 193, 215, 289, 389,
  398, 410-411, 449, 459, 481, 501, 532, 543, 546, 564, 586, 617, 621, 656, 690-694,
  698, 704, 731, 757, 772
  See also INFRINGING ACTIVITY
Not authorized (to register or use)   291, 294-295, 307, 332, 450, 512
Not making a bona fide offering   289, 382, 471
Not requested (referring to RDNH)   xx, 481, 684-685
Not within the scope of the Policy   250-251, 292, 437
  See also SCOPE OF THE UDRP

0

Objections (complainant objecting to)   145, 262, 266, 424
Objectively groundless complaint   xx, 663, 669
Objectively reasonable to maintain proceedings   666
Objectively unreasonable   xx, 25, 56, 177, 191, 194, 663, 666, 669, 673-674, 679
  See also REPUTATION
Obligation to avoid violating third-party rights   52-53, 77, 88, 156, 158, 172, 338,
  346, 483, 553
  See also SEARCH OBLIGATIONS, UDRP PARAGRAPH 2
Offering to sell domain name   xvii, 72, 161-163, 267, 275, 460, 497, 499-500, 507,
  720-721, 727, 751
  See also TARGETING, WHO CONTACTS WHOM
Oki Data Test   92-93, 95, 105, 445-450, 479, 513
  See also NOMINATIVE FAIR USE
Omitting letters (consequences for abusive registration)   192, 441, 528, 607
  See also CONFUSING SIMILARITY, COUNTING DIFFERENCES,
  TYPOSQUATTING
Opportunism (recklessly asserted)   486

Opportunistic Bad Faith   xvi, 142-143, 265, 336, 345, 408, 470, 484-487, 521, 547, 558, 631, 633, 707

Opt out rule (removing UDRP case to a court f competent jurisdiction)   39, 289, 298

Opt out rule (removing UDRP case to a court of competent jurisdiction)   39

Other rules and principles law (domesticating into UDRP jurisprudence   xii, 12, 21, 42, 106, 238, 256, 270, 272-273, 459, 554, 636, 669, 788

Out of pocket (demanding benefits in exchange of the domain name)   72, 90, 115, 170, 275, 452, 497-498, 502, 506, 523, 582, 600, 621, 688, 690, 719

Out of pocket(demanding benefits in exchange of the domain name)   72, 90, 115, 186, 275, 452, 460, 497, 502, 504, 582, 690, 720, 722, 728-729
See also UDRP PARAGRAPH 4(b)(i)

Overreaching mark owner *See* RDNH

Overreaching mark owner (US Senate Report)   17, 749, 758

Overreaching of mark owner (UDRP)   xxii, xxxi, 17, 19, 37, 84, 92, 94, 99, 129, 550, 599, 657, 672, 746, 749, 758

Overstating one's rights or reputation   164, 599
See also RDNH

Overview 1.0   68, 71, 99, 101, 237, 485

Overview 2.0   72, 96, 101, 110, 121, 485

Overview 3.0 (Jurisprudential Overview)   72, 96, 101, 123, 211, 284, 323, 402-403, 431, 434, 642

Ownership of rights to language (no ownership) *See* MONOPOLY OF LEXICAL CHOICES

Ownership right to language (no ownership)   181-182, 217, 395

Ownership right to language(no ownership)   179

Ownership rights to domain names   50
See also GODADDY

Ownership rights to language (no ownership)   179-180, 215

Ownership rights to language(no ownership)   7, 168, 180, 184, 191-192, 401, 476, 609, 696

Ownership rights to trade and service marks   145, 229

P

Panels' Role   21

Panels' Powers   30, 236, 288, 304
See also GENERAL POWERS, UDRP RULES 10, 12, 15(d)

Paragraph 2 (Representations of good faith)   52-53, 121-122, 126, 470, 496, 626

Paramountcy of Statutory rights   ix, 128, 132, 160, 269, 330, 376, 466, 490, 492, 716

Parking page   26, 241, 419, 421, 478-479, 481-483, 517, 576, 586, 667
  See also REGISTRAR PARKING PAGE
Parody and satire   xvi, 440-441, 736
Parties known to each other   xii, 36, 70, 129, 139, 150, 161, 165-166, 207, 246, 253,
  288, 290, 336, 378-379, 404, 408, 545, 570, 659, 719, 732
  See also STRANGERS
Partners   xiii, 42, 86, 126, 150, 155, 226, 228, 248, 253, 287, 289-291, 317-318,
  331, 338, 345-346, 355, 375-376, 415, 439, 549, 647, 666-667, 670, 718, 761
Passing off   71, 82, 91, 129, 153, 231, 364, 481, 515, 524, 605
  See also ABUSIVE REGISTRATION, CONCEPTUAL OVERLAP,
  COUNTERFEIT, TRADE AND SERVICE MARK INFRINGEMENT
Passive holding   xvi, xxvii, xxxi, 52, 71-72, 90, 94, 99, 117, 119, 155, 232, 379, 386,
  394, 400, 458-461, 477, 479, 499-500, 541, 580, 700
  See also CONCEIVABILITY TEST, TELSTRA, NON USE
Pattern of conduct   222, 394, 452, 508, 690
  See also HORIZONTAL, UDRP PARAGRAPH 4(b)(ii), VERTICAL
Pay Per Click   xv, 13, 156, 171, 186, 418, 474
  See also COMPETITIVE, HYPERLINK, PPC
Pejorative affixes   100, 107, 353, 428-429, 459
Pending applications (referring to trade and service mark applications *See* INTENT TO
  USE APPLICATION, SUPPLEMENTAL REGISTER
Pending applications (referring to trade and service mark applications)   xiii, 132, 137,
  312, 331, 339-340, 407, 410, 583, 741, 774
Pending court action   289, 298-299, 648
  See also COURT OF COMPETENT JURISDICTION, LEGITIMATE
  TRADEMARK DISPUTE, UDRP RULE 18
Permanent injunction   39, 262
Permission *See* AUTHORITY, UNAUTHORIZED
Permission (referring to grant of permission to use   68, 92, 111, 117, 121, 142, 167,
  246, 248, 259, 264, 295-296, 317, 319, 381, 422, 444-445, 465, 477, 496, 515, 554,
  578, 620, 625, 653, 740
Personal and family names (specializing in warehousing)   x, 162, 200, 205, 600, 651
  See also SURNAMES
Personal contact information   29, 439, 464
  See also GDPR, WHOIS DIRECTORY
Personal Jurisdiction   viii, xxi, 28, 44-47, 110, 302-303, 739-740, 743-745, 763, 765,
  772, 777
Personal knowledge proof *See* DECLARATION

Personal names (trademark rights)   viii, x, xiv-xv, xx-xxi, xxviii, 15, 17, 19, 28-29, 37, 39, 44-47, 60-61, 75-76, 79, 88, 103, 110, 126, 132, 134, 168, 170, 172, 180, 186, 193-194, 200-201, 204-205, 207, 212, 248-249, 289, 302-303, 315, 322-324, 327-328, 339, 369-373, 375-376, 381, 389, 394, 401, 405, 408, 426, 430, 439, 441, 451, 464, 469, 481, 486, 523, 525, 527, 540, 545, 548, 550, 553, 611-612, 614, 616, 623, 636, 676-677, 695, 700, 715, 728-729, 739-740, 743-745, 752, 763-765, 772, 777

Personalities (of such fame as to have common law rights)   xx, 17, 76, 88, 132, 193, 200, 327-328, 371, 373, 376, 700

Phishing   xvii, xix, 142, 248-249, 370, 423, 515-516, 522, 525-530, 540, 604, 606, 611-616, 744
See also SCAMMING

Phrases (common)   85, 94, 124-125, 147, 169, 200, 206, 208-209, 219, 287, 400, 423, 486, 502, 537, 624, 653, 688, 690, 695, 697, 725

Phrases (descriptive)   x, 66, 160-163, 168, 186, 194, 197, 213-214, 312, 326, 349, 567, 583, 593, 654, 670, 710, 714

Plan "B"   xx, 506, 659, 674, 679-680, 683
See also OBJECTIVELY UNREASONABLE, PRICING, RDNH

Plausible denial (referring to respondent's statements and totality of evidence)   76, 133, 170, 182, 188, 199, 370, 459, 477, 507, 513, 539, 546, 576, 670, 683, 699, 755
See also ACTUAL KNOWLEDGE, IMPLAUSIBLE DENIAL

Plausible inferences   554
See also INFERENCES

Pleadings   xvii-xviii, 41, 237, 255, 258, 310, 533, 536-540, 542, 553-554, 565-566, 596, 636, 665
See also CERTIFICATION OF PLEADINGS, EVIDENCE, SUMMARY JUDGMENT

Policy questions   vii, 15, 711

Political Speech   xvi, 59, 437, 441-442

Populate (Website)   284, 420, 470, 478-479, 481, 564, 748
See also CURATION, HYPERLINKS

Pornography   14, 205, 249, 435-436, 443, 462, 486, 610, 704, 774

Portfolio (ownership of a portfolio of domain names)   56, 61, 164, 195, 205, 229, 404, 499, 610, 627, 690, 696, 701-702

Postdating registration of domain name   xvii, xix, 40, 44, 89, 91, 113, 126, 131, 133, 142, 162, 168, 239, 305, 310-311, 313, 320, 336-339, 345, 386, 398, 455, 459, 462, 465, 476, 505, 538, 557, 559, 562, 564, 577, 579, 583-584, 605-606, 635, 644, 646-649, 652, 659, 663-664, 673-675, 679-680, 686, 700, 712, 714, 723, 734, 741,

754, 759, 764, 773, 790

See also NO ACTIONABLE CLAIM FOR CYBERSQUATTING

PPC links   xv-xvi, 13-14, 62, 144, 418-420, 469, 478-480, 532, 580, 595, 629, 667, 703, 709

See also HYPERLINKING

Precedent (precedential)   xix, xxviii, 28, 49, 67-68, 70-71, 73, 77-81, 83, 95, 223, 236, 255, 317, 327, 357, 440, 446, 590, 613, 617, 644-646, 681-682, 684, 696, 716, 759, 778, 785

See also CONSENSUS, CONSISTENCY, PREDICTABILITY

Predating (domain name registered before trade or service mark)   188, 210, 493, 595, 685

Predating disputed domain name   88, 137, 210, 239, 311, 313-314, 322, 328, 332, 334, 339, 466, 506, 647, 662, 675, 722, 781

See also FIRST USE OF MARK IN COMMERCE

Predictability   xxvi, 19, 67-68, 71, 73, 78, 84, 95, 106-107, 121, 255, 259, 587, 671, 690-691, 701

See also CONSISTENCY

Prefixes and suffixes   xiv, 140, 353-354, 367

Preponderance of Evidence   xviii, 40, 251, 256, 290, 365, 475-476, 516, 542, 550-552, 579, 583, 787

See also STANDARD OF PROOF

PRESUMPTION OF BAD FAITH   43, 131, 143, 149, 153, 165, 171, 215, 232, 239, 246-247, 255, 285-286, 289, 302, 305, 309, 335, 377, 380-383, 387-388, 392, 396, 501, 533, 552, 566-567, 579, 606, 630, 669, 718

Presumption of bad faith *See* NO PRESUMPTION. REBUTTAL

Presumption of bad faith (not conclusive of liability but open to rebuttal)   xii, 8, 39-40, 99, 206, 285, 309-310, 380, 453, 531

Presumptive evidence   xii, 39-40, 99, 285, 453, 531

Pretense   14, 290, 313, 411, 429, 445, 477, 511

See also IMPERSONATION

Pretextual   xv, 96, 107-111, 165, 198, 206, 227, 394, 428-429, 434, 437, 441, 450, 459, 532, 558

Prevailing in UDRP   18, 26, 36, 123, 188, 228, 253, 322, 466, 499, 535-536, 592, 676, 725, 749, 785-786

Preventing others from using common lexical material   185, 202-203, 232

Pricing *See* BUSINESS ASSETS, EXCESSIVE, EXTORTION, MARKET DRIVEN

Pricing of domain names   xxi, 64, 492, 499, 505-506, 544, 594, 598, 604, 637, 665, 678, 680, 716-717, 719, 721, 725, 729, 735, 738

Prima Facie *See* UDRP PARAGRAPH 4(a)(ii)

Prima Facie (lacking rights or legitimate interests)   xiv, 40, 53, 86, 94, 165, 209, 227, 244, 251, 253, 283, 305, 309, 320, 339, 346, 363, 365-366, 377-385, 387-388, 390, 392, 400, 411, 417, 426, 467, 471, 499, 501, 535, 540, 545-546, 552, 566-567, 570, 579, 606, 616, 625, 630, 632, 670, 697-698, 703

PRIMA FACIE CASE   40, 43, 140, 173, 309, 380, 383, 387, 476, 546, 579, 628

Primarily for the purpose   90, 107, 110-111, 124, 141, 143, 156-157, 171, 221, 250, 275, 300, 349, 353, 443, 452-453, 471, 474, 488, 497-498, 500-502, 504, 507, 511, 519, 539-540, 544, 549, 563, 578, 622, 627, 657, 664, 666, 684, 697, 699, 726, 729, 789

See also DISRUPTING THE BUSINESS OF A COMPETITOR, SELLING DOMAIN NAME TO COMPLAINANT

PRINCIPAL REGISTER   xiii, 100, 306, 312, 338-341, 741

Principal Register   19, 129, 311-312, 314, 560, 584

See also SUPPLEMENTAL REGISTER

Principles of law   viii, xii, xxvii-xxxi, 3, 8, 11-12, 14-18, 21, 27, 29, 36-37, 48, 56, 67-68, 70-74, 76-79, 81-84, 86-87, 89-90, 93-99, 101, 103, 107, 112, 119, 124, 134, 137, 144, 155, 179, 182, 210, 225, 232, 236, 238, 240, 245-246, 256, 259, 262, 270-272, 284, 300, 325, 339, 343, 350, 360, 372, 380, 402, 407-408, 410, 413, 427, 431-432, 436, 441, 449-450, 453, 457, 468, 472, 475, 516, 534, 548, 551, 554-555, 570, 590, 607, 617, 619, 693, 696, 700, 714, 726, 730, 737, 743, 762-763, 773, 788, 790

See also JURISPRUDENCE

Prior use (of mark in respondent's own business)   142, 780

Prior use (to support claim for common law rights)   312

See also COMMON LAW RIGHTS

Priority (of right or use)   xx, 32, 49, 162, 178, 181, 197, 207, 223-224, 290, 328, 336, 340, 391, 398, 400, 487-488, 500, 506, 520, 571, 577, 579, 650, 681, 690, 701, 703, 706

Privacy guard   288, 479, 592

Privacy service   xii, 23-24, 30-33, 42, 46, 61, 78, 81, 86, 104, 109, 114, 117, 120, 124, 126, 145, 151, 161, 163, 174, 180, 183, 191, 193, 197, 203, 209, 215, 217, 229-231, 233, 235, 240, 249, 251, 259-261, 263-265, 267, 277, 283-288, 295, 300, 316, 323, 329, 345, 347, 352, 364, 367, 370, 376, 384, 394-395, 401, 403, 405, 416, 420, 423, 426-427, 430, 434, 437, 439, 441, 451, 461, 463, 471, 473, 475, 479, 488, 500-501, 505, 507, 510, 515, 522, 526-528, 536, 539, 557-559, 563, 567, 573, 578, 583, 592, 594-595, 599-600, 609, 612-614, 616, 630, 637, 646, 648, 651, 653, 656, 663, 667-668, 672, 676, 681-682, 684, 687, 699, 702, 705, 709, 716, 724-725, 727

See also ANONYMOUS, PROXY SERVICE

Privileged communications   xviii, 580-582
See also SETTLEMENT DISCUSSIONS
Pro Se *See* UNREPRESENTED
Probabilities *See* BALANCE OF PROBABILITIES, STANDARD OF PROOF
Probative   85, 88, 145, 245, 390, 501, 623, 709
See also BURDEN OF PRODUCTION, BURDEN OF PROOF, NOT
PROBATIVE, STANDARD OF PROOF
PROCEDURAL EFFICIENCY   viii-ix, 37, 39, 104-106, 244, 246, 278, 282, 603
Procedural efficiency   ix, 42, 104, 106
Procedural Orders   xi-xii, 30, 175, 236, 240, 242, 244-245, 248, 260, 280-282, 548,
558, 560, 566, 671
See also UDRP RULE 12
Production (of evidence)   xiv, xviii, 22, 40, 42, 75-76, 143, 147, 152-153, 291, 294,
309, 319, 333, 346, 379, 381-387, 399-400, 411, 415, 451, 470, 524, 540-541, 543,
549, 570, 577, 579
Professional representatives   31, 43, 79, 126, 628, 635-636, 642, 644-646, 654-655,
662, 665, 681, 791
Proof   36, 249, 390, 426, 573, 606, 741
Proper party respondent   33
See also PROXY, WHOIS DIRECTORY
Property rights   15, 17, 20, 35, 50-51, 54-55, 88, 112, 298, 302, 603, 692, 711,
733-734, 756, 780
See also INTELLECTUAL PROPERTY
Protectability of marks *See* PROTECTABILITY OF MARKS (Issues Index)
Protected speech   xv, xxx, 7, 15, 31, 56, 100, 107-108, 110, 128, 130, 133, 137-138,
142, 155, 167, 181, 183, 194, 203, 212, 220, 231, 277, 291, 296, 322, 329, 353,
369, 374, 404, 408-409, 412, 428-431, 433, 435-437, 441-443, 445, 457, 486, 496,
526, 537, 561, 581, 604, 611, 613, 615-616, 691, 725, 748, 767, 770, 778
PROVIDED NO EVIDENCE   56, 342, 379, 501, 557, 573, 773
Provided no evidence   58, 91, 174, 196, 199, 239, 269, 506, 546, 572, 625
Providers (appointing panelists to adjudicate UDRP disputes)   xiii, xxx, 8, 11, 23,
30, 32-38, 41-42, 44-45, 47, 68, 112, 147, 197, 201, 234, 236, 243, 246, 251, 253,
256-257, 263, 272, 281-285, 287, 294, 296, 298-299, 337, 367, 369, 420, 447, 469,
513, 523, 586, 700, 711, 736, 788-789
Proving a negative (cannot prove facts known to respondent)   381, 385
See also UDRP PARAGRAPH 4(a)(ii)
Proxy as respondent   33, 283-284, 287
Proxy Registration *See* ANONYMOUS, PROXY AS RESPONDENT
Proxy registration   33, 283, 285, 287, 613

Proxy service   xii, 32, 233, 283-285, 287

Public auction   51, 58, 65, 124, 155-156, 195, 216-219, 396, 490, 492, 495, 533, 634, 672, 701, 703-705
See also DROPPED, HIGH BIDDER

Public domain (referring to free use of language)   xxv, 9, 102, 181, 221, 495, 634, 713
See also MONOPOLIZING COMMON LEXICAL MATERIAL, OWNERSHIP OF WORDS

Publish decisions) *See* RULE 16(B

Purpose for acquiring disputed domain name   52, 115, 146, 181, 204, 256, 386, 391, 414, 500, 514-515, 537, 622, 627
See also MOTIVATION

Q

Quintessential Cybersquatting   xix, 12, 490, 597, 603-606, 616, 644, 646, 711, 731, 748, 765-766

QWERTY keyboard   xix, 192, 348, 607-608, 646

R

RAA   30, 50-51, 284, 526, 614

Random Letters   xi, 94, 166, 213-214, 227, 258, 310, 690, 693, 714, 721, 757

Ransom   770, 777

Ransomware   614

Raw law   viii, 73
See also CONSTRUCTION

RDNH   xx, 126, 223, 265-266, 582, 638, 651, 657-659, 661, 664-665, 669, 680-682, 685-687, 749-750, 786
See also OVERREACHING MARK OWNER

RDNH (not requested)   xx, 481, 681, 684-685

Re-registration   xxii, 36, 53, 113, 401, 405, 455, 488, 628, 660, 730, 751-757, 759, 766, 785
See also RENEWAL OF REGISTRATION

Reactivation of domain name   749-750
See also SECTIONS 1114(2)(D)(4) and (5),

Reading across the dot (ignoring the dot separating the first and second domains)   xiv, 203, 347, 367

Reading across the dot (that is, ignoring the dot)   xiv, 203, 347, 367

Reasonable belief   19-20, 23, 25, 32, 38, 46, 60, 63-65, 81, 93, 112, 114-115, 118, 121, 149, 156, 170, 172, 175, 177, 196, 203, 228-229, 237, 242, 245-247, 251, 258, 260, 273, 279, 299, 302-303, 318, 355, 383, 386, 433, 444, 456, 458-459, 478, 493, 506, 517, 519-520, 542-543, 546, 551, 555, 557, 567, 569, 574, 578, 589, 595,

606, 620-621, 630-631, 636, 641, 649, 656, 659, 662, 664-666, 669, 672-676, 678, 680-681, 706-708, 714, 716-717, 719, 721, 723, 727, 737, 739-740, 744, 750, 766, 783-787, 790

Rebranding   x, 12, 91, 161, 164, 173-174, 226, 410-411, 439, 492, 622, 679, 708, 729, 741

Reclaiming dropped (lapsed) domain names   xvi, xxi, xxxi, 14, 50, 66, 137, 201, 328, 376, 471, 487-488, 490-492, 704-706
  See also DROPPED DOMAIN NAMES

Reconsideration   xviii, 12, 554-556, 559, 561
  See also REHEARING

Recusal of Panel   234-236

Redaction (omitting information from decision)   xii, 30-31, 33, 163, 175, 180, 248-249, 347, 403, 440, 475, 535, 682

Redirect domain name to one's own or infringing websites   xv-xvi, 80, 85, 145, 231, 416-417, 477-478, 525-527, 558, 588, 604, 613, 615-618
  See also INTERNET LOCATION, HYPERLINKING

Referential additions (that is referring back to the complainant)   xiv, 86, 140, 196, 219, 347, 353, 365-366, 394, 445

Refiled complaint dismissed   40, 245

Refiling Complaint   xviii, 12, 41, 70, 265, 288, 554-556, 558-560
  See also DISMISSED WITHOUT PREJUDICE, RECONSIDERATION, REHEARING

Refusing to register trade or service mark   584

Registered (domain name registrant)   11, 13, 22, 51, 107, 179, 186, 225, 227, 273-274, 277, 470, 600, 713, 728

Registered (Domain Name) *See* AUTHORITY, PERMISSION, SUBDOMAINS

Registering (justifying domain name registration)   563

Registrant representations   126, 454, 626
  See also GODADDY, REGISTRAR REGISTRATION AGREEMENT, UDRP PARAGRAPH 2

Registrar   9, 16, 30, 33, 283, 774

Registrar Accreditation Agreement   viii, 50
  See also RAA

REGISTRAR REGISTRATION AGREEMENT   xix, 35, 50, 625, 756

Registrar Registration Agreement   13, 32, 35, 626
  See also DROPPED DOMAIN NAMES, NON-RENEWAL OF REGISTRAR REGISTRATION AGREEMENT

Registration date versus Creation date   xxii, 745, 751

Registration in bad faith   xvi, 20, 36, 53, 64, 72, 91, 117, 136-137, 164, 174, 196, 260, 276, 283, 296, 313, 328, 401, 403, 421, 452, 455, 463-465, 469-470, 477, 493, 496, 506, 522, 568, 598, 626, 633-634, 656, 680, 682
See also CONJUNCTIVE BAD FAITH
Registrations incorporating two brands   131
Registry of dot com and dot net   7, 10-11, 13, 39, 165, 713, 733, 742-743, 745-746, 775
Rehearing   12, 554-555
See also REFILING, RECONSIDERATION
Relate back (referring to trade and service mark applications relating back to submission)   337, 407, 466, 584
See also COMMON LAW
Related Parties   402, 405, 487, 507, 756
See also CORPORATE FAMILY, LICENSEE; STRANGERS (UNRELATED PARTIES)
Related persons (parties)   xiii, xv, 316-317, 319, 401
See also CHAIN OF TITLE
Reliability (of evidence)   xvii, 255, 519, 537, 547, 623, 669
Remedies   12, 40
See also ACPA, STATUTORY REMEDIES, UDRP, URS
Removing to court of competent jurisdiction (respondent's action)   301
See also PARAGRAPH 4(k)
Renewal of Registration *See* RE-REGISTRATION
Renewal of registration   xxii, 4, 14, 36, 39, 50, 52, 80, 94, 113-114, 118, 120-122, 125-127, 260, 345, 455, 463, 471, 487-488, 639, 659-660, 665, 707, 730, 732, 751-752, 754, 756
Reopening Decided Case *See* REHEARING
Repackaging a rejected theory   ix, 122
Representations *See* REGISTRAR REGISTRATION AGREEMENT, UDRP PARAGRAPH 2
Representations (registration agreement and Paragraph 2)   viii, 36, 52, 118, 454
Represented by counsel   38, 126, 242, 247, 279, 327, 458, 567, 645-647, 651, 654, 660, 662, 664-665, 676, 681, 685, 734, 740
See also PRO SE
Reputation in the market   xx, 91, 149, 459-460, 568, 597, 604, 635, 677
See also EVIDENCE, GOODWILL, MISLEADING STATEMENTS OF FACT, MISSTATES THE LAW OR EVIDENCE
Reputation in the market/iW   17, 23, 63, 89, 133, 160, 163, 218, 228, 238, 332, 370, 397-398, 402, 464, 482, 497, 625, 630, 633, 655

Reputation of the complainant   151, 320-321, 667
See also NO REPUTATION
Reputation of the mark   26, 149, 182, 344, 458, 645
Reputation of the market   344
Res Judicata   12, 49, 555, 559-561, 749
Resale in the open market   62, 85, 125, 400, 605, 617, 688, 716, 718, 728
Researching   xi, 5, 29-30, 38, 60-62, 102, 126, 155, 225, 236-243, 245, 267, 270, 385, 408, 427, 431, 438, 499, 521, 533-534, 543, 546, 558, 560, 572, 578, 647, 664, 674-675, 681-682, 725, 789
See also UDRP RULE 10, RULE 12, WAYBACK MACHINE
Resellers (of domain names)   92-93, 146, 178, 198, 200, 202, 211, 215, 221, 230, 445-447, 450, 487, 501-502, 506, 574, 578, 689-690, 698, 709, 718, 759, 778
See also SECONDARY MARKET
RESOLUTION OF DOUBT   xii, xxvii, 62, 65, 89, 118, 175, 210, 234, 236, 241, 259, 261-262, 273, 287, 299, 319, 358-359, 361, 363, 371, 379, 405, 480, 489, 512, 517, 526, 536, 551, 607, 615, 617, 623, 669, 683, 725, 741, 789
Resolving Website   xxxii, 5, 10, 20, 70, 72, 82, 97, 99, 102, 109, 111, 145, 171-172, 225-226, 237, 242, 244, 250-251, 253, 284, 309, 327, 363, 396, 434, 440, 461-462, 502, 517, 521, 523-524, 602, 614, 618, 639, 736, 747, 760
Resolving website *See* CONCEIVABILITY TEST, PASSIVE HOLDING, TELSTRA
Respondent has neither a right nor a legitimate interest   40, 380, 383, 390, 392
See also RIGHTS OR LEGITIMATE INTERESTS, UDRP PARAGRAPH 4(a)(ii)
Respondent's rights   vii, xii, xx, 31-32, 85, 161, 163, 213, 216-217, 223, 283, 395, 400, 665-666, 683, 688
See also METES AND BOUNDS
Responding to complainant's inquiry to Purchase domain name *See* WHO CONTACTS WHOM
Responding to complainant's Inquiry to Purchase Domain Name   xxi, 727-728
Responding to complainant's inquiry to Purchase domain name   504
Responding to complainant's inquiry to purchase domain name   504, 715
Responding to complaint   162, 194, 254, 256, 390, 585
See also SUPPLEMENTAL SUBMISSION, UDRP RULE 5
Responsibility for Content (referring to respondent's website)   xii, xxx, xxxii, 32, 34, 38, 53, 58, 60-61, 95, 136, 173, 175, 248-249, 251, 264-265, 280, 290, 423, 455, 470, 483, 540, 626, 636, 643, 645, 655, 681, 684, 790
See also REDIRECT DOMAIN NAME TO ONE'S OWN OR INFRINGING WEBSITES
Retaining Jurisdiction over Dispute   61, 255, 292, 386

Retroactive bad faith   ix, xxviii, 14, 52, 69, 80, 88, 95-97, 113, 117-123, 125-127, 304, 395, 405-406, 453, 462, 465, 553, 571, 627, 633, 659, 669
See also RENEWAL OF REGISTRATION
Revenue Model Not Condemned   26, 328, 333, 417-418, 420, 469, 474, 478-480, 482, 506, 522, 546, 704, 768, 778
Reverse Domain Name Hijacking   xx, xxii, 11, 19, 38, 84, 92, 94, 126, 172, 215, 230, 264-266, 301, 338, 427, 457, 504, 506, 570, 582, 598, 635, 637-639, 641-643, 657-662, 664-671, 673-674, 676, 679-687, 700, 707, 712, 717, 742, 749-750, 758, 766, 782-783, 785-787
See also RDNH
Right by Priority   273, 307, 391, 400
See also PRIORITY
Right to a remedy   346
See also NO ACTIONABLE CLAIM, STANDING,
Rights or Legitimate Interests *See* INHERIT (NO BREAK IN CHAIN OF OWNERSHIP), NEITHER RIGHTS NOR, PRIMA FACIE, UDRP PARAGRAPH 4(a)(ii)
Rights or Legitimate Interests (have rights or legitimate interests)   8, 11, 66, 141, 188, 199, 206, 209, 224, 232, 291, 304, 336, 365-366, 380, 383-385, 388, 390, 434, 572, 660, 676
Rights or Legitimate Interests (lacks rights or legitimate interests)   8, 11, 18, 36, 40, 53, 89, 94, 161, 188, 206, 224, 291, 303-304, 309, 362, 365, 377, 379-380, 382-384, 388, 390, 396, 398-400, 416, 419, 434, 453, 455, 457, 476, 494, 534, 545, 552, 567, 579, 625, 642, 704
See also LACKS RIGHTS OR LEGITIMATE INTERESTS
Rights Protection Mechanisms (RPMs)   xxvi, xxviii-xxix, 18, 302
Rights to Lexical Elements in Design Trademark   xiv, 341, 344
Risk of others using the same term (where drawn from the common lexicon)   186-187, 262, 325-326, 522
ROLE OF DECISIONAL LAW   68, 82, 182, 258, 484, 508, 589
Role of decisional law   68, 82, 182, 258, 484, 508, 589
Role of local Law   79, 542, 736
Role of local law   106, 272
See also LOCAL LAW
Rule 408 of the Federal Rules of Evidence   581

S

Safe Harbor   27, 100, 411, 498, 531
Sanction   xx, 11, 19-20, 84, 92, 94, 126, 230, 241, 265-266, 271, 338, 407, 427, 457, 570-571, 595, 600, 636-637, 639, 642, 646-647, 650-651, 657-664, 667-669,

676-677, 680, 682, 684-685, 707, 717, 783

See also RDNH

Scamming   14, 100, 107, 436, 439, 449, 471, 481, 522, 524, 528-529, 540, 604, 612-615

See also FRAUD, PHISHING, SPOOFING

Schemes   xvii, xx, 14, 48, 70, 248-249, 277, 287, 370, 479, 481, 496, 525-527, 529, 531, 611-613, 615-616, 618, 662, 679-680, 762

Schmidheiny v. Weber   xxii, 404-406, 751-754, 756

Scope of the UDRP   xxviii, 8-9, 16-17, 27, 34, 71, 130, 165, 217, 250-253, 288-289, 291-294, 297, 300, 304, 434, 437, 524, 556, 566, 601, 619, 648, 651, 706, 732, 761

See also NOT WITHIN THE SCOPE

Scope of trademark   159, 225

Scope of trademark rights   123, 179-180, 219, 344, 350, 701

Screenshots   217, 329, 421, 492, 517, 545, 677

See also INTERNET ARCHIVE, WAYBACK MACHINE

Search obligations   53-55, 57, 66, 196, 664, 672

See also DUE DILIGENCE, OBLIGATIONS, PARAGRAPH 2 (REPRESENTATIONS OF GOOD FAITH), WIPO GLOBAL BRAND DATABASE

Search obligations (what is demanded?)   56-58, 404

Search procedures to assure hyperlinks not infringing   579

See also CURATION OF WEBSITE

Search processes to ensure no trade or service mark infringement   24

Searching (expected to search world databases)   53-54, 56, 59-60, 62-63, 98, 156, 219, 358, 464, 471, 534, 608, 626, 628-629, 631, 712, 789

Second Level Domain   59, 142, 178, 188, 220, 346-347, 367-368, 371, 425, 441, 476, 600, 607-608, 610, 641, 763

Second Staff Report   37, 69, 93, 120, 130, 250, 435, 440, 492, 675, 701

See also ICANN

Secondary Market   xx-xxi, 13, 154, 162-163, 399, 688-689, 693-694, 701, 703, 709, 711-712, 714, 729, 789-790

Secondary Meaning *See* COMMON LAW RIGHT, FUNCTIONING AS TRADEMARK

Secondary meaning   xx-xxi, 83, 132, 134, 190, 199, 314, 321-322, 325-326, 328, 330, 333, 335, 339, 341-342, 407, 416, 537, 584, 621, 688-689, 693, 709, 712, 714, 790

Secondary meaning (proof of)   323, 330, 333, 622

Selling domain name   142, 167, 386, 397, 400, 501, 503, 582, 653, 688-689, 691, 694, 698, 714, 721, 776

Semantic Value   7, 92, 393, 410-411, 441, 564, 591, 627, 630, 653, 714
Senate Report on the ACPA   19, 731-732
Senate Report on the ACPA, Anticybersquatting Consumer Protection Act   19, 731
Senior rights   167, 208, 258, 476
   See also FIRST USE OF MARK IN COMMERCE
Senior user   167, 208, 258, 476
Serial cybersquatter   510
   See also PATTERN OF SUCH CONDUCT, UDRP PARAGRAPH 4(b)(ii)
Service of Complaint and Notice   39, 47, 264, 275, 286, 321, 329, 585-586
Settlement discussions   xviii, 68, 103, 207, 580-582, 615, 710
Shifting burden rule   94, 305, 309, 365, 380, 382, 384, 387, 390, 484, 501, 550, 552, 579, 617, 624-625, 717
   See also REBUTTING COMPLAINANT'S CONTENTIONS
Silence   256, 258, 382, 444, 453, 456, 518, 541-542, 546, 552, 558, 565, 571, 580, 588, 623
   See also EVIDENCE
Similar and confusing   xiv, 348-350, 352, 357, 364
Similar But Not Confusingly Similar   xiv, 162, 172, 214, 218, 347-348, 357-360, 363, 365, 370, 578, 618
Sleeping on One's Rights   593, 652
   See also LACHES, STATUTE OF LIMITATIONS
Small Differences Matter   x, 172, 179, 191-192, 610
Social media   51, 131, 158, 207, 212, 238, 328, 333, 341, 398-399, 426, 486, 610, 764
Soliciting to sell   136, 142, 501-502
   See also BROKERS, UDRP PARAGRAPH 4(b)(i)
Sorkin, David E.   36
Source of value   ix, xxi, 147, 723
Speculating on domain names   xx, 211, 694, 697
Speculation (in a business sense)   xx-xxi, 211-212, 501, 623, 689-690, 694-698, 700, 702, 717, 722, 789
   See also ARBITRAGE
Speculation (in an evidentiary sense)   xviii, xx-xxi, 84, 115-116, 195, 211-212, 501, 516, 552, 596-597, 623, 665, 689-690, 694-698, 700, 717, 720, 722, 728, 789
   See also ABSENCE OF EVIDENCE, CONCRETE EVIDENCE, DOCUMENTARY EVIDENCE
Speculation in a business sense   211, 697, 699
Split of views   74, 97-98, 100-101, 103-104, 110, 113, 195, 289, 428, 430, 432, 443, 495, 632, 659, 730, 751, 761, 765-767, 785

Spoofing   xix, 14, 526, 604, 611-613, 615-616
  See also PHISHING, SCAMMING
Standard of Proof   xviii, 15, 40, 43, 53-54, 57, 62, 84, 93, 101-102, 114, 145, 196,
  202, 233, 236, 238, 251, 345, 352, 365, 396, 423, 430, 440, 446, 464, 484, 543,
  550-554, 579, 626, 631, 648, 665, 679, 687, 787
  See also BALANCE OF PROBABILITIES, CLEAR AND CONVINCING, MORE
  LIKELY THAN NOT, ON BALANCE
Standing but no actionable claim   340
Standing to maintain UDRP   xiii-xiv, 22-23, 27, 44, 85, 91, 94, 114, 133, 138, 191,
  239, 285, 291, 294, 302, 305-307, 309-311, 316-317, 319-321, 326, 329, 334-341,
  345, 347, 351, 363, 385, 391, 407-408, 416, 422, 440, 493, 546, 559, 568, 583,
  585, 619, 649, 656, 665, 677, 734, 741, 752, 761, 763-764, 767-768, 772, 775-776
  See also MARK PREDATES, MARK POSTDATES, REGISTERED MARK,
  UNREGISTERED MARK
Stare decisis *See* PRECEDENT
State trademarks   313-314
  See also US STATE REGISTRATIONS
Statute of limitations   xviii, xxvi, 42, 101, 105, 132, 177, 250, 272, 588, 590, 640,
  695
Statutory damages (over contract rights)   vii, ix-xi, xxi-xxii, 7, 10, 14, 19-21, 35,
  45-47, 73, 87, 128-129, 131, 160-161, 181-182, 204, 212, 224, 238, 250, 263, 391,
  396, 412, 457, 466, 484, 629, 713, 731-732, 734-736, 738, 748-751, 756-758, 763,
  766, 769-770, 774, 782-785, 787, 790
Statutory factors (good faith and bad faith)   736, 738
  See also ACPA
Statutory factors that define famous   129, 735-736, 738
Statutory remedies   181, 263, 750
  See also ACPA
Statutory rights   ix-x, 10, 14, 21, 87, 128, 160, 182, 224, 396, 466, 713
Stock ticker   307, 329
Stolen domain names   776, 778, 780
  See also FRAUDULENTLY TRANSFERRED
Strangers to each other (unrelated parties)   xii, 253-254, 288-290
  See also KNOWN TO EACH OTHER
Strength or Weakness of Mark   7, 17, 24, 351, 460, 515, 543, 705
  See also TRADEMARK
Structure   xiii, 190, 278, 303, 311, 318, 508, 664, 674, 747, 753, 773
Stylized mark   57, 341, 343-344, 506, 573
  See also DESIGN MARK, FIGURATIVE MARK

Subdomains   600

Subject Matter Jurisdiction   vii, xxi, 17, 19, 26-28, 45-49, 250-252, 302-303, 430, 600, 648, 733, 739, 763

Subjective bad faith intent   xiii, 25, 62, 177, 185, 207, 214, 223, 258, 328, 360, 518-519, 553, 678, 683
See also OBJECTIVE

Subjective intent   518, 553

Subsequent Bad Faith Use (ACPA jurisprudence)   455, 464, 515, 751, 755

Subsequent registrant   xv, 30, 32, 41, 208, 226, 260, 316, 394, 401, 404, 455, 559, 647, 730, 751
See also TRANSFEREE

substantial secondary   13, 324

Substitution of word or letter   xix, 119, 191, 233, 348, 355, 440, 608, 610

Substitution of words or letter *See* ADDING LETTERS OR WORDS TO DOMINANT ELEMENT

Successor registrants   29, 138, 162, 168, 171, 174-175, 177, 185, 210, 321, 401, 403-405, 493, 505, 592, 753

Suck cases   100, 102, 106-107, 306, 353, 429, 431, 436, 442, 459, 495
See also FAIR USE

Sufficient evidence   xiv, 144, 150, 195, 223, 227, 244, 270, 277-278, 312, 319, 329, 373, 375, 385, 387, 420, 427, 460, 477, 494, 516, 536, 548, 552, 567, 583, 593, 632, 647
See also INSUFFICIENT EVIDENCE

Suggestive (in the sense of evoking complainant's mark)   133, 140, 641

Summary judgment (UDRP pleading is equivalent to)   xviii, 5, 15, 17, 37-38, 41, 49, 68, 70, 203, 213, 293, 302, 369, 378, 408, 433, 541, 565, 576, 583, 739, 741, 744, 750, 755, 759, 764, 767, 770-771, 787
See also DOCUMENTARY EVIDENCE, PLEADINGS

Supplemental (supplementary or additional) submission   xii, 40-42, 236, 240, 242-244, 246-247, 305, 380, 469, 502, 533, 542, 566-567, 723, 744, 783

Supplemental Register   xiii, 100, 306, 312, 338-341, 741

Supplementary rules   243

Surnames   200, 216, 427, 716
See also FAMILY OF MARKS, PERSONAL NAMES

Suspending or terminating UDRP proceeding   299-300
See also PENDING COURT ACTION, UDRP RULE 18

T

Taking advantage (of trademark or mark owner)   15, 109, 148, 153, 166, 177, 182, 204, 206-207, 338, 368, 382, 397, 419, 458, 477, 497, 516, 524, 529, 606, 608-610, 625, 671, 688, 691, 701, 707, 724

Targeting the mark for its value   7, 150, 212, 391, 458, 575, 695
See also EXPLOITATION, NON-TARGETING OF COMPLAINANT OR ITS MARK

Tarnish (special meaning)   xv, 19, 107-108, 379, 385, 435-438, 516-517, 734

Telepathy, Inc.   22, 25, 39, 161, 185, 206-207, 228-229, 300, 313, 418, 421, 504, 576, 591, 597, 621, 676, 714-715, 717, 721

Telstra Corporation Limited v. Nuclear Marshmallows   99, 459, 461, 477, 670

Telstra test   90-91, 99, 232, 459, 461, 477, 670

Temporary specification   30, 239, 243

Temporary specification/iW *See* GDPR

Terminating proceeding   45-46, 263, 265-266, 294, 296, 299-300, 444, 745
See also WITHDRAW COMPLAINT

Territorial (referring to trade and service marks)   15, 20, 22, 59, 64, 183, 191, 321, 682, 711

Textual component (side by side comparison)   341, 343, 355, 362, 364
See also CONFUSINGLY SIMILAR, UDRP PARAGRAPH 4(a)(i)

The 3-Part Structure *See* STRUCTURE

The Marketplace (defining the strength of a mark)   ix, xxviii, 24, 49, 75-76, 128, 130-136, 141, 147, 158, 160, 163, 165-166, 184, 197, 203, 227, 231, 286, 321, 327, 343, 349-350, 371, 374-375, 398, 402, 412, 426, 440, 448, 541, 543, 583, 623, 625, 629, 631, 644, 655-656, 710, 738, 789

the parties supply   471

The right balance between the parties   16, 27-28, 62, 74, 195, 439, 736, 789

The UDRP Exploratory Group initiative   18, 36

Thief (purchasing from)   777
See also FRAUDULENT TRANSFER

Third and Ninth Circuit split   751-753, 755

Third Circuit   404-405, 730, 737, 751-753, 759

Third level domains   601

Third party links *See* CURATION OF WEBSITE

Threatening   103, 177, 296, 435, 587, 590, 661

Threshold   xviii, 40, 236, 250, 281, 285, 307, 320, 333, 338-339, 348, 351, 416, 559-562, 583, 604, 619, 677, 767-768
See also STANDING

Timing (as a significant issue in determining actual knowledge and bad faith)   ix, xiii, xvi, 44, 132, 135, 140, 149, 161, 190, 210, 264, 298, 306-307, 321, 324, 327, 390, 410, 462, 558, 577, 645, 655, 739

Timing (as a significant issue in determining actual knowledge)   168

Timing (as a significant issue in determining actual knowledgeand bad faith)   136, 476

Toeppen, Dennis   4, 99, 501, 690, 694, 731-732, 762-763

Tortious   vii, 3-4, 6, 14-15, 83, 108, 128, 132, 144, 309, 337, 518, 522-523, 548, 582, 588, 598, 603-604, 616, 627, 635, 663, 668, 683, 696, 717, 735, 761-762, 765, 779-780, 784

Totality of evidence or circumstances   26, 38, 89, 94, 99, 108-109, 111, 152, 174-175, 186, 194, 242, 259, 284-285, 349, 366, 388, 420, 442, 454, 456, 459, 471, 480, 502, 519-520, 605, 620, 622, 654, 701, 750, 759, 762, 771, 787
See also EVIDENCE, WEIGHT TO BE APPLIED TO THE EVIDENCE

Trade and Service Mark application and issuance of mark certification   xiii-xiv, xxxi, 10, 23, 59, 135, 159, 167, 173, 203, 210, 212, 239, 302, 312-314, 321, 330, 332, 336-337, 339-341, 355, 358, 370, 390, 399, 407-410, 415, 466, 508, 583-584, 597, 604, 651, 670, 682-683, 702, 731, 789
See also DESIGN MARK, PRINCIPAL REGISTER, SUPPLEMENTAL REGISTER, UNREGISTERED, WORD MARK

Trade and service mark infringement   xxv, 8-9, 130, 209, 219, 253, 289, 520, 590, 649, 668, 734-735, 768, 786

Trade and Service Mark value   92, 165, 194, 212, 296, 537, 591, 694-695, 703

Trade Name   xiv, 183, 224, 226, 238, 315, 325, 328, 335, 339, 371-375, 388, 457, 463, 570, 671
See also FUNCTIONING AS

Trade off third party trade or service marks   125, 196, 240, 382, 388, 426, 529, 580, 707

Trade-Related Aspects of Intellectual Property Rights   88

Trademark abandonment   395

Trademark Act of 1946 (Lanham Act)   6, 9, 12, 17-19, 48, 84, 99, 129, 312, 314, 323, 371, 419, 436, 501, 575, 584-585, 734-735, 737, 746, 748-749, 769, 776, 783

Trademark Clearinghouse   18

Trademark did not exist when the respondent registered to domain name   44, 292, 407, 549, 597-598, 651, 682, 787
See also NONEXISTENCE OF TRADEMARK AT THE TIME OF REGISTRATION OF THE DOMAIN NAME

Trademark registration   225, 306
See also USPTO AND NATIONAL REGISTRATIONS

Trademark Trial and Appeals Board   114, 286, 290, 299, 384, 472, 587, 589, 783

Traffics in   732, 748, 751, 766-767, 770

Transferee   29, 402, 404, 757

See also SUBSEQUENT REGISTRANT

Transferred (forfeiture of registration) to complainant   36, 38, 62, 156, 195, 218, 303, 356, 402, 434, 706, 737, 745, 753, 760, 766, 768, 780

See also REMEDIES, STATUTORY REMEDIES

Truthful   52, 83, 215, 259, 378-379, 382, 387, 424, 437, 441, 447, 449, 456, 537, 552, 623-624, 635, 639-640, 642, 670

See also CERTIFICATION OF PLEADINGS

TTAB   299

See also TRADEMARK TRIAL AND APPEALS BOARD

Typing errors   85, 209, 218, 607-608

Typosquatting   xix, 85, 88, 191-192, 203, 205, 218, 233, 349, 352, 355, 368, 426, 432, 527-528, 537, 588, 608-610, 616, 646

See also TYPING ERRORS

U

UDRP award vacated (annulled)   88, 768

See also SETTLEMENT

UDRP Elements *See* ELEMENTS

UDRP Jurisprudence   viii-ix, 8, 68, 82-83, 94-95, 98-99, 107, 121, 128, 233, 273, 325, 369, 375, 405, 445, 533-534, 603, 732, 793

UDRP PARAGRAPH 2   viii, xix, 24, 36-37, 51-54, 60, 72, 118-119, 389, 454-455, 492, 496, 625-626, 628, 631, 662, 671, 749

UDRP Paragraph 4(a)(i)   xiii, 27, 76, 87, 239, 258, 304, 306, 310-311, 313-314, 317, 340-341, 348-349, 355, 363, 373, 377, 392, 407, 412, 414, 520, 557, 607, 655-656

See also BYPASSING 4(a)(i) (UNNECESSARY TO ASSESS COMPLAINANT'S PROOF WHERE IT CANNOT PROVE BAD FAITH), STANDING

UDRP Paragraph 4(a)(ii)   xiii, 88-89, 171, 224, 258, 305, 307, 309, 362, 377-379, 383, 387, 392, 396-397, 417, 520, 535, 540, 552, 654, 656

See also RIGHTS AND LEGITIMATE INTERESTS

UDRP Paragraph 4(a)(iii)   xiii, 6, 72, 89, 113, 117-118, 120-122, 125, 259, 267, 296, 305, 307, 309-310, 349, 397, 400, 452-453, 456-457, 462-463, 468, 496, 508, 514, 519-520, 535, 540, 563, 654, 656, 723

See also REMEDIES

UDRP Paragraph 4(b)   90, 116, 119, 243, 406, 417, 459, 467, 496, 500, 574

UDRP Paragraph 4(b)(i)   xvii, 72, 78, 99, 119, 124-125, 137, 186, 197, 473-474, 490, 497-500, 502-503, 507, 519, 544, 563, 582, 604, 627, 729
See also PRIMARILY FOR THE PURPOSE OF SELLING
UDRP Paragraph 4(b)(ii)   xvii, 137, 267, 508-511, 519, 563, 604
See also ENGAGED IN A PATTERN OF PREVENTING OWNERS
UDRP Paragraph 4(b)(iii)   xvii, 405, 441, 465, 471, 511, 514-516, 563, 627
See also DISRUPTING THE BUSINESS OF A COMPETITOR
UDRP Paragraph 4(b)(iv)   xvii, 43, 59, 72, 78, 80, 117, 119-122, 126, 137, 152, 157, 171, 229, 304, 387, 428, 450, 453, 455, 457, 462, 465, 480, 495, 497, 514-516, 518-519, 528, 553, 563-564, 604, 618, 729
See also INTENTIONALLY ATTEMPTING TO ATTRACT FOR COMMERCIAL GAIN
UDRP Paragraph 4(c)(i)   xv, 116, 148, 188, 190, 211, 309, 378, 384, 387, 393, 396, 410-412, 414, 417-418, 454, 478, 490, 525, 531, 577, 585-586, 589-590, 596, 606, 697, 703-704
See also BEFORE ANY NOTICE OF CLAIM
UDRP Paragraph 4(c)(ii)   xv, 309, 378, 384, 392, 425, 508, 596, 610, 623
See also COMMONLY KNOWN BY
UDRP Paragraph 4(c)(iii)   xv, 7, 100, 107, 309, 379, 417, 427-428, 434-435, 463, 466, 478, 495, 516, 519, 525, 531, 588
See also MAKING A NONCOMMERCIAL OR FAIR USE
UDRP Paragraph 4(k) (10 business day stay of execution)   viii, 12, 28, 39, 45, 47-49, 106, 252, 298, 338, 405, 742, 745, 747
UDRP procedure   39, 42
UDRP proceedings   9, 37-40, 42, 250, 253, 552-553, 560
UDRP Rule 1 (Definitions)   21, 32, 37-39, 68, 84, 95, 104, 242, 255, 259, 261, 263, 284, 289, 537, 567, 789
UDRP Rule 2 (Communications)   36, 38
UDRP Rule 3 (The Complaint)   41, 44, 273, 277, 316, 565, 636, 681
UDRP Rule 3 (xiii) (Certification)   256, 636
UDRP Rule 3(c) (Consolidation)   273, 277
UDRP Rule 5 (The Response)   38, 254, 273, 640, 661
UDRP Rule 5 (viii) (Certification)   256, 273, 636
UDRP Rule 10 (General Powers of the Panel)   234, 236, 250, 254, 273, 288, 537, 547
UDRP Rule 10(b) (Fair opportunity to present its case)   234, 254, 268
UDRP Rule 10(c) (Consolidation)   268, 628
UDRP Rule 11 (Language of the Proceedings)   xii, 268, 636, 639, 669
UDRP Rule 12 (Further Statements)   xii, 236, 242-247, 264, 556, 567

UDRP Rule 14 (Default) 38, 175, 255-257, 259, 261, 543, 623

UDRP Rule 14(b) (Drawing inferences) 38, 175, 255-257, 259, 261, 543, 623

UDRP Rule 15(a) (Any rules and principles deemed applicable) xii, 21, 104, 238, 254, 256, 270-271, 405, 789

UDRP Rule 15(e) (Panel Decisions xx, 250, 266, 657-658, 667, 669, 681, 685-686

UDRP Rule 16(b) (Publication of decision) 68, 84

UDRP Rule 17 (Settlement or Other Grounds for Termination) 263

UDRP Rule 18 (Effect of Court Proceedings) 39, 289, 298

UDRP Rule 20 (Exclusion of liability) 36

UK Law 12, 48-49, 179, 270

Unauthorized *See* INCORPORATING TRADEMARK

Unauthorized (to register or use a mark) 4, 93, 107, 115, 291, 319, 371, 376, 386, 447, 449, 469, 525, 529, 589, 604, 606, 616-617, 697

Unbroken chain 401-403, 406
  See also CHAIN OF TITLE

Uncertain 3, 19, 38, 43, 47, 64, 113, 138, 210, 239, 259-260, 294, 307, 314, 349, 357, 363, 365, 456, 557, 659, 666, 701, 732, 747

Unclean hands 570

underlying ownership by a single person 401-402

UNFAIR COMPETITION x, xxi, xxv, 4, 67, 146, 149, 168, 186, 194, 197, 252, 271, 363, 405, 424, 447, 458, 465, 511-512, 602, 710, 730, 735

Unfair competition xxv, 186, 194, 252, 271, 363, 602, 730, 735
  See also UDRP PARAGRAPH 4(b)(iii)

Unfair use of domain name xxv, 102, 106-107, 186, 190, 194, 221, 232, 236, 240, 245, 248, 252, 265, 271, 286, 309, 363, 386, 428, 433, 435, 468, 483, 488, 522-523, 544, 602, 604, 678, 689, 706, 712, 730, 735, 764, 769, 786
  See also BAD FAITH, UDRP PARAGRAPH 4(b)(iv)

Uniform Rapid Suspension Policy (URS) 18, 527

Unintentional mistake (as to droping domain name) 705
  See also DROPPED DOMAIN NAMES

Unique (as a trade or service mark) 63, 75, 144, 157, 393-394, 494, 599, 632, 661

Uniquely associated (of a mark to its product or service) 632, 661

Uniquely within respondent's knowledge 379

Uniquely within the respondent's knowledge *See* SHIFT OF BURDEN RULE

Unitary *See* BINARY (CONJUNCTIVE)

Unitary (disjunctive) 118-119, 122

United Kingdom 132, 199, 225, 228, 261, 270, 332, 460, 503, 582, 626

United States iv, xxvi-xxvii, xxxi, 12, 15-16, 21-23, 53, 69, 77, 82, 103, 105, 108-111, 115, 129, 147-148, 151, 170, 174, 216, 226, 238-239, 248, 255, 270-272,

301, 325, 330, 333, 336, 341, 353, 366, 391, 422, 433, 435-436, 445, 452-453, 455, 484, 534, 561, 580, 584, 589, 599, 637, 653, 667, 677, 683, 692, 695, 707, 711, 718, 762, 772-773

Unknown (mark unknown outside its territory)   36, 70, 150
See also TERRITORIAL

Unlawful   xvii, 31, 52-53, 82, 94, 107, 131, 182-183, 211, 233, 258, 302, 389, 420, 445, 449, 454, 457, 463, 501, 511, 522, 546, 598, 606, 626-628, 688, 697, 710, 717, 747, 749-750, 761, 784

Unlawful purpose   52-53, 183, 454, 457, 522, 546, 606, 626, 628, 761

Unlikelihood   154, 600

Unprotected speech   xv, 110, 428, 431, 436

Unrebutted   94, 305, 309, 365, 380, 382, 387, 390, 501, 579, 617, 624, 717
See also BURDEN OF PRODUCTION

Unregistered marks   19, 75, 88, 114, 129, 134, 180, 184, 305-307, 313, 327-328, 338, 572, 579, 654, 741
See also COMMON LAW, STANDING

Unregistered trade or service mark   201, 225, 306, 313, 316, 329, 332, 371, 374-376, 471, 491
See also COMMON LAW RIGHTS

Unrepresented   36, 42, 637, 639, 649, 664-665

Unsolicited offers   xxi, 161, 243, 247, 285, 325, 503-504, 507, 651, 715, 721, 726-727
See also WHO CONTACTS WHOM?

Unsuitable defendant   xxi, 742-743
See also IN REM JURISDICTION

URS (Uniform Rapid Suspension System)   18, 527

US Circuit Courts
    Eleventh Circuit   xxii, 25, 45, 113, 455, 692, 751, 753, 755, 766, 768, 782
    Fourth Circuit   46, 102, 138, 433, 730, 736, 744-745, 754, 759, 767-768, 770
    Ninth Circuit   xxii, 45, 93, 97, 112-113, 138, 307, 404-405, 455, 730, 740, 745, 751-757, 759-760, 762-763, 766, 782, 785-787
    Second Circuit   735
    Seventh Circuit   113
    Tenth Circuit   759
    Third Circuit   404-405, 730, 737, 751-753, 755, 759, 785

US Constitution   21, 69, 101, 104-105, 238, 433, 517, 769, 783, 786
See also FAIR USE

US Court decisions   93, 179, 404

US Department of Commerce   4-5, 29, 711

US District Courts   xxii, 4, 8, 12, 15, 39, 45-47, 138, 236, 289, 300-301, 432-433, 442, 620, 730, 733, 737, 740, 742-747, 750-755, 757, 759-760, 763, 765-766, 769-770, 775-777, 782-787
  D. Utah   408, 759, 764
  District of Arizona   47, 138, 740, 744, 760
  District of Colorado   759
  District of Columbia   39, 301, 527, 733
  District of Florida   281, 777
  District of Nevada   740
  District of New York   199, 527
  District of Utah   408, 759, 764
  District of Virginia   620, 733, 742, 744, 760, 775, 782
  District of Washington   744
US House of Representatives
  House Report on the ACPA   10, 19, 603, 765
US law   xv, 21, 49, 88, 98-99, 101-102, 105, 110, 122, 132, 138, 162, 270, 272-273, 322, 404, 428, 432, 434, 441-442, 446-447, 547, 583, 696, 772
US PATENT AND TRADEMARK OFFICE   xvii, xxxi, 6, 14, 17, 23-24, 34-36, 38-39, 43-44, 51-55, 60, 63, 66, 75, 78, 84, 88-89, 91-94, 114, 118-119, 121, 124, 128, 131, 133, 135, 137, 145, 148-149, 151, 154-155, 162, 171, 173-174, 176, 188, 190, 202, 216, 232, 239, 245, 249, 254, 258, 275, 282, 285-286, 288, 291, 293, 295, 303, 305, 307, 310-311, 313, 320, 322-323, 328-341, 344-345, 347-348, 360, 371, 382, 384, 386, 388, 391-392, 394, 398, 401-402, 406, 408-409, 425, 427, 430, 434, 455, 458-459, 462, 464, 466-469, 471, 478, 482, 484, 488, 490-491, 493, 501, 505, 509, 511, 520-521, 524, 529, 533, 546-547, 550-551, 556, 558-559, 561-562, 564, 569, 572-574, 576-579, 584-585, 591, 593, 596, 599-602, 606, 618, 620, 626-628, 630-631, 633, 640, 642, 646-647, 651-655, 662-665, 671, 673, 675-677, 686-687, 690, 698-700, 702, 709, 712, 714-715, 719-720, 722, 732-735, 739, 741-742, 744, 748-749, 751-757, 759, 761, 763-764, 766-767, 769, 772-774, 778, 781, 784
US Senate
  Senate Report on the ACPA   6, 16-17, 19, 603, 690, 732, 748-749, 762, 765
US State Registrations   xiii, 314-315
  See also DEFERENCE
Use in connection with bona fide offering   314, 702
  See also NOT MAKING A BONA FIDE USE, UDRP PARAGRAPH 4(a)(i)
USPTO *See* UNITED STATES PATENT AND TRADEMARK OFFICE (USPTO)
USPTO and national Registrations   316, 652
USPTO Registrations *See* TRADE AND SERVICE MARKS

USPTO TRADEMARK MANUAL OF EXAMINING PROCEDURE   324, 330, 652

USPTO Trademark Manual of Examining Procedure 903.06   324, 330, 652

V

Valuable (referring to domain names)   xi, xx, xxviii, 7, 17, 26, 72, 90, 92, 105, 114-116, 130, 133, 135, 147, 149, 160, 168, 170, 174, 176, 180, 187, 197, 204, 207, 211, 214-215, 226, 228, 233, 271, 275, 332, 384, 400, 409, 415, 419, 440, 452, 468-469, 497-498, 500, 502, 506, 534, 564, 582-583, 585, 599-600, 605, 608-610, 621, 625, 650, 688, 690-691, 699-701, 708, 710, 714-716, 719, 723, 732, 736, 756
See also EXPLOITING THE VALUE OF MARKS, UDRP PARAGRAPH 4(b)(i)

Value, source of   ix, xxi, 147, 723

Value, source of (whether from mark or the descriptive or connotative domain name)   ix, xxi, 7, 88, 92, 106, 132, 142-143, 147, 197, 214, 221, 272, 409, 466, 498, 518, 688, 691, 697, 723, 728

Value, source of (whether from mark or the descriptive or connotative value of the domain name)   215, 400, 480

Vendor   xiii, 294, 296-297, 448, 521, 770
See also KNOWN TO

Verisign, Inc. (generally and registered domain names)   7, 10-11, 13, 39, 165, 713, 733, 742-743, 745-746, 775

Vertical pattern of conduct   191, 200, 233, 235, 287, 419-420, 426, 455, 508-510, 570, 591, 594, 609, 638, 662, 722

W

Wayback Machine   xi, 29-31, 37, 157, 175, 217, 237-238, 241-242, 260, 390, 543-545
See also ALLOWABLE RESEARCH, UDRP RULES 10 AND 12

Weak Marks   336, 630, 654, 693, 717, 724
See also LEXICAL COMMON, STRONG MARKS

Website Content   30, 362, 364, 436, 438, 470, 588
See also CURATION OF WEBSITE, HYPERLINK, PPC

Weight to be applied to the evidence   169, 516, 538, 551-552

Weslow, David   619

What law applies   viii, 22-23, 26, 67, 101

White Paper (NTIA)   5, 711

Who contacts whom?   xvii, 144, 162, 499, 502, 630, 707, 719, 722-723
See also ANONYMOUS OFFER (FROM COMPLAINANT), SOLICITING TO SELL, UNSOLICITED OFFERS

Who is the respondent *See* PROXY

Who owns what? (speaking of language)   xi, 170, 202
See also COMMODIFICATION

Whois Directory   vii, xxvii, 29-33, 38, 56, 88, 116, 142, 150, 175, 189, 191, 209, 231, 233, 238, 240, 244, 251, 260-261, 264, 272, 277, 282-288, 291, 318-319, 324, 335, 364, 375-378, 392, 401-402, 404, 416, 430, 445, 471, 480, 488, 492, 500, 526, 558-559, 566, 578, 582, 592, 594, 600, 609, 611, 613-616, 623, 637, 647, 652-653, 668, 673, 682, 699, 713, 724, 745, 771
See also GDPR

Wick, Brian   204, 433, 516

Widespread use of term   115-116, 128, 135, 141, 143, 167, 172, 187, 207, 226, 238, 240, 299, 371, 389, 393, 576, 578-579, 597, 599, 630, 696, 725, 789
See also MULTIPLY USED BY OTHER TO MARKET THEIR GOODS OR SERVICES

Widespread use of the term   393

Willful blindness   xvi, xix, 25, 59, 61-62, 96, 191, 262, 470, 484-486, 494, 606, 622-624, 626, 629-633, 676, 729, 735, 784, 786

WIPO Final Report   5-7, 10-11, 15-17, 20, 27-28, 34-35, 51, 54-55, 69, 78, 82, 84, 88, 92, 100, 104, 112, 161, 163, 250, 284, 300, 303, 336, 370, 392, 427, 432, 435, 462, 484, 550, 588, 593, 603, 625, 657, 692, 701, 711-712, 731

WIPO Global Brand Database   60, 66, 168

WIPO Overviews *See* OVERVIEW 1.0, 2.0, 3.0

WIPO Second Report   369, 371

Withdraw complaint   xii, 11, 28, 38, 138, 189, 234, 262-266, 495, 651-653, 658, 661, 663, 665-667, 679, 735, 745
See also DISMISSING COMPLAINT (AT COMPLAINANT'S REQUEST)

Without intent for commercial gain   7, 379, 428, 516

Without intent to take advantage of (or target)   207, 507, 694, 727

Without prejudice (complaint dismissed without)   xviii, 44, 51, 264-265, 277, 303, 356, 554, 556, 558, 560, 562, 581-582

Word combinations (compounds)   152, 157, 218

Word mark (distinguished from a word plus design mark)   129, 219, 231, 245, 342, 348, 506, 543

Word Plus Design Mark *See* DESIGN MARK

Words cannot be owned (or monopolized)   179, 194, 203
See also MONOPOLIZING COMMON LEXICAL MATERIAL

World Intellectual Property Organization   5-6, 67, 71, 112, 452
See also WIPO

ISSUES INDEX

A

A sufficient nexus to claim a right
  Standing to maintain proceeding   xiii, 315-316, 318-319, 401
ACPA
  Attorneys fees and statutory damages   784
  Creation date registration carries to successors Ninth Circuit   xxii, 745, 751
  Creation date registration does not carry to successor Third, Fourth, and Eleventh
    Circuits   xxii, 404-406, 751-754, 756-757
  Docket (challenges to UDRP awards and other cases)   xxii, 761
  Exceptional (to merit attorney's fees)   750, 784-785
  Factors in assessing bad faith   735-736, 738
  Federal Arbitration Act   737
  Fraudulent transfers   775-780
  In rem jurisdiction
    Abstention   746
    Requesting TRO   743
  Intent to Profit   733, 738, 745, 755, 770
  Registration date versus creation date test   732, 751-752, 755, 757-758
  Remedy for overreaching
    RDNH heavy and light   749
  Standing
    Not distinctive at the time of the registration of the domain name   733-734, 751,
    756, 761, 763
  Statutory damages   770, 782
  Subject matter jurisdiction   46
  UDRP award affirmed   25
  UDRP award vacated   88, 213
  Venue   744, 762
ACPA jurisdiction, the meaning of "transfer"   742
ACPA: Registration date versus creation date test   753-754
Acquiesced or consented to registration *See* AUTHORIZED (question as to whether or
  not) TO REGISTER DISPUTED DOMAIN NAME
Acquiring stolen domain names   777-778
See also FRAUDULENT TRANSFERS ACPA (Issues Index)
Acquisition of names from the common lexicon
  Generic, dictionary words, descriptive phrases   95, 161, 163, 200, 419, 506, 538
  Personal names   200

Acronyms *See* SHORT STRINGS OF LETTERS > COINCIDENTALLY CORRESPONDING TO ACRONYMS OF MARKS

Acronyms treated as generic words   172
  See also ACRONYMS (General Index)

Actionable claim (no actionable claim)   38

Active website not the only legitimate use *See* EMAIL, FTP AND OTHER DOMAIN NAME USES (Issues Index)

Actual knowledge   59, 62, 86, 115, 137, 143, 170, 172, 195, 232, 331, 365, 382, 388, 393, 410-411, 426, 471, 494, 507, 553, 699
  See also ANTICIPATORY INFRINGEMENT (Issues Index); TARGETING (Issues Index)

Actual knowledge versus *See* CONSTRUCTIVE NOTICE (General Index and Issues Index)

Addition of letters, words and phrases *See* PREFIXES AND SUFFIXES (General Index and Issues Index)
    Trademarks of more than one word   191, 352, 472

Addition of word *See* REINFORCES TARGETING COMPLAINANT'S MARK

Addition of word referential to complainant *See* REFERENTIAL
    Reinforces targeting complainant's mark   219-220, 350, 365-366, 458, 472, 586

Adversarial versus inquisitorial system   237, 536

Adverse inference   198, 259, 453, 460-461, 534, 654
  See also Rule 14(b) DRAWING INFERENCES (Issues Index)

Allowable research   241
  See also LIMITED RESEARCH, RULES 10 and 12 (Issues Index)

Altering use of a disputed domain name after notice of alleged infringement
    Discontinuing infringing use no cure for past use   146, 462, 531-532, 588, 770

Anonymity (guarded by privacy shield)   vii, 31-33
  See also PRIVACY SERVICE (General Index); RULE 1 HOLDER OF DOMAIN NAME (Issues Index)

Anticipatory infringement   xv, 44, 152, 305, 319, 335, 354, 407-409, 522, 579, 664
  See also ACTUAL KNOWLEDGE, INSIDER KNOWLEDGE (General Index)

Appeal of UDRP Award *See* DE NOVO "APPEAL" TO COURTS OF COMPETENT JURISDICTION

Approached by complainant *See* WHO CONTACTS WHOM? > NOT IN VIOLATION and VIOLATION (Issues Index)

Appropriating the value of the mark *See* ATTEMPTING TO ATTRACT (Issues Index); VALUE AS MEASURED BY THE WORTH OF THE DOMAIN NAME

Arbitraging domain names as a business   xv, 410-413
    Bona fide offering of goods   497, 501, 656, 690-691, 694
    Not condemned as violating 3rd-party rights   xxi, 727-728

Assessing strength of mark   129, 131, 134-136, 140, 142, 167, 262

Assessing the date from which 4(a)(ii) and 4(a)(iii) are measured   23, 113, 162, 174-175, 259, 398-400

Associated Exclusively with complainant   22, 82, 155, 171, 185, 188, 194, 207, 214, 239, 354, 359, 425, 441, 493-494, 496, 586, 604, 632, 678

Attempting to attract

Appropriating the value of the mark   103, 498, 518-519, 691

Attorneys (as associates, in-house, etc) *See* DEMAND FOR PROBATIE EVIDENCE > ATTORNEYS STATEMENTS NOT EVIDENCE

Names do not function as trademarks *See* CORPORATE OFFICERs AND ATTORNEYS

Attornies

Names do not function as trademarks   372

Authorized (question as to whether or not) to register disputed domain name

Authorized (acquiesced or consented)   445

Not authorized   295, 307, 331, 446, 496, 525, 529

Authorized (question as to whether or not)to register disputed domain name *See* NOMINATIVE FAIR USE

Awareness or knowledge of complainant or its mark   23, 124, 545

See also ACTUAL KNOWLEDGE

B

Backordering, earlier acquired by respondent   252

Bad faith use alone

Not actionable for abusive registration   439, 462-464

Beneficial owner   xii, 284

Better right theory

No better right to domain names registered in good faith   124, 176-178

Better right theory debunked   178

Binary version unitary   ix, 117, 120, 122

Binary versus unitary construction of 4(a)(iii) and 4(b)(iv)   121-122, 125-126, 453

Branding *See* REBRANDING PREDATING ACQUISITION OF DOMAIN NAME (Issues Index); REBRANDING SUBSEQUENT TO DOMAIN NAME (Issues Index)

Brands (separate and unrelated incorporated in domain name)   354-356

Building the law   77-80, 85, 400, 688

See also CONSENSUS (ACHIEVEMENT OF) (Issues Index)

Bulk transfers *See* HIGHER DUTY FOR BULK TRANSFERS, NO EXPLOITATIVE INTENT (Issues Index)

Burden of proof

Onus on complainant   83, 153, 206, 245, 247, 476, 567, 627

Proving respondent lacks rights or legitimate interests   xiv, 331, 378-380

Shifting burden   40, 140, 173, 206, 379, 381, 383, 387, 628

Business issues outside scope of Policy   250-251, 253, 291-293, 793

Business leaders (no trademark right no standing)   88, 370-371

Buying and selling domain names *See* ARBITRAGING DOMAIN NAMES AS A BUSINESS (Issues Index)

C

Cease and desist notice

Timing fixes date of awareness of trademark

Effective in favor of complainant   275, 517, 585, 587-588

Effective in favor of respondent   411, 595, 659, 674

Certification of pleadings   81, 638-640, 643, 645-646, 681

See also RULE 3 (xiii) AND RULE 5(c)(viii); RULE 3(xiii) AND RULE 5(c)(viii) > FALSE CERTIFICATION (OR NONE) (Issues Index)

Chain of title

Standing to maintain proceeding

Transfers of domain names between commonly-controlled entities   401-403

Changing website *See* ALTERING USE OF DISPUTED DOMAIN NAME AFTER NOTICE (Issues Index)

Choosing generic words and phrases

Registrations in good faith   64, 169-170, 467-468

Circuit Court split

Creation date jurisprudence   138, 753, 756-758

Re-registration date jurisprudence   752, 754-755

Circumstantial evidence   94, 488, 502, 539, 541, 617

Clear-cut cases of cybersquatting   9, 37, 253, 552

Click through traffic/revenue   156, 171, 186, 418, 474, 478, 480, 483, 778

See also PAY PER CLICK

Coined words *See* COINED WORD (ONE OF A KIND) (General Index)

Commentary and criticism   101, 104, 107, 109, 111, 429, 431, 434-435, 439, 444, 448, 495, 527, 736

Commercial gain

Creating or not creating likelihood of confusion   457, 479, 513, 517, 519, 538, 553, 561, 563, 625

Common and coined words *See* ONE OF A KIND VERSUS NONE OF A KIND

Common law right *See* UNREGISTERED RIGHTS MUST BE EARNED (Issues Index)

Registration of a domain name predating registration disputed domain name not evidence of common law right   321

Common versus coined words   149, 155, 165, 175, 195, 491, 633, 718
See also GENERIC, DICTIONARY WORDS, DESCRIPTIVE PHRASES
Common words and descriptive phrases
   No fixed association with mark   181, 183, 185, 678
Common words and expressions   167
Commonly known by *See* UDRP 4(c)(ii) (General Index and Issues Index)
Competitors (defining who they are)   125, 129, 170, 420, 482, 496, 512, 515, 539, 563, 580, 735
Complainant dismissing case
   Does not require permission   263, 745
Complainant's own evidence indicates that the Complainant was willing to purchase the disputed domain name for USD 10,000   499
Complainants do not own the lexical material of their marks *See* REGISTERING A TRADE OR SERVICE MARK NOT OWNERSHIP OF LEXICAL CHOICE (Issues Index)
   But have the right to claim legal relief against infringement   161, 206-207
complainants have the burden   153, 247, 476, 567, 627
Complex cases
   Inappropriate for UDRP
      Courts of competent jurisdiction   251, 253-254, 290, 292, 298, 300, 459, 554, 648, 667, 723, 793
Composition of domain name
   Qualifying for free speech protection   100-103
   See also FREE SPEECH
Concurrent court proceedings *See* RULE 18(a)
   Discretionary with Panel to terminate or proceed to determination   298-301
Confidential and privileged communications
   Not binding on Panels   581-582
Confusing similarity *See* UDRP 4(a)(i) (General Index and Issues Index)
Consensus *See* RISE AND DEVELOPMENT OF A JURISPRUDENCE (Issues Index)
Consensus (achievement of)   79-81, 681
Consequences of default
   Does not in itself constitute an admission   36, 198, 255-257, 658
Consistency and predictability   68, 70, 79-80, 84, 106, 110, 120, 259, 694
Consistency in the types of domain names acquired   718
Consolidation
   UDRP 4(f) and Rule 4(c)

Consolidating complainants   275

Many holders of domain names   275

See also COUNTERFEIT (General Index)

Puppeteer holder of domain names   277

See also CONSOLIDATION COMMON HOLDER (General Index)

Constructive notice   390, 412, 573, 575-576, 646

Consumer confusion and deception

Heavy protection as the distinctiveness of mark grows   20, 423, 526

See also LIKELIHOOD OF CONFUSION (General Index)

Narrow protection as the value of a mark declines   358

Contract disputes *See* BUSINESS ISSUES OUTSIDE SCOPE OF POLICY (Issues Index)

Contractual obligations to avoid infringement   52, 55, 57-59, 455, 470, 626

Copyright infringement

Digital Millennium Copyright Act

Take down notice   605

Copyright infringement evidence of bad faith   152, 252, 289, 463, 605

Corporate officers and attorneys

Names do not function as trademarks

No trademark, no standing   370-372

Counter and unsolicited offers   xxi, 161, 504, 507, 715, 721, 726-727

See also UDRP 4(b)(i) (Issues Index)

Counterfeit and pirated goods

Famous and well-known marks

Offering counterfeit goods   604, 617-618

Counteroffering when approached by complainant   161, 174, 726

See also WHO CONTACTS WHOM?

Creation-date respondent   xxii, 174-175, 455, 651, 655, 751, 757

Credibility (incredulity) of evidence   167-168, 549, 637, 643

See also EVIDENCE (OVERSTATING AND MISLEADING); RELIABILITY OF EVIDENCE (CREDIBILITY)

Credible   165, 169

Not credible   64, 169-171, 539, 547-548, 550, 633

Credible narrative   xvii, 547

Cross-fertilization   69

See also DOMESTICATING PRINCIPLES FROM US DECISIONAL LAW (General Index)

Curating content of website   171, 461, 709

Cybersquatters *See* DOPPELGANGERS OR CYBERSQUATTERS (DISTINGUISHED FROM DOMAIN NAME INVESTORS)

Cybersquatting *See* QUINTESSENTIAL (Issues Index)

D

De novo "appeal" to courts of competent jurisdiction   xxi-xxii, 742, 769, 771

Deceptive *See* DECEIVE, DECEPTION, DECEIT (General Index)

Default in responding *See* CONSEQUENCES OF DEFAULT (Issues Index)

Deficient of proof

   Failing to offer documentary evidence   21-24, 43, 56, 115, 150, 154, 165, 257, 395, 655, 671

Degree of distinctiveness in the market

   Value of mark vs value of domain name independent of mark   135, 477

Delay in giving notice *See* LIMITATIONS AND LACHES (Issues Index)

Delivery of malware

   Malicious registrations   xix, 526, 614-615

Demand for probative evidence   85, 245, 334, 540

  See also EVIDENTIARY DEMAND (Issues Index), PROBATIVE (General index)

   Attorneys statements not evidence   540

Demise of retroactive bad faith   ii, iv, vii, ix-xxii, xxv-xxxii, 3-26, 28-80, 82-86, 88-233, 238-242, 245, 247-265, 267-271, 273-323, 325-559, 561-635, 637-791, 793

Demonstrable preparations *See* UDRP 4(c)(i) (Issues Index)

   Some act(s) that demonstrates the assertion   98, 413-417, 478

Denial of having knowledge *See* IMPLAUSIBLE (Issues Index)

Denial of having knowledge of Complainant or mark *See* IMPLAUSIBLE, PASSIVE (Issues Index)

Deprive registrant of its registration   216

  See also RDNH AND RULE 15(e)

Derivative of the value of the mark   131-132, 157, 472

  See also APPROPRIATING THE VALUE OF THE MARK (Issues Index); IMPERSONATION TO BENEFIT FROM THE VALUE OF THE MARK (Issues Index); VALUE OF MARK VS VALUE OF DOMAIN NAME INDEPENDENT OF MARK (Issues Index)

Descriptive marks

  Distinctive   134, 212, 252, 311

  Not distinctive   63, 86, 92, 95, 135, 149, 157, 163, 179-180, 185-186, 203, 215, 219, 223, 262, 314, 325, 338, 340-341, 349, 358, 361, 367, 385, 394, 419, 458, 476, 506, 513, 572, 580, 650, 705, 715, 721

Descriptive marks for

  Everyday services   512-513, 547

Descriptive meaning undercuts exclusivity   13, 57, 92, 95, 135, 137, 139, 145, 149, 151, 163, 167, 186, 194, 203, 215, 219, 252, 262, 314, 322, 325, 333, 340-342,

347, 358, 361, 374, 394, 419, 458, 471, 476, 489, 506, 513, 538, 568, 573, 584, 597, 642, 654, 715, 720-721

Descriptive of a business
  Lawful registration   139, 361, 389, 450, 538, 578

Descriptive terms, narrow of protection   233, 348, 357-361

Development of a jurisprudence   77-81, 85, 88, 95, 400, 688

Different line of business   468, 470

Directing / Redirecting   xvi, 477

Disclaimer *See* DISCLAIMER (General Index)

Disclaiming association
  Effective disclaimer   424-425
  Not effective disclaimer   xv, 422-424

disinclination of the courts to take words of ordinary meaning out of common usage
  See REPUTATION > WHAT MAKES A MARK DISTINCTIVE? (Issues Index)

Dismissing complaint without prejudice   560-562
  See also REFILING COMPLAINT

Distinctive and distinctiveness   135, 139, 219

Distinctiveness in the market (coined terms)   x, 149, 154-155, 176, 220, 718

Distinctiveness measured by market presence   129, 156, 189

Distributor and dealership agreement
  Within or outside scope of Policy   293, 645

Diverting domain name to a competing website   379, 417, 457, 478, 515-516, 525

Divesting registrants of their domain names
  Justified by concrete evidence of bad faith   117, 225, 460, 465, 753
    See also EVIDENTIARY DEMANDS

Divesting, not justified   225, 460, 465-466, 753

DMCA take down of websites   605

Doctrine of first come first served *See* FIRST COME FIRST SERVED

Domain names incorporating two marks   356

Domestication of domestic law   21, 68, 82, 99, 270, 445, 603, 788

Dominant element generic or descriptive *See* FIGURATIVE MARKS (Issues Index)

Doppelgangers or cybersquatters (distinguished from domain name investors)   xix, 12, 14, 90, 153, 164, 627

Dropped domain name   xxi, 14, 50, 66, 195, 201, 487-488, 490, 702, 705-708
  See also PUBLIC AUCTION (General Index and Issues Index)

Dropped domain names *See* RECOVERING DROPPED DOMAIN NAMES (Issues Index)

Due diligence (failure by complainant)   638, 722

Due diligence search to avoid infringement   25, 56, 58, 63-66, 404, 485, 493, 627, 631, 638
See also DUE DILIGENCE (General Index); WILLFUL BLINDNESS (Issues Index)
Duping Internet users   451, 524-528, 612, 615
See also PHISHING, SPAMMING AND RELATED FRAUDULENT SCHEMES (Issues Index)
Duty to search (when does the duty arise?)   25, 53, 56-57, 60, 66, 404

E

Earlier registered domain names no evidence of common law rights   330
Email, FTP and other domain name uses
   Domain names not exclusively used for website   xv, 388, 406-407, 460
Employees holding in their own names with permission   296, 444, 477
Employees, vendors, and service providers
   Unauthorized registration   294-296, 522
Error before consensus   75, 164, 172, 195, 232, 244, 457, 576, 696
Evidence (overstating and misleading)   164, 539, 599
   See also RULE 15(e) RDNH
Evidence of bad faith
   Copying complainant's page, trademark, and or copyright logos   605
Evidentiary demands
   Significantly greater the weaker the mark   43, 258, 562, 635
   Speculation or conjecture   149, 247, 258, 456, 539, 542, 544, 568-569, 596
Expired Registration Recovery Policy ("ERRP")   14
Exploitative intent *See* NO EXPLOITATIVE INTENT; UDRP 4(a)(iii)
Exploitative intent (UDRP 4(b))   12, 108, 116, 146, 148, 166, 458, 506, 513, 699, 716
Extensions of time to submit responses (only if reason is exceptional)   628

F

Fabricated evidence   523
   See also CONSUMER CONFUSION AND DECEPTION
Failure to prove one of the elements makes further inquiry into the remaining elements unnecessary   310
Fake goods *See* COUNTERFEIT AND PIRATED GOODS, OFFERING FAKE GOODS OF COMPLAINANT (Issues Index)
False association with mark owner *See* COMMON WORDS AND DESCRIPTIVE PHRASES, DISCLAIMING ASSOCIATION, NOMINATIVE FAIR USE (Issues Index); UDRP 4(b)(iv)

Fame as marker of knowledge   23-24, 43, 129, 135, 141, 144, 151, 212, 310, 388, 564, 570, 572, 714
  See also VALUE OF MARK VS VALUE OF DOMAIN NAME INDEPENDENT OF MARK
Fame defined   129, 142, 144, 147, 310, 370
Family of marks   x, 158-159
Famous marks (defined in Lanham Act)   140
  See also ASSESSING STRENGTH OF MARK
Fan site   427, 439, 594
Fanciful *See* STRENGTH BY LEXICAL INVENTION
Figurative marks
  Word and design combination
    Dominant element   xiv, 340-342
First come first served
  Doctrine of   167, 225
First come first served doctrine *See* FIRST TO REGISTER
First come-first served
  Doctrine of   161, 163, 195, 197, 292, 321, 330, 333, 680, 712
First to register
  First come-first served
    Doctrine of   163, 223-226, 476
    Doctrine of first come-first served *See* EXPLOITATIVE INTENT
First use in commerce
  Alleged date not evidence   329-330
Forfeiting domain names *See* DIVESTING REGISTRANTS OF THEIR DOMAIN NAMES (Issues Index)
Fraudulent schemes *See* PHISHING, SPAMMING AND RELATED FRAUDULENT SCHEMES (Issues Index)
Fraudulent transfers UDRP   619-620
Free speech   ix, 98, 100, 103, 107-109, 431, 438, 442, 495
Further statements *See* SUPPLEMENTAL SUBMISSIONS

G

General Data Protection Regulation   vii, 29, 31
  See also GDPR
General powers of the Panel   234, 242, 247, 284-285, 534
  See also RULE 12 PROCEDURAL ORDER (Issues Index)
Generic words
  Combined into distinctive phrases   134-135
Generic words creating generic phrases

Noninfringing   23, 65, 115, 155, 189, 209, 216, 218, 697

Generic, Descriptive *See* GENERIC WORDS CREATING GENERIC PHRASES (Issues Index)

Geographic location of services *See* UDRP 4(b)(iv)

GoDaddy Registration Agreement *See* OWNERSHIP OF DOMAIN NAMES > NO OWNERSHIP

Good faith registration *See* BETTER RIGHT THEORY > NO BETTER RIGHT TO DOMAIN NAME REGISTERED IN GOOD FAITH

Good faith registration followed by bad faith use   464-466

Goodwill and reputation   143-144

Goodwill and reputation (does not travel outside of its market)   150, 390, 678
    See also REPUTATION > WHAT MAKES A MARK DISTINCTIVE?

Goodwill and reputations *See* MARKS ASSOCIATED WITH A PARTICULAR OWNER

Grammar *See* PUNCTUATION, HYPHENS, AND SPACES

H

Heritable *See* RIGHTS SURVIVING DEATH (Issues Index)

Higher duty for bulk transfers   60-63, 626

Historical information redacted (lack of creation-date registrant and registration date of successor)   29-31

I

Identity theft *See* NAME REDACTED

Impersonation (false impression of an association)   xv-xvi, 88, 101, 431, 433, 437, 440, 451, 485, 495-496, 524-525, 527-528

Impersonation and pretextual *See* IMPERSONATION, PRETEXTUAL (General Index)

Impersonation to benefit from the value of the mark *See* ATTEMPTING TO ATTRACT (Issues Index)

Impersonation to commit fraud *See* PHISHING AND OTHER FRAUD (Issues Index)

Implausible
    Denial of having knowledge of complainant   26, 55, 143, 166, 173, 467, 542, 546, 573, 631-632, 790

Implausible reason for acquiring the domain name   546, 699, 755

In mind *See* MARK "IN MIND" AND TARGETING (Issues Index)

In rem jurisdiction   xxi, 19-20, 39, 45-46, 138, 544, 619, 733, 742-746, 765, 778-780

in the record   63, 145, 159, 173, 258, 269, 278, 294, 309, 317, 372, 401, 456, 505, 542, 570, 580, 625

Inadvertent failure to renew domain name *See* DROPPED DOMAIN NAME (General Index and Issues Index)

Increased recognition of Panel's Obligation under Rule 15(e)   xx, 666, 675-676, 680-681

Inferences (drawing from material and/or circumstantial evidence *See* RULE 14(b) DRAWING INFERENCES

Infringement, but not of this complainant *See* UNRELATED THIRD PARTY (Issues Index)

Initial interest confusion   xvi, xxviii, 100-102, 365, 422, 442-444

Initiating contact *See* WHO CONTACTS WHOM?

   Offering to sell disputed domain name *See* UDRP 4(a)(iii) and UDRP 4(b)(i) (Issues Index)

Injunctive relief *See* EX PARTE INJUNCTION (General Index); INJUNCTION (General Index); SUING FOR INJUNCTIVE RELIEF (Issues Index); SUING FOR INJUNCTIVE RELIEF (Issues Index)

Insufficiency of proof   332, 453, 534

   See also EVIDENTIARY DEMANDS; FAILING TO OFFER DOCUMENTARY EVIDENCE (Issues Index)

Intent to profit   732-735, 738-739

Internet archive *See* WAYBACK MACHINE (Issues Index)

Investing in domain names   394, 503

   See also ARBITRAGING DOMAIN NAMES AS A BUSINESS (Issues Index)

Invitation to refile complaint   557, 560-562

   See also Refiling complaint

J

Jurisprudential Overview   67-68, 70, 99

   See also WIPO OVERVIEW 1.0, WIPO OVERVIEW 2.0, WIPO OVERVIEW 3.0

K

Knowledge *See* ACTUAL KNOWLEDGE VERSUS CONSTRUCTIVE NOTICE (Issues Index)

L

Laches *See* LIMITATIONS AND LACHES

Landing page   xvi, 479, 481, 483

Laundering past infringement 146
See also ALTERING USE OF A DISPUTED DOMAIN NAME AFTER NOTICE
OF ALLEGED INFRINGEMENT
Lawful offers to sell, rent, etc. 499
See also UDRP 4(b)(i) RESPONDENT
Legitimate interests *See* RIGHTS OR LEGITIMATE INTERESTS, UDRP 4(a)(ii),
REBUTTING PRIMA FACIE CASE (General Index, Issues Index)
Leverage 769
leverage *See* LEVERAGE (General Index)
Lexical choices associated with one particular mark owner 148, 176-177
Lexical commonplace *See* MONOPOLIZING (General Index and Issues Index)
Liability of Domain Name Registrar
No liability 763
Licensee *See* A SUFFICIENT NEXUS TO CLAIM A RIGHT (Issues Index)
Likelihood of Confusion xvii, 520-522
Limitations and laches
Effect of delay in giving notice or commencing proceedings 132
Favoring Complainant 588-590
Favoring Respondent xviii, 590-591, 593-595
Limited Panel research
Rules 10 and 12 30, 237-239, 242
Limits to speech? 437-439, 464
Local law 21, 105-106, 110, 272
See also RULE 15(a)

M

Mark "in mind" and targeting
Intentional (bad faith) conduct 86, 149, 206, 349, 457-458, 468-469
Mark "in mind" and targeting *See* TARGETING EXCUSED BY FAIR USE
Mark associated with a particular owner xiii, 327
Marks associated with a particular owner 134-135, 137-142, 144, 148, 152-153, 155,
158
See also LEXICAL CHOICES ASSOCIATED WITH ONE PARTICULAR MARK
OWNER
Marks having no association with any particular owner 24, 137, 145, 150, 154, 229
Mind ("in mind") and targeting 466
Misleading or omission of evidence 639
See also EVIDENTIARY DEMANDS > SIGNIFICANTLY GREATER THE
WEAKER THE MARK; RULE 15(e) RDNH
Misreading the Policy terms *See* RULE 4(b)(i) (Issues Index)

Monopolizing

Registering a trade or service mark not ownership of lexical choice   180, 182, 184

Monopolizing (law against)   95, 123, 186, 194, 203, 701, 767

Registering a trade or service mark not ownership of lexical choice   83, 95, 179-184, 186, 194, 203-204

Monopoly *See* OF WORDS (General Index and Issues Index); REGISTERING A TRADE OR SERVICE MARK NOT OWNERSHIP OF LEXICAL CHOICE (General Index and Issues Index)

Mutual jurisdiction   44, 49, 101, 106, 110, 405, 740

See also RULE 3(b)(xii) Mutual Jurisdiction (Issues Index); UDRP PARA. 4(k) (Issues Index)

MX exchanger records and other techniques for committing fraud   529-530

N

Name redacted

Identity theft   248-249

Narrow class of complaints *See* OUTSIDE SCOPE OF POLICY

More appropriate for court of court of competent jurisdiction   28-29, 35, 38-39, 69, 91, 251-252, 289, 292, 298, 323, 366, 437

Outside scope of Policy   8-9, 21

Within scope of Policy   253

Negotiations over domain names

Without prejudice   582

No actionable claim

No reason to grant complainant standing   336, 345, 656

No exploitative intent *See* UDRP 4(b)(i)

No exploitative intent (UDRP 4(c)(i))   167

Nominative fair use

Not fair where website conveys a false impression of association or sponsorship   450-451, 524

Referential use permissible but limited   xvi, 445-448, 450-451

Non distinctive marks demand greater proof of targeting   24, 146, 148-150, 153-154, 458

Non use of Domain Name   176

Noncommercial use (Trademark law)   731

Nonexclusive remedy for cybersquatting   28

not an intuitive combination of words   157

Not currently in active use *See* ASSESSING THE DATE FROM WHICH 4(a)(i) AND 4(a)(ii) ARE MEASURED

O

Objective assessment of the facts   19, 25, 156, 177, 360, 491, 519, 568, 663, 732
Objective test of intent *See* SUBJECTIVE / OBJECTIVE INTENT (Issues Index)
Offering fake goods of complainant
    Famous and well-known marks
        Fake not counterfeit goods   618
Offering for sale following registration   461
    See also WHO CONTACTS WHOM? (Issues Index)
One of a kind versus none of a kind   148, 155, 184, 188, 208, 490, 493
Outside of scope of Policy
    Complaint dismissed   251, 253, 293, 761
Outside scope of Policy
    Subdomains   601
Overreaching mark owner *See* DE NOVO "APPEAL" TO COURTS OF
COMPETENT JURISDICTION (Issues Index)
Overreaching mark owner's rights   750
Overstates goodwill and reputation   655
    See also EVIDENCE (OVERSTATING AND MISLEADING)
Ownership
    No ownership of domain names   14, 50
Ownership of language *See* MONOPOLIZE (Issues Index); REGISTERING A
TRADE OR SERVICE MARK NOT OWNERSHIP OF LEXICAL CHOICE
(Issues Index)
    No exclusivity   x, 184-186, 188-189
    No ownership   x, 179, 184, 692
Owning what (grammatical parts)?   202-204, 350

P

Paragraph 4(k), the meaning of transfer   742
Paramountcy of statutory rights over contract rights   129-130, 135
Parties geographically separated
    Does reputation travel to distant markets?   23-25, 154, 177, 320
Parties' requests
    Suspend or terminate proceedings   263
Passive holding *See* TELSTRA TEST
    Inconceivable to be used in good faith   459
    No presumptive bad faith   394, 459-460
    Not possible to conceive of any plausible use   90, 119, 155, 458-459, 788
    Plausible legitimate use   406, 459-460

Passive use, an oxymoron?   90
  See also PASSIVE HOLDING
Pattern of bad faith conduct   62, 267, 394, 452, 503, 508-510, 513, 771
  See also UDRP 4(b) (Issues Index); UDRP 4(b)(ii) (Issues Index)
Pattern of Conduct   267, 363, 394, 503, 508, 510-511, 698, 771
Pay Per Click
  Is hyperlinking permissible?   xv-xvi, 13, 418, 478-479, 481, 483
    See also REGISTRAR LANDING PAGE (General Index)
Pay per click
  Errant links insufficient to prove cybersquatting   420-421
  Meaning consistent with word(s)   418-420, 703
Pending application or supplemental register *See* STANDING TO MAINTAIN
  PROCEEDING (Issues Index)
Personal names   75-76, 88, 103, 134, 186, 200-201, 204-205, 207, 323, 326,
  369-370, 374, 677, 752
  See also SCHMIDHEINY (General Index)
Personalized email *See* ACTIVE WEBSITE NOT THE ONLY LEGITIMATE USE
  (Issues Index)
Phishing, Spamming and Related Fraudulent Schemes   248
  See also DELIVERY OF MALWARE
    Payment instruction fraud   525-527, 612-614
Plausible acquisition   26, 76, 170, 187, 199, 369, 459, 539, 571
Pleadings
  But for it would have prevailed   537
    See also REFILING COMPLAINT (Issues Index)
  Deficiencies of proof   537, 641-642
Political speech   441
  See also UDRP 4(c)(iii) (Issues Index)
Politician (Merely a)   376
Postdating *See* UDRP 4(a)(iii) and 4(b) RESPONDENT (Issues Index)
Postdating domain name registration   476
Precedential but not precedent   67-68, 74-75, 79
Predates (mark postdates domain name registration)   91, 167, 174, 226, 322, 333,
  391, 427, 476, 493, 544
Prejudice *See* NEGOTIATIONS OVER DOMAIN NAMES, WITHDRAWING
  COMPLAINT WITH OR WITHOUT PREJUDICE (General Index, Issues Index)
Pretextual purpose   xvi, 107, 109, 198, 434, 437, 441, 532
Pricing of domain names
  Evidence of targeting   497-498, 691
    See also WHO CONTACTS WHOM? (Issues Index)

Not an issue   161

Pricing, a misconceived issue   499, 505, 721-722, 726-727
  Not a determinative factor of bad faith   xxi, 161, 174, 499, 505, 518, 544, 604, 680, 717, 719, 721, 723, 726-727
Prima facie case, Defining   378-380, 382
Primary market   688
  See also SECONDARY MARKET
Privileged communications *See* CONFIDENTIAL AND PRIVILEGED COMMUNICATIONS (Issues Index); IMPERSONATION (Issues Index)
Profit from complainant's goodwill
  Evidence of   4, 35, 111, 116, 138, 146, 163, 206, 212, 252, 296, 419, 424, 433, 497, 501, 506, 512, 709, 738-739
  No evidence of   92, 161, 165, 211, 216, 503, 689, 697
Protectability of marks   213, 225, 227, 320, 349, 374, 390, 492, 678
  See also CONSUMER CONFUSION AND DECEPTION > NARROW PROTECTION AS THE VALUE OF A MARK DECLINES
Protection of mark, degree of protection   6, 20, 123, 135, 137, 157-158, 180, 183, 213, 303, 310, 334, 340, 342, 349, 358, 371, 376, 701-702, 748, 784
Protection of trademark (to what extent?)   129, 135, 137, 142
provides a fruitful source of precedent   77
Proving contentions   81, 258, 453-454, 456-458, 535, 539-540, 542, 548, 638, 681
Public auction *See* DROPPED DOMAIN NAME (General Index and Issues Index)
Public auctions *See* DROPPED DOMAIN NAMES
  Challenging registration and use   65, 155-156, 195, 217-218, 396, 490, 495, 634, 672, 705
Punctuation, hyphens, and spaces   191-192, 368, 607-608

Q

Quintessential
  Cyberquatting   12, 490, 604, 616, 765

R

RDNH heavy and light *See* OVERREACHING MARK OWNER'S RIGHTS (Issues Index)
RDNH not requested *See* RULE 15(e) RDNH
  But sanctionable conduct but found in the record   xx, 685, 687
Rebranding predating acquisition of domain name
  No better right   175, 260
Rebranding subsequent to domain name

No better right   40, 91, 161, 173-174, 756
  See also BETTER RIGHT THEORY (Issues Index)
Reclaiming domain names from employees, vendors, and Providers   294, 296
Recovering dropped domain names   193, 702, 705
  See also DROPPED DOMAIN NAMES (General Index and Issues Index)
Redacted name *See* IDENTITY THEFT (Issues Index)
Redaction   248-249
Referential *See* ADDITION OF WORD REFERENTIAL TO COMPLAINANT
  Reinforces targeting complainant's mark   33, 285, 352
Refiling complaint
  Rules for reconsideration   40, 245, 288, 554-561, 673
    See also RES JUDICATA (General Index)
Registering a trade or service mark not ownership of lexical choice   131, 182
Registrar Registration Agreement
  Registration for a renewable term
    Right to use domain name dissolves on nonrenewal of agreement   50
  Representations of lawful registration   50-52, 54, 59, 61-63, 66, 135, 455, 470, 626,
    631
Registration *See* UNBROKEN CHAIN OF POSSESSION
Rejected arguments (Complainants)   56, 97, 113, 127, 138
Rejected arguments (Respondents)   25, 82, 105, 158
Related persons or entities *See* STANDING TO MAINTAIN PROCEEDING (Issues
  Index)
Reliability of evidence (credibility)   187, 255, 519, 541-542
Remedy for overreaching
  ACPA
    RDNH heavy and light   750
  RDNH heavy and light   749
Renewal of registration
  Measuring the date from which to determine bad faith   14, 80, 113, 122, 126, 455,
    463, 659
Reputation
  Niche market   75, 144, 169, 226
  What makes a mark distinctive?   xvi, 63, 82, 129, 133-135, 137-138, 143, 147, 150,
    157, 159, 180, 194, 477, 628, 630, 653, 655, 710, 724
Reputation is a matter of proof
  Standard of proof   xviii, 516, 550-554
Request to withdraw complaint   xii, 264, 653, 661
  See also WITHDRAW COMPLAINT

Res judicata *See* REFILING COMPLAINT > RULES FOR RECONSIDERATION
(Issues Index)

Researching history *See* WAYBACK MACHINE (Issues Index)

Respondent
  Offers to sell to specific parties   498

Respondent disclosed (also see Anonymity)   32-33

Respondent's consent to transfer
  Transferred without assessment of Para. 4(a) elements   263, 267-268, 276, 470

Retroactive bad faith (debunked theory of)   ix, 69, 80, 88, 97, 113, 117-119,
  121-123, 127, 304, 395, 627, 633, 669

Reverse Domain Name Hijacking *See* RULE 15(e) (Issues Index)

Reversing, transposing, omitting letters   367
  See also TYPOSQUATTING (General index, Issues Index)

Rights or legitimate interests
  Has rights or legitimate interests   85, 172, 193, 377-378, 382, 390-391, 394-395,
    400, 476, 553, 587, 650, 656, 688, 716
  Lacks rights or legitimate interests   379, 382, 399, 433, 485, 631

Rights surviving death
  Legal transfer of rights   404

Rise and development of a jurisprudence
  Construing the Policy
    Building consensus around multiple issues   67-75, 77, 80-81, 83, 112
  Law as process   83

Risk of harm by those who intend to inflict it
  Unlawful and dishonest purposes   522-523, 525-527, 613, 615

Rule 1 Holder of domain name
  Proxy listed as registrant in Whois directory
    Proxy stands in as registrant   32-33

Rule 3(b)(xii) Mutual Jurisdiction
  Condition for maintaining UDRP
    Complainant "will submit" to personal jurisdiction if UDRP award
      challenged   44-46, 740, 745

Rule 3(xiii) and Rule 5(c)(viii)
  False certification (or none)   594, 636-638, 640, 643

Rule 4(b)(i)
  Misreading the Policy terms   124

Rule 11(a)
  Default language is English   268-269

Rule 12
  Procedural Order

Discretionary not to order   xii, 245

Discretionary to Panel

To be used with caution   175, 240, 243-246, 260

Unrequested discouraged   xii, 242-246, 305

Unrequested submissions

Discretionary to Panel accept supplemental submission

Only in exceptional circumstances   243, 245, 248

Rule 14(b) Drawing inferences

Absence of direct evidence

Reasonable to draw inferences   59, 77, 206-207, 621-622, 729

Rule 15(a)

UDRP law not centric to any national laws

Domestication of principles deemed applicable   xii, 21, 68-69, 104-105, 270, 404

Rule 15(e) RDNH

Conduct that constitutes abuse

Misleading the Panel   676-677, 683

Plan B conduct   659, 674, 679

Preexisting rights   405, 474, 642, 650, 658, 663, 669, 671-673, 675, 679

Conduct that supports RDNH

Definition   676, 680

General considerations   657, 660-661, 667, 669, 684-685

Misleading or omission of evidence   xx, 635, 677-678, 683, 687

Not requested

Found based on the clear evidence   682

Found based on the clear evidence in the record   81, 658, 681-682, 684

Definition   657-658, 663, 674-676

Obligation to rule

Whether or not requested or respondent appears   81, 661, 681-682, 685-687

Rule 17

Consent to transfer overridden   263, 266-267

Transferring domain name as requested by the parties   267

See also RESPONDENT'S CONSENT TO TRANSFER

RULE 18(a)   xiii, 298

Rules 4(a)(iii) and 4(b)(iv) *See* BINARY VERSUS UNITARY

S

Sales and advertising figures   322, 324, 329, 332, 622, 645, 654

See also ADVERTISING AND SALES FIGURES (Issues Index)

Scope *See* NARROW CLASS OF COMPLAINTS (General Index and Issues Index)

Scope of Policy *See* NARROW CLASS OF COMPLAINTS (Issues Index)

Limited to cybersquatting   8-9, 17, 21, 252, 429, 435, 604

Outside of scope *See* TRADEMARK INFRINGEMENT AND OTHER CLAIMS OUTSIDE SCOPE OF POLICY

Outside scope of Policy   xxxi, 16-17, 34-35, 93, 123, 179-180, 203, 250-252, 342, 349, 428, 468, 521, 601-602, 700-702, 761, 774

Secondary market   222, 712, 714

Secondary meaning *See* SALES AND ADVERTISING FIGURES (Issues Index)

Secondary meaning for common law rights

Required evidence   xiii, 307, 313, 315, 320, 322, 324, 326-327, 329, 331, 333-334, 338, 374, 598, 654-655

Selling on the secondary market   13, 211, 688-689, 692-694, 696-697, 716, 718, 720

Selling would require respondent to rebrand   174

Settlement discussions   582

See also NEGOTIATIONS OVER DOMAIN NAMES (Issues Index)

Shifting burden *See* BURDEN OF PROOF

Short strings of letters

Coincidentally corresponding to acronyms of marks

Favor respondents except evidence of targeting   227-228, 230-231

Corresponding to acronyms of marks

Favor mark owners on evidence of targeting   231-232

Similar and confusing vs Likelihood of confusion

Distinction between the two   520-522

Small differences

Adding, subtracting letters or words or doing nothing to common words

Very limited protection   x, 172, 179, 191-193, 201, 608, 610, 646

Small differences and confusing similarity   172

See also SMALL DIFFERENCES MATTER (Issues Index)

some have drawn a line in the sand when the tenor of the website content changes   436

Speculation *See* ARBITRAGING DOMAIN NAMES AS A BUSINESS (Issues Index)

Standard of proof *See* BLACK'S LAW DICTIONARY; REPUTATION IS A MATTER OF PROOF (Issues Index)

Standing

Not distinctive at the time of the registration of the domain name   734-736, 741-742

Standing regardless of different national jurisdictions *See* A SUFFICIENT NEXUS TO CLAIM A RIGHT

Outcomes depend on the facts   22-26

Standing to maintain proceeding

Pending application or supplemental register

Rights not matured to mark   338-340

State registrations   313-314

Statute of limitations   132, 588

  See also EFFECT OF DELAY IN GIVING NOTICE OR COMMENCING
  PROCEEDINGS (General Index and Issues Index); LACHES (Issues Index)

Stock ticker symbol   307, 328

Strength by lexical invention

  Fanciful   57

Sub and other domains out of Policy's scope   357, 600-601

Subdomains   600-601

Subject matter jurisdiction (UDRP)   vii, 17, 26, 28, 48, 250, 750

Subjective / Objective Intent   25, 177, 258, 518, 553, 683

Suing for injunctive relief

  For order directing registrars to transfer domain names   733

  Is it premature to commence an action if "transfer" has not taken place?   742

Supplemental register

  No actionable claim   686, 741

    See also STANDING TO MAINTAIN PROCEEDING

Supplementary submissions   245-247, 534

Swiftness of offering a domain name for sale *See* OFFERING FOR SALE
  FOLLOWING REGISTRATION

T

Taking (not taking) advantage of trademark value   458, 691

Taking advantage of trademark value   367, 516, 609

  See also CAPITALIZE (General Index)

Targeting (No targeting) *See* DIFFERENT LINE OF BUSINESS. "IN MIND" AND
  TARGETING

Targeting excused by fair use   428, 466

  See also MARK "IN MIND" AND TARGETING

Telstra test

  Inconceivable to be used in good faith   76, 459-460, 534, 543, 672

They are acts that on an objective accounting are intentionally designed   606

Third level domains   600-601

Timing of first use in commerce   xiii, 326

to require bad faith at the time of registration or acquisition of the disputed
  domain   121

to which the mark is entitled   179-180

Tort (continuing) see Laches   132

Trade and service mark

  What makes a mark distinctive? *See* MARKET VALUE (General Index)

Trade names functioning as trade or service marks   xi, xiv, 187, 212, 227, 338, 369, 654
  Protected rights   372-373
Trade names functioning as trademark *See* COMMON LAW RIGHTS, SECONDARY MEANING (General Index and Issues Index)
Trademark infringement
  Outside scope of Policy   186, 194, 253
Trademark infringement and other claims *See* NARROW CLASS OF COMPLAINTS > OUTSIDE SCOPE OF POLICY
Trademark infringement and other claims outside scope   9, 619
  See also SCOPE OF POLICY > OUTSIDE THE SCOPE OF POLICY
Trademark Manual of Examining Procedure   324
Trademark rights to words   135
  See also MONOPOLIZING (Issues Index)
Trademarks protected (distinctive in the marketplace)   82
Transferring domain names *See* DIVESTING REGISTRANTS OF THEIR DOMAIN NAMES (Issues Index)
Typosquatting
  Inverted or revered   367
  Inverted or reversed   354
  Omissions of letters   367, 609
  Qwerty keyboard   192, 608
  Substitution   192, 347

U

UDRP 4(a)(i) 1st factor
  What evidence satisfies common law rights?   xiii-xiv, 7, 88, 129, 224, 238, 313-314, 320-321, 324, 326-327, 333-334, 338, 347, 369-370, 372-374, 457, 598, 654, 786
  When do trade and service marks ripen?   xiii, xv, 310, 312, 315-316, 318, 401, 665
UDRP 4(a)(i) 2nd factor
  Low bar
    Failing to clear the bar   xiii, 307, 309, 749
  When does totality of facts inform confusing similarity?   362
  When is similar confusing?   xiv, 172, 347, 352, 357, 359
UDRP 4(a)(ii) Complainant
  Proving prima facie case   xiv, xvi, xviii, 147, 381, 385, 387, 415, 450, 570, 579
UDRP 4(a)(ii) Respondent
  Rebutting prima facie case   xiv-xvi, xxviii, 7, 93, 143, 365, 388, 392, 425, 427, 445-446, 448-451, 496, 509, 511, 739
UDRP 4(a)(iii) and 4(b) Respondent   193, 716

Good faith registration   xvii, xxi, 14, 50, 66, 487, 505, 706

UDRP 4(a)(iii) and UDRP 4(b)(i) Initiating contact

Offering to sell disputed domain name   xvii, 136, 144, 162, 499, 719, 723

UDRP 4(a)(iii) and UDRP 4(b)(iii) Complainant

Who are competitors?   515, 563

UDRP 4(a)(iii) and UDRP 4(b)(iv) Complainant

What is "likelihood of confusion"   xvii, 520, 529

UDRP 4(a)(iii) Complainant

Proving conjunctive bad faith   xvi-xvii, xxvii, 90, 94, 99, 232, 457-460, 468,
477-478, 484, 516, 520, 580, 700

See also CONJUNCTIVE BAD FAITH (General Index)

UDRP 4(a)(iii) Respondent

Lack of abusive registration evidence   xvi, 489

UDRP 4(b)(i) Complainant

Contractual obligations to avoid infringement

Exploitative registrations of domain names   62, 145, 501, 629, 709

UDRP 4(b)(i) Complainant or Respondent *See* WHO CONTACTS WHOM? (Issues
Index)

UDRP 4(b)(i) Respondent *See* LAWFUL OFFERS TO SELL, RENT, ETC.

Avoiding infringement

No exploitative intent   63, 628, 630, 633

Complainant initiatives and no suggestion of infringement   499-500, 630

Offers to sell to specific parties   498-499, 518, 691

Who among many have a better right?   123-125, 701

UDRP 4(b)(ii) Complainant

Evidence of bad faith   509, 511

UDRP 4(b)(ii) Respondent

Not Commonly known by

Fails to satisfy rebuttal burden   425

UDRP 4(b)(iii)   xvii, 514

UDRP 4(b)(iv)   xvii, 453, 498, 516, 518-520, 691

Factors determining bad faith   516

Geographic location of services   512-513, 547

UDRP 4(c) Respondent *See* DEMONSTRABLE PREPARATIONS (Issues Index)

Alternative defenses, anyone of which

Satisfies rebuttal burden   392

Common lexicon

Alternative defenses, anyone of which

Satisfies rebuttal burden   393, 425, 427

UDRP 4(c)(i) *See* DEMONSTRABLE PREPARATIONS (Issues Index)

Mala fide use   396-397

UDRP 4(c)(i) Before notice
  Bona fide use   384, 393-396, 672

UDRP 4(c)(ii) Complainant
  Does not satisfy rebuttal burden   392

UDRP 4(c)(ii) Respondent *See* UDRP 4(c)(ii) RESPONDENT (Issues Index)
  Commonly known by business name
    Satisfies rebuttal burden   426
  Commonly known by nick name
    Satisfies rebuttal burden   393, 426
  Commonly known by personal name
    Satisfies rebuttal burden   392, 427

UDRP 4(c)(iii)
  Legitimate noncommercial or free speech
    Protected if conveyed in the right form
      Abusive registration if in wrong form   429, 432, 434
      Right form if not pretextual
      Abusive registration if in wrong form   ix, xxviii, 78, 107, 109-111, 387, 431, 434-435, 438, 442, 448, 495
  Political speech
    Not sufficient to overcome respondent's intentions   441

UDRP 4(c)(iii) Respondent
  Legitimate noncommercial or free speech
    Good faith registration   100, 304, 427
    Protected if conveyed in the right form
      Abusive registration if in wrong form   431

UDRP 4(f) and Rule 4(c)
  Consolidation
    Puppeteer holder of domain names   278

UDRP Para. 4(k)
  Respondent's right to challenge award in Court of Competent jurisdiction
    At venue of Mutual jurisdiction   vii-viii, 20, 28-29, 45-49, 104, 405, 742, 745, 765, 769

Unbroken chain of title *See* CHAIN OF TITLE

Uncommon combinations of words *See* ONE OF A KIND VERSUS NONE OF A KIND (Issues Index)

Unlawful, Deceitful, and dishonest purpose   522

Unlawful, Deceitful, and Dishonest Purposes   451, 522-524

Unprotected speech *See* FREE SPEECH (Issues Index); UNPROTECTED (Issues Index)

Unregistered marks (culture creators fighting back)   75-76, 374, 492
Unregistered rights must be earned   239, 321-322, 324, 326, 329, 332, 622
Unrelated third party (if there is infringement it is not of this complainant)   469
Untimely filing of response *See* EXTENTIONS OF TIME TO SUBMIT
  RESPONSES (ONLY IF REASON IS EXCEPTIONAL) (Issues Index)
Unusual or creative combination of words   175
US State Registrations   313
US trademarks versus UK and EU registrations   132

V

Value of mark vs value of domain name independent of mark   25, 139-140, 149, 177,
  778
  See also FAME AS MARKET OF KNOWLEDGE
Venue in US District Court   303, 762-763

W

Wayback Machine
  Proof or lack of it historically   217, 241-242, 545
What law applies?
  From narrative to legal principles   95, 167, 339, 538, 547, 549-550, 651
What level of due diligence satisfies the burden to avoid infringement?   64, 66, 161
What makes for distinctive in the market   134-135, 139, 149-150, 157, 458
When is similar confusing? *See* UDRP 4(a)(i) 2ND FACTOR
Who contacts whom? *See* UDRP 4(b)(i) (Issues Index)
  Not in violation   503-505, 715, 720, 726
  Violation   145, 499-503, 709
Who is the respondent? *See* RULE 1 (Issues Index)
Willful blindness   xvi, 154, 484, 630-632
  See also DUE DILIEGENCE SEARCH TO AVOID INFRINGEMENT (Issues
  Index)
WIPO in its legislative role
  The "travaux preparatoires" of the UDRP   5, 10, 17, 67
WIPO Overview 1.0   99, 485
WIPO Overview 2.0   72, 101, 110, 485
WIPO Overview 3.0   72, 123, 211, 284, 322, 402-403, 431, 434, 642
  See also JURISPRUDENTIAL OVERVIEW
Withdraw complaint *See* REQUEST TO WITHDRAW COMPLAINT
Withdrawing complaint
  With or without prejudice   263-266

TABLE OF UDRP CASES

5 PRE VIE W AB v. Diego Manfreda, D2013-1946 (WIPO December 27, 2013)   246

6 Société Du Figaro S.A. v. Cut Company, DTV2013-0007 (WIPO February 2, 2014)   403

21 Club Inc. v. 21 Club, D2000-1159 (WIPO November 22, 2000)   587

24 Hour Fitness USA, Inc. v. veronica rosignoli / veronicareidweb design.com, FA1512001653945 (Forum January 28, 2016)   367

978 Tech N. V. v. seo, Senh Sam, D2023-4092 (WIPO November 10, 2023)   410

1066 Housing Association Ltd. v. Mr. D. Morgan, D2007-1461 (WIPO January 18, 2008)   106, 272

636275 Canada, dba eResolution v. eResolution.com, D2000-0110 (WIPO April 13, 2000)   77

360training.com v. DNS ADMIN / BEST WEB LIMITED, FA2110001968877 (Forum November 24, 2021)   213

3M Company v. Above.com Domain Privacy, FA1604001668805 (Forum May 4, 2016)   527

4IMPRINT, INC. v. richard olivo / rockpoint apparel inc., FA2104001942146 (Forum May 18, 2021)   480

7Spiliadis v. Androulidakis, FA0708001072907 (Forum October 17, 2007)   566

A

A & F Trademark, Inc. and Abercrombie & Fitch Stores, Inc. v. Justin Jorgensen, D2001-0900 (WIPO September 19, 2001)   440

A & F Trademark, Inc., Abercrombie & Fitch Stores, Inc., Abercrombie & Fitch Trading Co., Inc. v. Party Night, Inc., D2003-0172 (WIPO May 28, 2003)   280

A Mediocre Corporation v. Domain Admin / Domain Registries Foundation, FA190600 1849931 (Forum July 27, 2019)   646

AAA Employment, Inc. v. Ahearn and Associates, FA0507000520670 (Forum September 6, 2005)   259, 319

Abbvie, Inc. v. James Bulow, FA1611001701075 (Forum Nov. 30, 2016)   526

ACE Limited v. WebMagic Ventures, LLC c/o WebMagic Staff, FA0802001144016 (Forum April 8, 2008)   182, 548, 596, 638, 698

Acko Technology & Services Pvt. Ltd. v. Shashank Singh, D2017-0821 (WIPO June 13, 2017)   373

Acqua Minerale San Benedetto S.p.A. v. Privacy Administrator, Anonymize, Inc. / MACROSTEN LTD   151

Adam Summers v. Georgina Nelson, CEO and Founder of truRating Limited, D2015-0592 (WIPO May 24, 2015)   425

Adaptive Molecular Technologies, Inc. v. Machines & More, D2000-0006 (WIPO February 28, 2000)   445

ADITO Software GmbH v. Domain Admin, Mrs. Jello LLC   213

Admiral Insurance Services Limited v. Mr. Adam Dicker, D2005-0241 (WIPO June 4, 2005)   418

Advance Magazine Publishers Inc. v. Christian Sopke, SOPI-Media, D2020-3490 (WIPO April 14, 2021)   85-86

Advance Magazine Publishers Inc. v. Domain Admin, Privacy Protect, LLC (Privacy Protect.org) / Tarun Suri, D2021-2923 (WIPO December 2021)   85-86

Advance Magazine Publishers Inc. v. Premier Models International Inc., D2013-0757 (WIPO July 5, 2013)   85-86

Advanced Personnel Systems, Inc. v. Domain Admin / Mighty Products, Inc., FA1804001780243 (Forum May 25, 2018)   419

Adventure SAS v. Mike Robinson, BlackHawk Paramotors USA Inc., D2019-2489 (WIPO December 12, 2019)   645, 653

Adventurous Entertainment LLC v. Marco Pirrongelli, FA2209002013597 (Forum November 9, 2022)   292

Advice Group S.P.A. v. Privacy Administrator, Anonymize, Inc. / Michele Dinoia, Macrosten LTD., D2019-2441 (WIPO December 2, 2019)   651, 699

Aerogroup International, Inc. v. Brave New Consultants, Inc., D2006-1216 (WIPO November 11, 2006)   180, 182

AF Gloenco, Inc. v. CT PACKAGING SYSTEMS, INC   595

AFMA, Inc., v. Globemedia, D2001-0558 (WIPO August 23, 2001)   148, 504

Agfa-Gevaert N.V. v. Pascal Olaf Schubert, Schubert UG, D2020-1413 (WIPO July 27, 2020)   43

Agile Software Corporation v. Compana LLC, D2001-0545 (WIPO July 23, 2001)   144, 474

Air Serbia a.d. Beograd Jurija v. Domains By Proxy, LLC / Meijun Lu, D2017-1986 (WIPO December 18, 2017)   169

Air Serv International, Inc. v. Stu Willcuts, FA1902001831670 (Forum March 31, 2019)   328

AirDNA, LLC v. ding zhi qiang / bei jing yi rui sheng wu ji shu you xian gong si, FA2207002006430 (Forum August 29, 2022)   123

Airpet Animal Transport, Inc. v. Marchex Sales, Inc / Brendhan Hight, FA121100 1470056 (Forum January 2, 2013)   673

Airpromote Limited v. Nick Sunnar, D2021-1544 (WIPO July 13, 2021) (<airpromote.com
)   8

Airtron, Inc. v. Domain Admin / Whois Privacy Corp., FA1812001822308 (Forum February 4, 2019)   209, 261, 578

AIRY GreenTech GmbH v. Privacydotlink Customer 3050720 / Samsu Sempena   680

Akamai Technologies, Inc. v. Cloudflare Hostmaster / Cloudflare, Inc., FA220100 1979588 (Forum March 9, 2022)   246, 410

Al-Dabbagh Group Holding Company v. Leo Radvinsky / Cybertania Inc, FA2009001913317 (Forum November 3, 2020)   352

Alaska Health Fair, Inc. v. Chris Jacobson, FA1305001500868 (Forum June 24, 2013)   297

Alfa Laval Corporate AB v. VNET Informatique, Vincent Lagacé, D2023-1972 (WIPO September 4, 2023)   257

Allen Fagin v. Crystal Cox, D2011-0678 (WIPO June 30, 2011)   372

Allianz SE v. Domain Admin, Whois protection/Domain Administrator, Radio plus, spol.s r.o   231

Allocation Network GmbH v. Steve Gregory, D2000-0016 (WIPO March 24, 2000)   56, 91

Alloy Rods Global, Inc. v. Nancy Williams, D2000-1392 (WIPO January 31, 2001)   114, 574

Alphalogix, Inc. v. DNS Services, FA0506000491557 (Forum July 26, 2005)   691

Alstom v. NetSupport AskMySite, AskMySite.com LLC, D2020-3206 (WIPO March 2, 2021)   312, 477

Altametrics, Inc. v. Ryan Sveinsvoll, FA1008001343628 (Forum November 11, 2010)   666

Alticor Inc. v. Domain Admin, Whois Privacy Corp., D2021-4157 (WIPO February 28, 2022)   363

Altiplano Voyage v. Terra Holding Ltd. / Pierre Boyer   648

Altron Limited, Altron TMT Limited v. ALTRON LIMITED DOOEL export-import Skopje, D2022-4163 (WIPO February 26, 2023)   165, 248

Altru Health System v. Altruism Network c/o Doug West, FA0805001195584 (Forum July 15, 2008)   676

Amadeus IT Group, S.A. v. Domains By Proxy, LLC / Narendra Ghimire, Deep Vision Architects, DCO2022-0040 (WIPO July 25, 2022)   59, 124, 195, 551, 706

Amazon Technologies, Inc. v. Robert Nichols, FA1609001693499 (Forum October 20, 2016)   724

America Online, Inc. v. Intellectual-Assets.com, Inc., D2000-1043 (WIPO December 22, 2000)   224, 311, 417, 478

America Online, Inc. v. John Deep d/b/a Buddy USA Inc., FA0103000096795 (Forum October 3, 2001)   224, 311, 417, 478

America Online, Inc. v. Tencent Communications Corp., FA 93668 (Nat. Arb. Forum Mar. 21, 2000)   224, 311, 417, 478

American Airlines, Inc. v. Registration Private, Domains By Proxy, LLC / Online Resource, Online Resource Management Ltd., D2021-3234 (WIPO November 22, 2021)   601

American Automobile Association, Inc. v. 555 Metro Airport Transportation Service LLC., D2011-0588 (WIPO May 17, 2011)   700

American Civil Liberties Union of New Mexico v. Vilma Morales/e:boom, S.A., D2004-0473 (WIPO August 23, 2004)   319

American Family Health Services Group, LLC v. Logan, FA 220049 (Forum Feb. 6, 2004)   319

American Funds Distributors, Inc., and the Capital Group Companies, Inc. v. Eunice May, D2011-0361 (WIPO April 25, 2011)   536

American Home Products Corporation v. Haymont Veterinary Clini, D2000-0502 (WIPO July 31, 2000)   334, 416

American Home Shield Corporation v. Domains By Proxy / Morris Chera, D2017-1142 (WIPO September 3, 2017)   103, 139, 333

American Honda Motor Co. Inc. v. Piazza Management Company   395

AmeriPlan Corp. v. Gilbert, FA0203000105737 (Forum April 22, 2002)   298

Ampol Management Services Pte. Ltd. v. Australia Online, D2022-3942 (WIPO January 5, 2023)   571

Amylin Pharmaceuticals, Inc. v. Watts Guerra Craft LLP, D2012-0486 (WIPO April 29, 2012)   436, 448

Anchor Drilling Fluids USA, Inc. v. anchordf, anchor drills, D2012-0385 (WIPO April 12, 2002)   525

Andrew Etemadi, Founder and Chief Technology Officer for Eyemagine Technology LLC v. Clough Construction and Deanne Clough, D2012-2455 (WIPO February 14, 2013)   646, 681

Anglotopia, LLC v. Artem Bezshapochny, D2013-0168 (WIPO March 13, 2013)   619

Antonio de Felipe v. Registerfly.com, D2005-0969 (WIPO December 19, 2005)   285

Anyclean Premium Limited v. Jethro Denahy, Any-Clean, D2017-0581 (WIPO April 28, 2017)   643

AOL LLC v. Joe DiMarco, FA0907001275978 (Forum September 9, 2009)   535, 569

AOL Time Warner Inc. v. John Zuccarini, D2002-0827 (WIPO December 1, 2002)   205, 508

Aperam S.A. v. Rowan Koepp Kirschner, D2021-1504 (WIPO August 21, 2021)   530

Apnea Sciences Corporation v. Private Domain / Above Privacy, FA2310002065870 (Forum December 24, 2023)   727

Apple Computer, Inc. v. DomainHouse.com, Inc., D2000-0341 (WIPO July 18, 2000)   115, 691

Aqua Engineering & Equipment, Inc. v. DOMAIN ADMINISTRATOR / PORTMEDIA HOLDINGS LTD, FA1805001785667 (Forum June 25, 2018)   421

ArcBest IP Holdings LLC v. Azinue Bamu, FA2206001999386 (Forum July 6, 2022)   356

Archipelago Holdings LLC, v. Creative Genius Domain Sales and Robert Aragon d/b/a/ Creative Genius Domain Name Sales, D2001-0729 (WIPO September 7, 2001)   279

Argenta Spaarbank NV v. Argenta, Mailadmin Ltd., D2009-0249 (WIPO June 8, 2009)   702

Argento Wine Company Limited v. Argento Beijing Trading Company, D2009-0610 (WIPO July 1, 2009)   269

Arla Foods Amba v. ESMM EMPIRE staincollins, CAC 101578 (ADR.eu August 14, 2017)   527, 612

Armor v. Ozguc Bayraktar, Rs Danismanlik, D2019-1803 (WIPOSeptember 17, 2019)   718

Arnold Clark Automobiles Limited v. Registration Private, Domains By Proxy, LLC / Carolina Rodrigues, Fundacion Comercio Electronico, D2021-3924 (WIPO January 22, 2022)   530

Art-Four Development Limited v. Tatiana Meadows, D2019-1311 (WIPO July 29,2019)   647

Art4Now, Inc. v. Gerald Waggoner / The Waggoner Law Firm, FA2312002074746 (Forum January 9, 2024)   560

Arturo Salice S.p.A. v. Paul Izzo & Company, D2000-0537 (WIPO August 17. 2000)   255

Asbach GmbH v. Econsult Ltd., d.b.a. Asbach Communities and Whois-Privacy Services, D2012-1225 (WIPO August 7, 2012)   416

Ascension Health Alliance v. Prateek Sinha, Ascension Healthcare Inc., D2018-2775 (WIPO January 25, 2019)   289

Aspect Capital Limited v. Fluder (aka Pierre Fluder), D2015-0475 (WIPO April 14, 2015)   367

Aspen Grove, Inc. v. Aspen Grove, D2001-0798 (WIPO October 5, 2001)   338, 597, 670

Aspen Grove, Inc. v. Aspen Grove,D2001-0798 (WIPO October17, 2001)   338, 597, 670

Aspen Holdings Inc. v. Christian P. Vandendorpe, D2009-1160 (WIPO October 16, 2009)   63, 580

Aspen Holdings Inc. v. Rick Natsch, Potrero Media Corporation, D2009-0776 (WIPO August 20, 2009)   63, 580

Asphalt Research Technology, Inc. v. National Press & Publishing, Inc., Case No. D2000-1005 (WIPO November 13, 2000)   225, 270

Asset Mktg. Sys., LLC v. Silver Lining, D2005-0560 (WIPO July 22,2005)   418

Associated Newspapers Limited v. Makhdoom Babar, Mail Group, D2019-0049 (WIPO February 25, 2019)   587

Association Francaise Contre les Myopathies v. Yemliha Toker, CAC 102229 (ADR.eu January 3, 2019)   169, 171

Association pour la défense et la promotion de l'œuvre de Marc Chagall dite "Comite Marc Chagall" v. Miri & Isaac Shepher, D2021-4216 (WIPO February 14, 2022)   726

Assurity Life Insurance Company v. DOMAIN MAY BE FOR SALE, CHECK AFTERNIC.COM Domain Admin / Whois Foundation, FA1911001872882 (Forum December 21, 2019)   652

Athena Infonomics India Private Limited v. Registration Private, Domains By Proxy, LLC / Renji Mathew, D2017-1779 (WIPO November 1, 2017)   297

Atlas Copco Aktiebolag v. Accurate Air Engineering, Inc., D2003-0070 (WIPO March 24, 2003)   92

ATVTracks.net Property, LLC v. Domains By Proxy, LLC, DomainsByProxy.com / Chad Green, FPNW, D2021-1774 (WIPOOctober 4, 2021)   185, 194

Audiopoint, Inc. v. eCorp., D2001-0509 (WIPO June 14, 2001)   211, 697

Aurelon B.V. v. AbdulBasit Makrani, D2017-1679 (WIPO October 30, 2017)   222, 420, 580, 712

Aurora Cannabis Inc., Aurora Marijuana Inc., Aurora Cannabis Enterprises Inc. v. Byron Smith, D2019-0583 (WIPO July12, 2019)   655

Austin Area Birthing Center, Inc. v. CentreVida Birth and Wellness Center c/o Faith Beltz and Family-Centered Midwifery c/o June Lamphier   198

Australian Stock Exch. v. Cmty. Internet (Australia) Pty Ltd., D2000-1384 (WIPO November 30, 2000)   509

Autobuses de Oriente ADO, S.A. de C.V. v. Private Registration / Francois Carrillo, D2017-1661 (WIPO February 1, 2018)   622, 729

AutoNation Holding Corp. v. Rabea Alawneh, D2002-0581 (WIPO May 2, 2002)   8

AutoZone Parts, Inc. v. Ken Belden, FA1811001815011 (Forum Dec. 24, 2018)   144

Avaya Inc. v. Holdcom, FA0806001210545 (Forum August 9, 2008)   397, 591, 675

Avaya Inc. v. Moayyad Hamad, FA1207001456063 (Forum September 14, 2012)   397, 591, 675

Aveve N.V. v. Privacy Administrator, Anonymize, Inc. / Dennis Koorn, D2020-1115 (WIPO September 2, 2020)   740

Avomex, Inc. v. Barry Pierce / Tina D. Pierce Widow of Barry E. Pierce, D2011-1253 (WIPO September 23, 2011)   404

Avomex, Inc. v. Tina D. Pierce Widow of Barry E. Pierce, D2011-1253 (WIPO September 23, 2011)   404

AXA SA v. Nanci Nette, Name Management Group, D2022-4885 (WIPO February 9, 2023)   510

B

B&V Associates, Inc. v. Internet Waterway, Inc., FA0303000 147531 (Forum April 15, 2003)   584

B2B CFO, LLC v. Code Mentor, Ken Sipe, D2023-2746 (WIPO September 5, 2023)   354

B2BWorks, Inc. v. Venture Direct Worldwide, Inc., FA0104000097119 (Forum June5, 2001)   184

Banc of California, N.A. v. kevin heckemeyer, FA1903001836223 (Forum April 25, 2019)   20

Banca Monte dei Paschi di Siena S.p.A v. Charles Kirkpatrick, D2008-0260 (WIPO April 14, 2008)   228

Banco Bradesco S.A. v. FAST-12785241 Attn. Bradescourgente.net / Name Redacted, D2009-1788 (WIPO March 7, 2010).   249

Banco de Chile S.A. v. Eric S. Bord, Esq., D2001-0695 (WIPO August 14, 2001)   222

Bank of Am. Corp. v. InterMos, FA0006000095092 (Forum August 1, 2000)   608

Bank of Scotland Plc v. Shelley Roberts, Diversity Network, D2015-2310 (WIPO February 15, 2016)   502

Bankwell Financial Group, Inc. v. Whois Privacy Protection Service, Inc. / Domain Manager, Affordable Webhosting, Inc., Advertising, D2015-1664 (WIPO November 13, 2015)   401

Banque Cantonale de Geneva v. Primatex Group S.A., D2001-0477 (WIPO June 29, 2001)   495

Banque Cantonale de Geneve v. Primatex Group S.A., D2001-0477 (WIPO June 21, 2001)   101

Barlow Lyde & Gilbert v. The Business Law Group, D2005-0493 (WIPO June 24, 2005)   228, 719, 721

Barnes & Noble College Bookstores, Inc. v. Leasure Interactive, D2001-1216 (WIPO March 25, 2002)   359

Barnesandnoble.com, LLC v. Rosenblum, FA071000 1089020 (Forum November 15, 2007)   214, 359

Barnesandnoble.com, LLC v. Rosenblum, FA0710001089020 (Forum November 15, 2007)   214, 359

Bartko Zankel Bunzel & Miller v. Perfect Privacy, LLC / Jan Bartko, D2022-0043 (WIPO March 17, 2022)   426, 600, 646, 651

Bauhaus AG, Zweigniederlassung Mannheim v. Robert Desideri, D2001-1177 (WIPO December 3, 2001)   577

Beautiful People Magazine, Inc. v. Domain Manager / PeopleNetwork ApS / Kofod Nicolai / People Network Aps / Nicolai Kofod / People Network, FA1502001606976 (Forum May 4, 2015)   648

Beijing Pernot Ricard Winery Co. Ltd. v. Capital Enterprises Group, Inc., AF-0177 (eResolution June 1, 2000)   380

Belmond Management Limited v. Roman Dopita / GrowSmart s.r.o., D2023-3323 (WIPO October 3, 2023)   256

Bentley Systems, Incorporated v. Anton Rodyanskiy, FA2212002022830 (Forum January 26, 2023)   515

BeReal v. osama abotamim, D2023-1189 (WIPO May 24, 2023)   146, 168

bet365 Group Limited v. Domains by Proxy, Inc. / Steve Prime, D2011-1242 (WIPO September 14, 2011)   347

BHE GT&S v. SS Ruprai, FA2306002048675 (Forum July 25, 2023)   318

BHP Billiton Innovation Pty Ltd v. Domains By Proxy LLC / Douglass Johnson, D2016-0364 (WIPO April 21, 2016)   529

Bialetti Industrie S.p.A. v. Gary Valenti Inc.,D2019-0190 (WIPOMarch 25, 2019)   386

Bible Study Fellowship v. BSF.ORG / Vertical Axis Inc.,D2010-1338 (WIPO November 29, 2010)   722

Billy Bob's Texas IP Holding LLC v. Domain Administrator, Name Administration Inc. (BVI), D2016-1221 (WIPO)   224

BinckBank N.V. v. Silue Tiessolikaabdoul, D2011-1980 (WIPO December 29, 2011)   248

BioClin B.V v. MG USA, D2010-0046 (WIPO March 22, 2010)   120

bioMérieux v. Registration Private, Domains By Proxy, LLC / Milton Bardmess, D2020-3499 (WIPO February 17, 2021)   530

BioSafe Systems LLC v. Donald Clark, FA1907001853762 (Forum August 24, 2019)   342

Birgit Rausing, AB Tetra Pak v. Darren Morgan, D2008-0212 (WIPO April 5, 2008)   376

Bitrise Limited and Bitrise Inc v. BitRise Network, David Koeman, Lora Mutner, [Chinese characters] (Lei Shi), Emmanuel Ewusi, Leland Li and Danny Harris, D2021-4051 (WIPO March 10, 2022)   278

Bitrise Limited v. Dalton Kline, Bitrise Trade Ltd., D2020-0835 (WIPO May 29, 2020)   175, 278

Bittrex, Inc. v. Wuxi Yilian LLC, FA1711001760517(Forum Dec. 27, 2017)   524

Black Foodie, Inc. v. Braxston Richmond, Black Chef / Black Foodie Finder, D2022-3536 (WIPO November 10, 2022)   340

Bloomberg Finance L.P. v. Nexperian Holding Limited, FA1804001782013 (Forum June 4, 2018)   352

Blue Mountain Coffee, Inc. v. Fundacion Private Whois / Domain Administrator, FA 1204001439829 (Forum May 21, 2012)   318

Blue On Highland LLC v. Matthew Sullivan, D2021-3168 (WIPO November 8, 2021)   295

Blue Ridge Fiberboard, Inc. v. Domain Administrator / Domain Asset Holdings, LLC, FA1602001661150 (Forum March 29, 2016)   576

BMEzine.com, LLC. v. Gregory Ricks / Gee Whiz Domains Privacy Service, D2008-0882 (WIPO August 21, 2008)   403, 749, 782

BMW AG v. Loophole, D2000-1156 (WIPO October 26, 2000)   148

Boehringer Ingelheim Pharma GmbH & Co. KG v. Ilgam Nurtdinov, CAC 105197 (ADR.eu March 24, 2023)   105

Bold Limited v. Toni Georgiev / Outsourcing International Ltd.,FA1709001749693 (Forum November 3, 2017)   387, 472, 545-546, 695

Bolex International SA v. Kurt Hall & Nathan Lafionatis, D2019-2650 (WIPO December 16, 2019)   592

Boller, Winkler AG v. Craig Schlossberg, Image Info, LLC., D2022-2222 (WIPO August 9, 2022)   666

Booked Ltd v. Privacydotlink Customer 251836 / Dominic Hulewicz, D2014-1937 (WIPO January 14, 2015)   161

Boot Barn, Inc. v. Domain Protection Services, Inc., D2022-3018 (WIPO October 10, 2022)   524

Bootie Brewing Company v. Deanna D. Ward and Grabebottie Inc.,D2003-0185 (WIPO May 28, 2003)   253, 290, 552

Bosco Prod., Inc. v. Bosco email Servs., FA0005000094828 (Forum June 29, 2000)   593

Brabners LLP v. Privacy Service Provided by Withheld for Privacy ehf / Saracens Saracens, D2021-3547 (WIPO January 26, 2022)   616

Breazy Inc. v. Domains by Proxy, LLC, DomainsByProxy.com / VR PRODUCTS I LLC., D2021-1486 (WIPO July 6, 2021)   570, 668

Breezy Inc. v. Domains by Proxy, LLC, DomainsByProxy.com / VR PRODUCTS I LLC, D2021-1486 (WIPO July 6, 2021)   632

Bremer Toto und Lotto GmbH v. Birrell Nigel, Cavour Ltd., D2019-2391 (WIPO December 24, 2019)   390

Bridgestone Firestone, Inc., Bridgestone/Firestone Research, Inc., and Bridgestone Corporation v. Jack Myers, D2000-0190 (WIPO July 12, 2000)   102, 431

Bright Horizons Family Solutions Inc., Allmont Limited, Bright Horizons Limited Partnership and Bright Horizons Family Solutions Ltd. v. Vertical Axis, Inc, D2007-0795 (WIPO October 12, 2007)   287

Britannia Building Society v. Britannia Fraud Prevention, D2001-0505 (WIPO July 6, 2001)   102, 234-236, 429-430, 432, 435

British Heart Foundation v. Harold A Meyer III, AF0957 (eResolution November 13, 2001)   306, 331

British Sky Broadcasting Limited v. Domain Reservations, D2000-0507 (WIPO July 14, 2000)   143

Broadway Trading, LLC. v. Gene Weissman, FA000300094310 (Forum April 25, 2000)   140

Brooke Bollea, a.k.a Brooke Hogan v. Robert McGowan, D2004-0383 (WIPO June 29, 2004)   259

Brooks Sports, Inc. v. Domain Admin / Whoisprotection.cc, FA2102001932380 (Forum March 15, 2021)   284

Brooksburnett Investments Ltd. v. Domain Admin / Schmitt Sebastien, D2019-0455 (WIPO April 16, 2019)   116, 569, 678, 699, 716

Bruce Molzan v. Mitar Miric, FA2002001883442 (Forum March 24, 2020)   601

Bruce Springsteen v. Jeff Burgar and Bruce Springsteen Club, D2000-1532 (WIPO January 25, 2001)   76, 375

Bryn Mawr Communications, LLC v. Linkz Internet Services, D2016-0286 (WIPO March 29, 2016)   506

BSH Home Appliances Corporation v. Michael Stanley / Michael Sipo, D2014-1433 (WIPO October 6, 2014)   316

BTCDRAFT INC. v. Brian Boyer, D2018-0613 (WIPO June 1, 2018)   152

Buhl Optical Co v. Mailbank.com, Inc., D2000-1277 (WIPO March 1, 2001)   200

Bulbs 4 East Side Inc., d/b/a Just Bulbs v. Fundacion Private Whois/ Gregory Ricks, D2013-1779 (WIPO January 13, 2014)   559, 771

Bulmers Limited and Wm. Magner Limited v. (FAST-12785240) magnersessions.com 1,500 GB Space and 15,000 Monthly Bandwidth, Bluehost.Corn INC/Jason LaValla, D2010-1885 (WIPO January 17, 2010)   539

Bunge Limited, Bunge SA and Bunge Deutschland GmbH v. eric ochoki, FA2208002009194 (Forum September 22, 2022)   317

Burn World-Wide, Ltd. d/b/a BGT Partners v. Banta Global Turnkey Ltd., D2010-0470 (WIPO May 19, 2010)   336, 345

BYLT Performance LLC v. Grant Vollmer, BYLT, D2019-1851 (WIPO October 14, 2019)   165

C

C. Brewer and Sons Ltd. v. Vertical Axis, Inc., D2009-1759 (WIPO April 11, 2010)   591

Caesars World, Inc. v. Lester Bakator, D2005-0125 (WIPO)   609

Caldsoft Way3D Sistemas Eireli EPP v. JInsoo Yoon, D2016-2514 (WIPO January 23, 2017)   373

Caleb Marshall v. c/o Weebly Domains, FA1901001826454 (Forum March 4 2019)   328

California Public Employees' Retirement System v. Nette, Nanci, FA2207002006055 (Forum August 24, 2022)   242

Calzaturificio Buttero SRL. v. Yang Chao Wei, CAC v. 103520 (ADR.eu February 23, 2021)   728

CAM London Limited and Comgest Asset Management International Limited v. Cam LondonLtd, D2013-2190 (WIPO February 4, 2014)   41, 244, 246

Camon S.p.A. v. Intelli-Pet, LLC., D2009-1716 (WIPO March 12, 2010)   465

Camper, S.L. v. Detlev Kasten, D2005-0056 (WIPOMarch 3, 2005)   721

Candy Cloud IP LLC v. Mike Morgan, D2022-3368 (WIPO November 14, 2022)   544

Capital One Fin. Corp. v. Howel,FA0406000289304 (Forum August 11, 2004)   525

Cappuccine Specialties, INC. v. Domain Administrator, NameFind LLC., D2023-3244 (WIPO October 20, 2019)   665

Capt'n Snooze Management Pty Limited v. Domains 4 Sale, D2000-0488 (WIPO July17, 2000)   343

CareerBuilder, LLC v. Stephen Baker, D2003-0493 (WIPO August 5, 2003)   611

CareerBuilderLC v. L. Azra Kha, D2003-0493 (WIPO August 5, 2003)   609

Careflight Australia Limited v. Domain Admin, Protection Service INC d/b/a Protect. org / CareFlight Australia Limited, D2016-1624 (WIPO December 5, 2016)   291

Carso S.A. de C.V. v. RusliCyber.com and Trisakti University, Mr. Ahmad Rusli, D2008-1767 (WIPO January 5, 2009)   587

Cartoon Network v. Mike Morgan, D2005-1132 (WIPO January 5, 2006)   268

Carvana, LLC v. Privacy Administrator, Anonymize, Inc., D2022-3657 (WIPO December 19, 2022)   155, 557-559

Caterpillar Inc v. Roam the Planet, D2000-0275 (WIPO)   352, 509

Caterpillar Inc. v. Miyar, FA 95623 (Forum December 14, 2000)   352, 509

CBS Broadcasting, Inc. v. Dennis Toeppen, D2000-0400 (WIPO July 11, 2000)   500, 502, 762

CBS Broadcasting, Inc. v. Gaddoor Saidi, D2000-0243 (WIPO June 2, 2000)   500, 502, 762

CECIA v. Abid, AbidNetwork.com   200, 543-544

Celebrity Signatures International, Inc. v. Hera's Incorporated Iris Linder, D2002-0936 (WIPO January 3, 2003)   386

Celilo Group Media, Inc. v. Domain Administrator, D2010-1119 (WIPO Aug. 19, 2010)   127

Cellular One Group v. Paul Brien, D2000-0028 (WIPO March 10, 2000)   149

CEMEX UK Operations Ltd. v. Privacy Service Provided by Withheld for Privacy ehf / Cargo Logistics Transportation Services, Cargo Logistics Transportation Services; South Coast Shipping Company, South Coast Shipping Company; and Cargo Logistics, Cargo Log   559

Centroamerica Comercial, Sociedad Anonima de Capital Variable (CAMCO) v. Michael Mann, D2016-1709 (WIPO October 3, 2016)   475, 724

Century Time Gems Ltd v. Century Aluminum SysAdmins, Century Aluminum, D2023-3480 (WIPO December 21, 2023)   491

Certamen Miss España, S.L. v. P1ESOFT.COM, D2006-0679 (WIPO September 12, 2006)   588

Certified Financial Planner Board of Standards, Inc. v. Career Professionals, Inc., FA0106000097354 (Forum July 12, 2001)   350

CGU Insurance plc v. Irving Remocker, D2000-1515 (WIPO February 19, 2001)   660

Champagne Lanson v. Development Services/MailPlanet.com, Inc., D2006-0006 (WIPO March 20, 2006)   703

Channel 5 Broadcasting Limited v. PT Pancawana Indonesia, FA0107000098415 (Forum October 3, 2001)   498

Charles E. Runels, Jr. v. Domain Manager / Affordable Webhosting, Inc., Advertising, FA1709001749824 (October 23, 2017)   127, 226, 476

Charles Schwab & Co., Inc. v. Simon Schwab, FA2210002017845 (Forum January 23, 2023)   677

Charter Fund, Inc., d/b/a Charter School Growth Fund v. Withheld for Privacy Purposes, Privacy service provided by Withheld for Privacy ehf / Jackson Mike, Right Consultation, D2021-2855 (WIPO October 13, 2021)   616

Chernow Communications, Inc. v. Jonathan D. Kimball, D2000-0119 (WIPO May 18, 2000)   531, 606

Chesterfield Valley Investors, L.L.A dba Gateway Classic Cars of St. Louis v. Brock Winters, D2019-1380 (WIPO August 16, 2016)   108, 437

Chicago Bd. Options Exch. Inc. v. Private, FA 804703 (Forum Nov. 29, 2006)   447

Chisholm Chisholm & Kilpatrick LTD v. SuZhi Hong, D2018-1357 (WIPO July 29, 2018)   346

Choice Courier systems, Inc. v. William H. Kirkendale, 2002-0483 (WIPO July 23, 2002)   377

Chopard International SA v. Patrick Lam, D2015-1277 (WIPO September 21, 2015)   549

Christian Dior Couture v. Kianna Dior Productions, D2009-0353 (WIPO May 2009) 346

Chrome Bones / CB Luxury Brands, LLC v. Laursen, Shawn / Shawn's pasta & bake shop, FA1805001787926 (Forum June 27, 2018) 188

Chuan Sin Sdn. Bhd. v. Internet Admin (not for sale), Reflex Publishing Inc., D2014-0557 (WIPO May 29, 2014) 686

CircleBack Lending, Inc. v. Andy Tang, FA1603001667870 (April 28, 2016) 372

Citigroup Inc. and Primerica Financial Services, Inc. v. Brian Allman, FA0708001066738 (Forum October 16, 2007) 69

Citigroup Inc. v. Andrew Robert Wilson, Andrew Robert Wilson, D2021-1058 (WIPO June 1, 2021) 63, 69, 159, 189

Citigroup Inc. v. LYON LESHLEY, FA1805001788603 (Forum June 29, 2018) 63, 69, 159, 189

CitiusTech Healthcare Technology Private Limited v. Anthony Moussa, Moo Companies, Inc., D2022-3813 (WIPO November 22, 2022) 545

CitiusTech Healthcare Technology Private Limited v. Rex Kersey, D2022-3773 (WIPO December 28, 2022) 545

City Views Limited v. Moniker Privacy Services / Xander, Jeduyu, ALGEBRALIVE, D2009-0643 (WIPO July 3, 2009) 117-118

Clad Holdings Corporation v. Administration Local, D2005-0124 (WIPO May 9, 2005) 364

Clinomics Biosciences, Inc. v. Simplicity Software, Inc., D2001-0823 (WIPO September 10, 2001) 297

Clockwork IP LLC, One Hour Air Conditioning Franchising, LLC v. Elena Wallace, D2009-0485 (WIPO June 1, 2009) 253

Cloudfm Group Limited v. Barry Garner, MyMailer Ltd., D2021-3251 (WIPO December 14, 2021) 707

Club Jolly Turizm ve Ticaret A. v. Whois Agent, Whois Privacy Protection Service, Inc. / Fred Millwood, D2016-1256 (WIPO August 12, 2016) 500, 724

CMG Worldwide, Inc. v. Eric Dluhos, FA0005000094909 (Forum October 2, 2000) 737

CNR Music B.V. v. High Performance Networks, Inc., D2005-1116 (WIPO January 23, 2006) 458

CNRV, Inc. v. Vertical Axis Inc., FA0912001300901 (Forum May 3,2010) 419

Coachella Music Festival, LLC v. Michael Gonzalez, FA2306002050418 (Forum July 25, 2023) 449

Cognate Nutritionals, Inc. v. Martin Zemitis / Entria.com, FA1602001660055 (Forum March 17, 2016) 681

COLAS v. Domain Administrator, Daruna, LLC., D2020-0560 (WIPO June 6, 2020) 339, 595

Coles Myer Limited and Myer Stores Limited v. Dominic Main and Mr. William Savage t/a SAV. Trading, D2002-0124 (WIPO MAY 6, 2002)   274

Colin LeMahieu v. NANO DARK, FA1805001786065 (Forum June9,2018)   153

Collective Media, Inc. v. CKV / COLLECTIVEMEDIA.COM, D2008-0641 (WIPO July 31, 2008)   675

CollegeNET, Inc. v. Mark Roxberry, Drive Technology, LLC, D2023-1538 (WIPO June 21, 2023)   572

Columbine JDS Systems, Inc., v. Jin Lu, AF-0137 (eResolution March 15, 2000)   261

Comfort Window Co., Inc. v. AL-SADEQOUN LIL-TASWEEQ LLC, FA1206001447758 (Forum July 25, 2012)   600

Commonwealth Communications Group, Inc. v. David Lahoti dba eSecure, FA0109000100124 (Forum November 5, 2001)   637

CommScope, Inc. of North Carolina v. Chris Lowe / comm-scope / Chris Lowe / comm-scopes / Chris Lowa / commmscope, FA1707001742149 (Forum September 7, 2017)   611

Compact Disc World, Inc. v. Artistic Visions, Inc., FA0107000097855 (Forum August 15, 2001)   485, 589

Compagnie Generale des Matieres Nucleaires v. Greenpeace Int'l, D2001-0376 (WIPO May 14, 2001)   103

Compañía Logística de Hidrocarburos CLH SA v. Privacy Administrator, Anonymize, Inc. / Sam Dennis, Investments.org Inc.,D2018-0973 (WIPO June 25, 2018)   656

Compañía Logística v. Privacy Administrator, Anonymize, Inc./ Sam Dennis, Investments.org inc., D2018-0793 (WIPO June 14, 2018)   230, 656

Compaq Computer Corporation v. Boris Beric, D2000-0042 (WIPO March 28, 2000)   82, 459

Compart AG v. Compart.com / Vertical Axis, Inc., D2009-0462 (WIPO July 9, 2009)   570

Concierge Auctions LLC v. Registration Private, Domains By Proxy, LLC / Wesley Donehue, Donehue Direct, D2020-1020 (WIPO August 17, 2020)   436

Consensys Software Inc. v. Justin Pietroni, Netymology Ltd., D2021-3337 (WIPO December 9, 2021)   664, 672

Consuela, LLC v. Alberta Hot Rods, FA1306001504547 (Forum August 3, 2013)   671

ConsumerDirect, Inc. v. BARRY WALTERS, FA2304002041457 (Forum August 7, 2023)   126

Cooper's Hawk Intermediate Holding, LLC v. Tech Admin / Virtual Point Inc. FA2010001916204 (Forum November 17, 2020)   582, 680

Coöperative Univé U.A. v. Ashantiplc Ltd/ c/o Domain Privacy LLC, D2011-0636 (WIPO June 30, 2011)   676

Corbis Corporation v. Zest, FA0107000098441 (Forum September 12, 2001)   489

Corinthians Licenciamentos LTDA v. David Sallen, Sallen Enterprises, and J. D. Sallen Enterprises, D2000-0461 (WIPO July 17, 2000)   45, 746

Corning Incorporated v. Domain Admin, HugeDomains.com, D2021-0549 (WIPO July 2, 2021)   192

Corporacion Empresarial Altra S.L. v. Development Services, Telepathy, Inc., D2017-0178 (WIPO May 15, 2017)   504

Costa Crociere S.P.A. v. Yoshiki Okada, D2018-1632 (WIPO September 27, 2018)   511, 723

County Bookshops Limited v. Guy Loveday, D2000-0655 (WIPO September 22, 2000)   321

CouponCabin LLC v. Charles Martin, Net Exclusive LLC., D2021-0244(WIPO March 18. 2021)   155

Course Hero, Inc. v. Julius Njeri, FA2105001945579 (Forum June 29, 2021)   157

Courtney Cox, Ivy Lane Living v. Domain Admin, Privacy Protect, LLC (PrivacyProtect.org) / Betsy Riot, Betsy Riot, D2018-1256 (WIPO August 16, 2018)   104, 441

Courtney Love v. Brooke Barnett, FA 944826 (Forum May 14, 2007)   253

Craft Multimodal LTDA. v. Alexandre Guandalini, ALGX CORP, D2023-1691 (WIPO July 5, 2023)   296

Crayola Properties, Inc. v. Domain Contact, Protected WHOIS @INR, D2018-2091 (WIPO December 2, 2018)   526, 615

Cream Holdings Limited v. National Internet Source, Inc., D2001-0964 (WIPO September 28, 2001)   391, 662

Credit Agricole Indosuez Luxembourg s.a. v. Patrick G O'Regan, D 2000-1300 (WIPO November 28, 2000)   43, 720

Credit Industriel et Commercial S.A. v. Demand Domains, Inc., D2009-1184 (WIPO October 19, 2009)   177

Credit Lyonnais v. Jehovah Technologies Pte LTD., D 2000-1425 (WIPO December 29, 2000)   364

Creo Products Inc & anor v. Website in Development, D2000-0160 (WIPO May 1, 2000)   539

Crew International v. crew.com, D2000-0054 (WIPO April 20, 2000)   75, 114, 696

Critter Control, Inc. v. Lori DeMoor, D2023-0838 (WIPO June 2, 2023)   513, 547

Croatia Airlines d.d. v. Modern Empire Internet Ltd., D2003-0455 (WIPO August 21, 2003)   380

CRS Technology Corporation v. Condenet, Inc., FA0002000093547 (Forum March 28, 2000)   245, 636

CSI Leasing Mexico, S. de R.L. de C.V. v. Withheld for Privacy Purposes, Privacy Service Provided by Withheld for Privacy ehf / Cristina Montalvo, D2021-2962 (WIPO November 16, 2021)   613

CSP International Fashion Group S.p.A. v. Domain Administrator, NameFind LLC, D2018-0163 (WIPO March 13, 2018)   621, 692

CW & Associates Consulting and Recruiting Inc. v. Lynda Pitchford / ITSR, FA1505001619758 (Forum June 29, 2015)   332

Cyberbit Ltd. v. Mr. Kieran Ambrose, Cyberbit A/S, D2016-0126 (WIPO February 26, 2016)   663

D

Daily Racing Form LLC v. na and Virtual Dates, Inc., D2001-1032 (WIPO November 6, 2001)   490

Dakota Access, LLC (c/o Energy Transfer LP) v. John Saldis, FA1906001849464 (Forum August 6, 2019)   655

Darryl Davis Seminars, Inc. v. Privacydotlink Customer 656889 / Domain Admin, Abstract Holdings International Ltd., D2018-2238 (WIPO January 21, 2019)   215

Datacap Systems, Inc. v. Domain Admin, XYZ Invest LLC., D2023-0858 (WIPO May 2, 2023)   60, 578

Datapath Limited v. Naveed Ahmad, D2018-2362 (WIPO February 15, 2019)   209, 219

Dating Direct.com Ltd. v. Aston, FA0511000593977 (Forum December 28, 2005)   515

DatingDirect.com Limited v. Michael Turner, FA0410000349013 (Forum December 16, 2004)   22

David Foox v. Bill Hicks, D2008-0397 (WIPO May 30, 3008)   88, 433

David Foox v. Kung Fox & Bill Hicks, D2002-0472 (WIPO July 25, 2002)   88, 433

David Michael Bautista, Jr. v. Quantec LLC / Whois Privacy Services Pty Ltd / Lisa Katz, Domain Protection LLC   375

David Pecker v. Mr. Ferris, D2002-0184 (WIPO January 15, 2007)   371

David Robinson v. Brendan, Hight / MDNH Inc., D2008-1313 (WIPO October 27, 2008)   675

DaVita Inc. v. Cynthia Rochelo, FA1706001738034 (Forum July 20, 2017)   615

DealerX Partners, LLC v. Domain Manager, Visionamics/Citytwist Inc. / Lyndon Griffin, D2017-1680 (WIPO December 26, 2017)   670

Dealhunter A/S v. Richard Chiang, D2014-0766 (WIPO July 17, 2014)   593

Dean Hill Systems Ltd. v. Gregory Santana d/b/a Invicta, D2002-0404 (WIPO September 20, 2002)   251

Debbie Morgan Macao Commercial Offshore Limited, Missguided Limited v. Samir Vora, D2013-0737 (WIPO June 14, 2013)   299

Decathlon SAS v. Nadia Michalski, D2014-1996 (WIPO January 27, 2015)   355

Decathlon v. Doug Gursha, D2023-0987 (WIPO May 12, 2023)   355, 483

Decision Analyst, Inc. v. Doug C. Dohring, D2000-1630 (WIPO February 6, 2001)   321, 684

Deep Focus Inc. v. Domain Admin, Abstract Holdings International LTD., D2018-0518 (WIPO June 6, 2018)   185, 677

Degani Designs, LLC v. Chris Morling / Dot Zinc Limited, FA1603001664293 (Forum April 13, 2016)   326

Delbert R. Terrill Jr. v. Domain Admin / Privacy Protect, LLC (PrivacyProtect.org), FA1803001775784(Forum April 2, 2018)   217

Dell Inc. v. ali zaheri / deliran / Mitra Haman, FA2310002067046 (Forum December 18, 2023)   245

Delta 9 Bio-Tech Inc. v. N trading BV, UDRP-17880 (CIIDRC July 28, 2022)   362

Delta Air Lines, Inc. v. Chad Meyerson, FA1509001636800(Forum October 19, 2015)   369

Delta Air Transport NV (trading as SN Brussels Airlines) v. Theodule De Souza, D2003-0372 (WIPO August 5, 2003)   6

Delta Dental Plans Association v. Domains By Proxy, LLC / Kwangpyo Kim, D2022-0566 (WIPO May 25, 2022)   60, 217

Dentless, LLC v. Dent Guys, Inc., and Bill Swartwout, Beaches and Towns, Network, Inc., D2023-1547 (WIPO June 27, 2023)   240, 640

Derivados, S.A. de C.V. v. Apple Inc., D2017-1351 (WIPO October 23, 2017)   570

Desert Community College District aka College of the Desert v. Christopher Parman, FA2210002015615 (Forum November 21, 2022)   442

Deutsche Bank Aktiengesellschaft v. New York TV Tickets Inc., D2001-1314 (WIPO)   485

Deutsche Messe AG v. Kim Hyungho, D2003-0679 (WIPO November 13, 2003)   268

Deutsche Post AG v. NJDomains, D2006-0001 (WIPO March 1, 2006)   578, 675

Deutsche Telekom AG v. Britt Cordon, D2004-0487 (WIPO September 13, 2004)   266, 384, 601

Dewberry Engineers Inc. v. Dewberry IT, Dewberry Group, D2022-5016(WIPO March 13, 2023)   247

Dialoga Servicios Interactivos, S.A. v. Finlead AG, D2018-2768 (WIPO February 8, 2019)   178, 215, 598

Diamond Hill Investment Group, Inc. v. Carole Elkins, D2015-1191 (WIPO September 12, 2015)   528

Diamond Hill Investment Group, Inc. v. Richard Stroud, D2016-0510 (WIPO April 25, 2016)   528

Diamond Trust Consultancy (UK) Limited v. Kim, James, D2015-2051 (WIPO January 27, 2016)   505, 705

Diet Center Worldwide, Inc. v. Jason Akatiff, D2012-1609 (WIPO October 5, 2012)   105

DigiPoll Ltd. v. Raj Kumar, D2004-0939 (WIPO February 3, 2005)   316, 414

Digital City, Inc. v. Smalldomain, D2000-1283 (WIPO November 6, 2000)   310, 348

Digital Vision, Ltd. v. Advanced Chemill Systems, D2001-0827 (WIPO September 23, 2001)   309, 336

Digitronics Inventioneering Corporation v. @Six.Net Registered, D2000-0008 (WIPO March 2, 2000)   425

Diners Club International Ltd. v. Mark Jenkins, FA0906001266752 (Forum July 27, 2009)   185, 481

Diners Club International Ltd. v. O P Monga, FA0603000670049 (Forum May 22, 2006)   185, 481

DIRECTV, LLC v. michal restl c/o Dynadot, FA 1788826 (Forum July 5, 2018)   510

DISH Network L.L.C. v. Alon Garay Garay, D2022-3437 (WIPO November 14, 2022)   613

Disney Enterprises, Inc. v. Elmer Morales, FA0505000475191 (Forum June 24, 2005)   268

Displays Depot, Inc. v. GNO, Inc., D2006-0445 (WIPO June 29, 2006)   488

Ditec International AB / Global Preservation Systems, LLC v. ADAM FARRAR / HOSTGATOR / FRITS VERGOOSSEN / DITEC INTERNATIONAL CORPORATION / Christopher Alison, FA1712001763998 (Forum Feb. 1, 2018)   510

Diversified Mortgage, Inc. v. World Fin., FA0208000118308 (Forum October 30, 2002)   374

DK Company Vejle A/S v. Blend Sports Ltd., D2023-2100 (WIPO June 23, 2023)   335, 652

DK Company Vejle A/S v. Cody Favre, C4 Squared, D2019-2676 (WIPO December 17, 2019)   335, 652

DME Company LLC v. unknown unknown / DME Online Services, Ltd., FA1711001759818 (Forum January 19, 2018)   172, 553

DNA (Housemarks) Limited v. Tucows.com Co., D2009-0367 (WIPO May 5, 2009)   255, 298

DNC Services Corporation v. Donald Peltier / 021web design, FA2006001901303 (Forum July 22, 2020)   591

Do The Hustle, LLC v. Monkey Media   379, 468, 476

Do The Hustle, LLC v. Tropic Web, D2000-0624 (WIPO August 23, 2000)   379, 468, 476

Document Technologies, Inc. v. International Electronic Communications Inc., D2000-0270 (WIPO June 6, 2000)   453

Dollar Bank, Federal Savings Bank v. Paul Stapleton, The New Media Factory, D2016-0518 (WIPO April 24, 2016)   389, 502

Dolopain LLC (an Ariz. Co.) v. T. J. Griffin Sr., Griffin IT Media, inc., D2021-1776 (WIPO August 17, 2021)   339

Dominique Tillen v. Administrator Administrator, D2018-2181 (WIPO November 12, 2018)   624

Don Algodon H, S.A. v. Miguel Garcia Quintas, D2000-1042 (WIPO December 27, 2000)   238

Donald J. Trump and Trump Hotels & Casino Resorts, Inc. v olegevtushenko a/k/a Oleg Evtushenko, FA0110000101509 (Forum December 11, 2001)   443

Donna Karan Studio v. Raymond Donn, D2001-0587 (WIPO June 27, 2001)   489

Dover Downs Gaming & Entertainment, Inc. v. Domains By Proxy, LLC / Harold Carter Jr, Purlin Pal LLC, D2019-0633 (WIPO May 22, 2019)   78, 109, 434, 637

Dow Jones & Company, Inc. and Dow Jones LP v. John Zuccarini, D2000-0578 (WIPO September 10, 2000)   42, 609

Dr. Arlen Lyle Salte, Break Forth Ministries Society v. Power to Change, D2019-1806 (WIPO October 10, 2019)   293

Dr. Frank Lipman, Be Well Health & Wellness, LLC v. Be Well by Dr. Frank Lipman Company, Be Well by Dr. Frank Lipman Media, Brett Sandman Sandman, D2022-0753 (WIPO April 30, 2022)   562

Dr. Ing. h.c. F. Porsche AG v. Kentech, Inc. a.k.a. Helois Lab a.k.a. Orion Web a.k.a. Titan Net a.k.a. Panda Ventures a.k.a. Spiral Matrix and Domain Purchase, NOLDC, Inc., D2005-0890 (WIPO September 25, 2005)   275, 509

Dr. Muscle v. Michael Krell, FA1903001833036 (Forum April 19, 2019)   212, 564, 695

Draw Tite Inc.,v. Plattsburg Spring Inc., D2000-0017 (WIPO March 20, 2000)   385

Draw-Tite, Inc. v. Plattsburgh Spring Inc., D2000-0017 (WIPO March 14, 2000)   45

Drayton Nay v. Ice Inc., FA 400432 (Nat. Arb. Forum Mar. 16, 2005)   251

Drone Genius, Inc. v. Paul Peterson, D2022-3525 (WIPO December 2, 2022)   174

Dryvit Systems, Inc. v. Texas International Property Associates, D2008-0599 (WIPO June 17, 2008)   268

DSN Software, Inc. v. Rob Bay, FA1910001865961 (Forum December 10, 2019)   653

DSPA B.V. v. Bill Patterson, Reserved Media LLC., D2020-1449 (WIPO August 13, 2020   149, 707

Dumankaya Yapi Malzemeleri SAN. VE TIC. A.S v. Domain Administrator, Name Administration Inc. (BVI), D2015-1757 (WIPO December 15, 2015)   209

Duoserve, Inc. d/b/a ScheduFlow v. Paul Tyrrell / ScheduleFlow Pty Ltd., FA1711001759845 (Forum January 17, 2018)   172

DuWop, LLC v. Jayson Online, D2001-1315 (WIPO December 19, 2001)   330

Dynamic Visual Technologies (Pty) Ltd v. Direct Privacy, Savvy Investments, LLC Privacy ID# 14448338   217, 405

Dynamic Visual Technologies (Pty) Ltd v. Direct Privacy, Savvy Investments, LLC Privacy ID# 14448338, D2018-0738 (WIPO June 6, 2018)   217, 227, 405

E

e-Duction, Inc. v. John Zuccarini, d/b/a The Cupcake Party & Cupcake Movies, D2000-1369 (WIPO February 5, 2001)   463

E. Remy Martin & C° v. Ali Hameed, D2020-3439 (WIPO February19, 2021)   183, 472

E*Trade Financial Holdings, LLC v. Alex Drown, FA2209002013318 (Forum Oct. 21, 2022)   356

Eastman Sporto Group LLC v. Jim and Kenny, D2009-1688(WIPO March 1, 2010)   122

Easyjet Airline Company Ltd. v. Andrew Steggles, D2000-0024 (WIPO March 17, 2000)   141

EAuto, L.L.C. v. Net Me Up, D2000-0104 (WIPO April 14, 2000)   95, 167, 346, 383, 538

EAuto, L.L.C. v. Triple S. Auto Parts d/b/a Kung Fu Yea Enterprises, Inc., D2000-0047 (WIPO March 24, 2000)   95, 167, 346, 383, 538

ECCO Sko A/S v. ShiHua Ren / RenShiHua, D2017-0225 (WIPO April 10, 2017)   451

Edmunds.com, Inc. v. WWWEDMUNDS.com and DMUNDS.com, D2001-0937 (WIPO August 31,2001)   274

EDP - Energias de Portugal, S.A. v. Huhan, Yuming Zhong, D2016-1536 (WIPO October 28, 2016)   620

eDreams, Inc. v. CK Ventures Inc., D2009-1508 (WIPO January 8, 2010)   348

Educational Testing Service (ETS) v. Morrison Media LLC., D2006-1010(WIPO December 5, 2006)   412

Educational Testing Service v. Domains By Proxy, LLC / M S, D2022-0867 (WIPO May 16, 2022)   250, 353, 379, 412, 497-498, 691

Educational Testing Service v. Netkorea Co., D2000-0087 (WIPO April 7, 2000)   250, 353, 379, 412, 497-498, 691

Educational Testing Service v. TOEFL, D2000-0044 (WIPO March 16, 2000)   250, 353, 379, 412, 497-498, 691

eGalaxy Multimedia Inc. v. ON HOLD By Owner Ready To Expire, FA0305000157287 (Forum June 26, 2003)   518

Elan, LLC v. Al Perkins, FA1705001731999 (Forum June 26, 2017)   373

ELCOMAN Srl v. Marc Ellis, D2020-1628 (WIPO September 7, 2020)   399

Electronic Arts Inc. v. Abstract Holdings International LTD / Sherene Blackett, FA1111001415905 (Forum January 4, 2012)   145, 229

Electronic Frontier Foundation v. WhoisGuard Protected, Whoisguard Inc. / Jan Hasko, D2017-1355 (WIPO September 13, 2017)   445

ElectronicPartner Handel GmbH v. Antonio Loffredo, D2007-0380 (WIPO April 24, 2007)   482, 564

Element Logic AS v. Lane Allen, D2023-4411 (WIPO December 11, 2023)   687

Elkem ASA v. Ray Chiamulera, D2021-0452 (WIPO April 30, 2021)   188

Elvstrom Sails A/S v. Moniker Privacy Services, D2008-0393 (WIPO June 2, 2008)   42

Emadeldin Abdelfattah Mohamed Elakshar v. Kareem Fouad / Ahmed Yossef, Crius Solutions, D2018-2262 (WIPO December 28, 2028)   253

Emazing B.V. v. Joe Pierce, D2015-1252 (WIPO August 25, 2015)   677

eMedicine.com, Inc. v. Aspen Grove Consulting, D2001-0147 (WIPO June 19, 2001)   137

Emilio Pucci SRL v. Mailbank.com, Inc., D2000-1786 (WIPO March 27, 2001)   216

Empire Engineering LTD v. Liamuiga LLC, FA1906001847862 (Forum July 22, 2019)   654

Empire Flippers, LLC v. Ansh Gupta / Jamkain Media Ventures, FA2012001925050 (Forum January 21, 2021)   554, 586

Empire Flippers, LLC v. Ansh Gupta / Jamkain Media Ventures, FA2012001925050 (Forum January 27, 2021)   554, 586

Empire Wine & Spirits, LLC v. Domain Administrator, See PrivacyGuardian.org / Telesphore TETA, D2022-0543 (WIPO April 19, 2022)   315

Empower Media Partners, LLC v. M. Jarrar, FA2301002030007 (Forum March 7, 2023)   330

Encyclopaedia Britannica, Inc. v. John Zuccarini and The Cupcake Patrol, D2000-0330 (WIPO June 7, 2000)   77

Endeavors Technology, Inc. v. Dick In Jar,D2001-0770 (WIPO July 21, 2001)   373

Endo Pharmaceuticals Inc. v. Tanzim Ahmad, D2021-0511 (WIPOApril 19, 2021)   226

Energysquare v. Management Team, Easy Property, D2021-1219 (WIPO June 15, 2021)   511

Enrique Bernat F., SA v. Marrodan, D2000-0966 (WIPO October 6, 2000)   454

Enuygun Com Internet Bilgi Hizmetleri Teknoloji Ve Ticaret Anonim Sirketi v. Kamran Agali, Ornek Teknoloji AS, D2023-0770 (WIPO April 28, 2023)   489

Epitec, Inc. v. EPITEC, FA1209001463139 (Forum October 24, 2012)   570

Equality Charter School v. Mona Davids / A Happy DreamHost Customer, D2011-1226 (WIPO September 20, 2011)   428

Equentia SCF Technologies Private Limited v. Huang ShaoHuai (WIPO D2023-4724)   719

Erase Technologies, LLC v. Web Presence LLC, NetReputation.com, D2022-3797 (WIPO January 2023)   315

eSnipe, Inc. v. Modern Empire Internet, Ltd., D2009-0719 (WIPO August 5, 2009)   339

ESPN, Inc. v. Danny Ballerini, FA0008000095410 (Forum September 2000)   417, 478

Estate of Gary Jennings and Joyce O. Servis v. Submachine and Joe Ross, D2001-1042 (WIPO October 25, 2001)   427

Estee Lauder Inc. v. estelauder.com, estelauder.net and Jeff Hanna, D2000-0869) (WIPO September 25, 2000)   609

Etam, plc v. Alberta Hot Rods, D2000-1654 (WIPO Jan. 31, 2001)   474, 720

Etechaces Marketing and Consulting Private Limited v. Bhargav Chokshi / IR Financial Services Pvt. Ltd., D2015-0563 (WIPO May 15, 2015)   365

ETH Zürich (Eidgenössische Technische Hochschule Zürich) v. Andre Luiz Silva Rocha, Construtora Norberto Odebrecht S/A, D2016-0444 (WIPO April 18, 2016)   230

European Monitoring Centre for Drugs and Drug Addiction (EMCDDA) v. Virtual Clicks / Registrant ID:CR36884430, Registration Private Domains by Proxy, Inc., D2010-0475 (WIPO July 7, 2010)   706

Everytown for Gun Safety Action Fund, Inc. v. Contact Privacy Inc., Customer 1249561463 / Steve Coffman, D2022-0473 (WIPO April 4, 2022)   78, 109, 362-363, 434

Everytown for Gun Safety Action Fund, Inc. v. IGI NA / IGI NA CORP   78, 109, 362-363, 434

Expedia, Inc. v. Mandanice, FA0302000146598 (Forum April 7, 2003)   352

Express Scripts, Inc. v. Windgather Investments Ltd. / Mr. Cartwright, D2007-0267 (WIPO April 26, 2007)   640

F

F. Hoffmann-La Roche AG v. PrivacyProtect.org, Domain Admin and Mark Sergijenko, D2007-1854 (WIPO March 11, 2008)   32

Fabricas Agrupadas de Muñecas de Onil S.A. (FAMOSA) v. Gord Palameta, D2000-1689 (WIPO March 23, 2001)   621, 660, 684

Fabricators & Manufacturers Association, International v. NameFind, FA 1728625 (Forum June 1, 2017)   183

Facebook, Inc. and Instagram, LLC v. WhoisGuard Protected, WhoisGuard, Inc. / Phishing Operations, Wombat Security Technologies, D2020-3218 (WIPO January 25,2021)   142

Facele SPA v. Jason Owens, D2019-0140 (WIPO July 28, 2019)   654

Factory Direct Wholesale, LLC v. decai fu, FA2111001971788 (Forum November 30, 2021)   774

Fair Isaac Corporation v. Doan Van Quang, FA2310002068237 (Forum November 28, 2023)   469

Fairmont Hotel Management L.P. v. Puts, D2001-0431 (WIPO May 17, 2001)   351, 473

Family Watchdog LLC v. Lester Schweiss, D2008-0183 (WIPO April 23, 2008)   299

Farouk Systems, Inc. v. QYM, D2009-1658 (WIPO January 19, 2010)   269, 618

Faster Faster, Inc. DBA Alta Motors v. Jeongho Yoon c/o AltaMart, FA1612001708272 (Forum February 6, 2017)   598

Fasthosts Internet Ltd v. Jamie Scott, Smudge It Solutions Ltd., D2008-0841 (WIPO July 24, 2008)   244

Federación Nacional de Cafeteros de Colombia v. Vince Harasymiak, Domain Capital, D2022-4022 (WIPO January 18, 2022)   342, 361

Federación Nacional de Cafeteros de Colombia v. Vince Harasymiak, Domain Capital, D2022-4022 (WIPO January 18, 2023)   342, 361

Femida a/k/a International Legal Counsels PC v. Reserved for Customers / MustNeed. com, FA190600 1847829 (Forum July 25, 2019)   647

Fenix International Limited v. DAVID STABOLITO, XTREME, D2022-0343 (WIPO March 15, 2022)   485

Fetish Factory, Inc. v. The Fetish Factory a/k/a Stanford Stuart a/k/a Pamela Hancock a/k/a Internetwork Partners, FA0108000099610 (Forum November 8, 2001)   344

Fiberstar, Inc. v. Merlin Kauffman, FA1602001663188 (ForumApril 11, 2016)   506

Fieldd Pty Ltd v. Jessica Duarte, D2022-4980 (WIPO March 22, 2023)   405

Fifth Street Capital LLC v. Fluder (aka Pierre Olivier Fluder), D2014-1747 (WIPO November 8, 2014)   367

Fine Tubes Limited v. Tobias Kirch, J. & J. Ethen, Ethen Rohre GmbH, D2012-2211 (WIPO January 30, 2013)   341

Finter Bank Zurich v. Shumin Peng, D2006-0432 (WIPO June 12, 2006)   269

Finwise BV v. Anne-Jan Hempenius, NameAvenue, D2020-3135 (WIPO January 19, 2021)   49

First American Funds, Inc. v. Ult.Search, Inc., D2000-1840 (WIPO May 1, 2001)   123, 393, 701

Firstgate Internet A.G. .v. David Soung, D2000-1311 (WIPO February 28, 2001)   307, 456

Fitness Anywhere LLC v. au tuu, FA2210002016615) (Forum November 11, 2022)   760

Fleetstar Information Systems Ltd. v. Stephen Morris, D2001-0518 (WIPO May 25, 2001)   162

Flexspace No 2 LLP v. Cem Arslan, DNU2022-0001 (WIPO June 6, 2022)   475

Flexspace No 2 LLP v. Michael Angelo Justiniano, Flexspace AS., D2021-4135 (WIPO February 29, 2021)   475

Florim Ceramiche S.p.A. v. Domain Hostmaster, Customer ID: 2439 1572426632, Whois Privacy Services Pty LTD / Domain Administrator, Vertical Axis Inc   233, 609

Florim Ceramiche S.p.A. v. Domain Hostmaster, Customer ID: 24391572426632, Whois Privacy Services Pty LTD / Domain Administrato, Vertical Axis Inc., D2015-2085 (WIPO February 11, 2016)   233, 609

Fluke Corporation v. Erwin Bryson / fixmyfluke / Nelson Bryson, FA2203001988399 (Forum July 6, 2022)   513, 592

Flying Dog Brewery, LLLP v. WhoIs Privacy Protection Services, Inc. / Phil Allen, Flying Dog Enterprises, D2018-1683 (WIPO September 22, 2018)   594, 637

Fondation Le Corbusier v. Monsieur Bernard Weber, Madame Heidi Weber, D2003-0251 (WIPO July 4, 2003)   361-362

Food and Wine Travel Pty Ltd v. Michael Keriakos, Keriakos Media Ventures, D2016-1953, (WIPO November 21, 2016)   489

Force Therapeutics, LLC v. Patricia Franklin, University of Massachusetts Medical School   9

Forest Laboratories, Inc. v. Natural Products Solutions LLC, D2011-1032 (WIPO July 29, 2011)   191

FormLinc Information d/b/a GroupLink v. Credit Suisse Group, FA0102000096750 (Forum April 25, 2001)   57

FOSS A/S, FOSS NIRSystems INC v. fossnirsystems.com c/o Whois IDentity Shield / Admin, Domain, D2008-1256 (WIPO October 10, 2008)   88

Franke Technology and Trademark Ltd v. hakan gUlsoy, CAC 101464 (ADR.eu May 11, 2017)   447

Franki Global Inc. v. Privacy service provided by Withheld for Privacy ehf / Golden Dream, The Stay Gold Co / Samantha Jurashka, D2021-2901 (WIPO December 13, 2021)   473, 475

Franklin Mint Federal Credit Union v. GNO, Inc., FA0612000860527 (Forum March 9. 2007)   229

Fraternal Order of Moai, Inc v. Tim Glazneraim, FA1607001686147(Forum August 30, 2016)   430

FreedomCard, Inc. v. Mr. Taeho Kim, D2001-1320 (WIPO January 20, 2002)   718

Fresenius Kabi S.A. v. Domain Manager, D2018-0491 (May 24, 2018)   190

Fresh Intellectual Properties, Inc. v. 800Network.com, D2005-0061 (WIPO March 21, 2005)   70, 80, 97

Frisby S.A. v. Registration Private, Domains by Proxy LLC / Michael Appolonia, D2020-0706 (WIPO May 12, 2020)   667

Fulham Football Club (1987) Limited, Tottenham Hostpur Public Limited, West Ham United Football Club PLC, Manchester United Limited, The Liverpool Football Club And Athletic Grounds Limited v. Domains by Proxy, Inc./ Official Tickets Ltd., D2009-0331 (May 12, 2009)   279

Function 4, LLC v. Michael McGrath, D2020-2725 (WIPO January17, 2021)   566

Fundación EOI v. Kamil Gaede, D2021-3934 (WIPO December 21,2021)   63, 157, 494

Future France v. Name Administration Inc., D2008-1422 (WIPO December 8, 2008)   490, 704

Futuris Automotive Interiors (Australia) Pty Ltd v. X9 Interactive LLC, D2011-0596 (WIPO June 20, 2011)   675

FXCM Global Services LLC v. WhoisGuard Protected, Whoisguard Inc. / Jenny Sohia   231

G

G.D. Searle v. Martin Mktg., FA0208000118277 (ForumOctober 1, 2002)   387

Gainvest Legal Corporation v. John Sozanski, Gainvest, LLC., D2020-2958(WIPO December 22, 2020)   549

Galvanize LLC, dba Galvanize v. Brett Blair / ChristianGlobe Network, FA1405001557092 (Forum June 26, 2014)   729

Gamesville.com, Inc. v. John Zuccarini, FA0007000095294 (Forum August 30, 2000)   416

Ganz v. Schuessler Enterprises, Inc., FA0810001230809 (Forum December 10, 2008)   423

Gapardis Health and Beauty, Inc. v. Frantz Boulos, FA2010001917653 (Forum November 23, 2020   391

Gary Chupik v. Shant Sarkuni, FA1910001868583 (Forum November 18, 2019)   650

Gary J. Player and Gary Player Enterprises, LLC v. Domains Admin / Gary Player Group, Inc   247, 566

Gary L. Pifer d/b/a Colchester Rubber Co., Inc. v. M.A. Stenzel, FA0510000588409 (Forum December 27, 2005)   741

Gazey and Partners LLP trading as Privacy Partnership v. Privacy service provided by Withheld for Privacy ehf / Muthu Balasubramaniam, One Trust, D2022-3138 (WIPO October 7, 2022)   667

Gen. Mach. Prods. Co. v. Prime Domains, FA0001000092531 (Forum March 16, 2000)   418

General Electric Company v. Estephens Productions, D2009-1438 (WIPO December 17, 2009)   275, 445, 470, 629

General Electric Company v. Marketing Total S.A., D2007-1834 (WIPO May 18, 2007)   275, 445, 470, 629

General Growth Properties, Inc., Provo Mall L.L.C. v. Steven Rasmussen/Provo Towne Centre Online, D2003-0845 (WIPO January 15, 2004)   408

General Machine Products Company, Inc. v. Prime Domains (a/k/a Telepathy, Inc., FA0001000092531 (Forum March 16, 2000)   597, 714, 717

General Machine Products Company, Inc. v. Prime Domains (a/k/a Telepathy, Inc.), FA0001000092531 (Forum March 16, 2000)   597, 714, 717

General Media Communications, Inc. v. Crazy Troll c/o CrazyTroll.com, FA0602000 651676 (Forum May 26, 2006)   671

Geniebooks.com Corporation v. William E. Merritt, D2000-0266 (WIPO July 27, 2000)   512

Genomatix Software GmbH v. Intrexon Corporation, D2010-0778 (WIPO July 8, 2010)   671

Genting Berhad v. Tan Kim Sin, FA0005000094735 (FORUM June 28, 2000)   415

Geo Global Partners, LLC v. Ruby Administrator / Ruby Advertising, FA180700 1797850 (Forum August 29, 2018)   647

George Pataki v. Trend Black, FA2112001978698 (Forum January 25, 2022)   376

Gibson Brands, Inc. v. Domain Administrator, AssuredPartners Inc., D2022-2678 (WIPO September 29, 2022)   549

Gigglesworld Corporation v. Mrs Jello, D2007-1189 (WIPO November 16, 2007)   679

Gilbert R. Armenta and Armenta Realty Holdings, LLC v. Robert Andre, FA1505001621195 (Forum June 29, 2015)   102

Givelify LLC v. Name Redacted, D2023-2406 (WIPO July 31, 2023)   249

Given Goods, Inc. v. Domain Administrator, Tiburon Holdings, Inc.,D2021-2589 (WIPO October 1, 2021)   187

Glimcher University Mall v. GNO, Inc., FA0107000098010 (Forum August 23, 2001)   264, 661, 685

Global Car Group Pte Ltd., Cars24 Services Private Limited v. Scott Simmons, ilearn-Project   49, 546

Global Personals, LLC v. Daniel Carvallo, Skyloop Digital Ltd., FA22050019 95514 (Forum July 18, 2022)   126, 194

Glory Ltd. V. MicroStrategy Inc., D2017-1900 (WIPO January 3, 2018)   169

Glovoapp23, S.L. v. Wang Shun, D2019-1986 (WIPO September 30,2019)   651

GO IN GmbH v. SpiritOfLogic GmbH, D2022-2752 (WIPO October 5, 2022)   176

GoDaddy in BzzAgent, Inc. v. Bzzing, Inc., Diego Berdakin, D2009-0295 (WIPO April 22, 2009)   605

Gold Coast Tourism Corporation Ltd. v. Digimedia.com L.P., D2013-1733 (WIPONovember 13, 2014)   499

Gold Fields Limited v. Vivek Narayan, D2018-2920 (WIPO February 9, 2019)   209

Goldline International, Inc. v. Gold Line, D2000-1151 (WIPO January 4, 2001) (<goldline.com
)   424, 641, 685

Goldmasters Precious Metals v. Gold Masters srl, FA0007000095246 (Forum August 21, 2000)   222

Goodr LLC v. Michael Rader, Brandroot, D2018-1171 (WIPO August28, 2018)   492

Goodwin Procter LLP v. Gayle Fandetti, FA1706001738231 (Forum August 8, 2017)   527, 612, 614

Google Inc. v. 1&1 Internet Limited, FA170800 1742725 (Forum August 31, 2017)   192, 485, 612, 614

Google Inc. v. Andrey Korotkov, FA120900 1463221 (Forum October 31, 2012)   192, 485, 612, 614

Google Inc. v. Blue Arctic LLC, FA1206001447355 (Forum July 25, 2012)   192, 485, 612, 614

Gordon Sumner, p/k/a Sting v. Michael Urvan, D2000-0596 (WIPO July 24, 2000)   459

GoSecure Inc. v. Billa Bhandari, FA2107001954083) (Forum August 19, 2021)   668

Government of Canada v. David Bedford a.k.a. DomainBaron.com, D2001-0470 (WIPO June 30, 2001)   388, 406

GPZ Technology, Inc. v. Aleksandr Vedmidskiy / Private Person, FA1504001612935 (Forum May 11, 2015)   619

Graftex Prodcom SRL and Graffitti – 94 R.B.I. Prodcom S.R.L. v. Piazza Affari srl, Michele Dinoia, D2017-0148 (WIPO March 22,2017)   694

Granite Gear, LLC v. Cameron Douglas, FA2311002069170 (Forum December 7, 2023)   232

Grasso's Koninklijke Machinefabrieken N.V., currently acting as Royal GEA Grasso Holding N.V. v. Tucows.com Co., D2009-0115 (WIPO April 10, 2009)   695

Green Bay Packers, Inc. v. Moniker Privacy Services / Montgomery McMahon, D2016-1455 (WIPO October 21, 2016)   594-595

Green Tyre Company Plc. v. Shannon Group, D2005-0877 (WIPO October 5, 2005)   633

Greenfort Partnerschaft von Rechtsanwälten mbB v. CheapYellowPages.com, D2016-0796 (WIPO June 16, 2016)   718

Gregg M. Mashberg v. Crystal Cox, D2011-0677 (WIPO June 30, 2011)   372

Gridiron Fiber Corp. and Lumos Telephone LLC d/b/a Lumos Networks v. Yui Quan, FA2110001970005(Forum December 20, 2021)   145

Grove Broadcasting Co. Ltd. v. Telesystems Commc'ns Ltd., D2000-0703 (WIPO November 10, 2000)   12, 40, 70, 245, 554

Grundfos A/S v. Texas International Property Associates, D2007-1448 (WIPO December 14 2007)   470

Grupo Costamex, S.A. de C.V. (COSTAMEX), Operación y Supervisión de Hoteles, S.A. de C.V. (OPYSSA) v. Vertical Axis Inc., D2013-1829 (WIPO February 10, 2014)   235

Grupo Costamex, SA de C.V. v. Stephen Smith and Oneandone Private Registration / 1&1 Internet Inc., D2013-1829 (WIPO February 10,2014)   412

Grupo Nacional Provincial, S.A. v. Privacydotlink, Customer 4270030 / Yancy Naughton, D2021-1136 (August 25, 2021)   24, 145, 154, 231

Grupo Televisa SA v. Party Night Inc, D2003-0796 (WIPO December 2, 2003)   316

GSL Networks Pty Ltd. v. Domains By Proxy, LLC / Alex Alvanos, Bobservers, D2021-2255 (WIPO September 27, 2021)   535, 682

Gstaad Saanenland Tourismus v. Domain Administrator, PrivacyGuardian.org / Dimitri Dimitriadis, D2016-2601 (WIPO May 19, 2017)   263

Guardian News & Media Limited v. Giovanni Laporta, Yoyo.email, D2014-1656 (WIPO November 21, 2014)   111

Guccio Gucci S.p.A v. Andrea Hubner, et al., D2012-2212 (WIPO February 8, 2013)   276

Gunther Marktl, and StepsApp GmbH v. Privacy service provided by Withheld for Privacy ehf / Michael Smirnov (or Michael Smirnoff), D2022-1746 (WIPO August 9, 2022)   203

Guru Denim Inc. v. Ibrahim Ali Ibrahim abu-Harb, D2013-1324 (WIPO September 27, 2013)   125, 455

H

H & M Hennes & Mauritz AB v. Whois Privacy Protection Service, Inc. / Dvl Den, D20162474 (WIPO January 31, 2017)   286

Hale Law, P.A v. Roger Hale, D2023-0084 (WIPO April 20, 2023)   266, 652

Halifax plc v. Sontaja Sanduci, D2004-0237 (WIPO June 3, 2004)   611

Hallmark Licensing, LLC v. EWebMall, Inc., D2015-2202 (WIPO February12, 2016)   389, 623

Hallmark Licensing, LLC v. Jarod Hallmark, FA2101001929310 (Forum February 22, 2021)   389, 623

Halo Innovations, Inc. v. Name Administration Inc. (BVI), FA1009001344653 (Forum November 3, 2010)   185

Handa Medical Group, Inc. v. anthony oyogoa / Oluwa Clothing, FA1404001552182 (Forum May 5, 2014)   561

Handy Guy Inc. v. Merlin Kauffman, FA 1998214 (Forum July 20, 2022)   330

Happy as Clams, Inc., a California Corp., DBA Date Like a Grownup v. Heather Dugan, D2014-1655 (WIPO November 1, 2014)   660

Harcourt, Inc. v. Fadness, FA0007000095247 (Forum September 8, 2000)   509

Harima Chemicals Group, Inc. v. Domain Administrator, DomainMarket.com, D2021-3512 (WIPOJanuary 31, 2022)   332, 486

Harry Winston Inc. and Harry Winston S.A. v. Jennifer Katherman, D2008-1267 (WIPO October 18, 2008)   441

Harvard Lampoon, Inc. v. Reflex Publishing Inc., D2011-0716 (WIPO July 26, 2011)   584

Harvest Dispensaries, Cultivations & Production Facilities, LLC v. Rebecca Nickerson / Rock City Harvest, FA2004001892080 (Forum June 26, 2020)   411, 577

Hästens Sängar AB v. Jeff Bader / Organic Mattresses, Inc., FA2005001895951 (Forum July 31, 2020)   512

HDT Software Limited v. Bryan Graves, D2022-0998 (WIPO April 21, 2022)   666

Healthgrades Operating Company, Inc. v. Erick Hallick, FA160400 1672836 (Forum June 9, 2016)   292

Healthyr, LLC v. Jonathan Curd, D2023-1802 (WIPO June 26, 2023)   683

Hearst Communications, Inc. and Hearst Magazines Property, Inc. v. David Spencer d/b/a Spencer Associates, and Mail.com, Inc., FA0093763 (Forum April 13, 2000)   696

Heaven Hill Distilleries, Inc. v. Contact Privacy Inc. Customer 0157950512 / Andrea Latimer, Latimer, D2020-1612 (WIPO September 14, 2020)   351

Herbalife Int'l v. Farmaha, D2005-0765 (WIPO October 3, 2005)   637

Hershey Chocolate & Confectionery LLC v. tedd cor, D2023-3924 (WIPO November 13, 2023)   146

High-Class Distributions S.r.l. .v. Onpne Entertainment Services, D2000-0100 (WIPO May 4, 2000)   344

Hill-Rom Inc. v. Jyoti Bansal, FA1703001724573(Forum May 3, 2017)   612

Hoffmann-La Roche Inc. v. Alan Truskowski, FA0609000808287 (Forum November 14, 2006)   481

Homer TLC, Inc. v. Andy Dorrani / HomeDept.com Inc., FA1202001429319 (Forum March 28, 2012)   233, 360

Hôpitaux Universitaires de Genève v. Aydin Karadeniz, D2016-1620 (WIPO October 10, 2016)   586

Hopscotch Group v. Perfect Privacy LLC/Joseph William Lee, D2015-1844 (WIPO January 20, 2016)   163

Horizon Publishing, LLC v. Opulence Communications Ltd., FA1302001487500 (Forum April 2, 2013)   675

Hostelworld.com Limited v. huangbo, huangbo, D2022-3341 (WIPO November 11, 2022)   436

Houlberg Dev. v. Adnet Int'l, FA0009000095698 (Forum October 27, 2000)   113

Howard Jarvis Taxpayers Association v. Paul McCauley, D2004-0014 (WIPO April 22, 2004)   80, 104, 442

HPD Software Limited v. Dvlpmnt Marketing, Inc., D2022-0269 (WIPO April 4, 2022)   220

HQUK Limited v. Head Quarters, D2003-0942 (WIPO February 5, 2004)   316

HSIL Limited, Somany Home Innovation Limited / SHIL Ltd., Brilloca Limited v. GOTW Hostmaster, Get On The Web Limited   646

HSM Argentina S.A. v. Vertical Axis, Inc., D2007-0017 (WIPO May 1, 2007)   455

Human Resource Consulting Inc. v. Konstantinos Zournas, D2007-1425 (WIPO November 23, 2007)   149, 627, 706

Humble Bundle, Inc. v. Domain Admin, Whois Corp., D2016-0914 (WIPO June 21, 2016)   614

I

I@D International v. Monica Da Costa, D2022-0033 (WIPO March 29, 2022)   296

IAFT International LLC v. Managing Director / Eutopian Holdings, FA 1577032 (FORUM Oct. 9, 2014)   9

iCommand Ltd v. Johnny Gray, ArtWired, Inc., D2020-1438 (WIPO August 11, 2020)   65, 723

Idaho Home Realty LLC v. Michael James Ohlson / Michael Ohlson / Bob Adams, VVG, D2021-2768(WIPO November 18, 2021)   337

Ideal Nutrition, LLC v. Khaled Alshahri / Khaled Group, LLC, FA2306002048379 (Forum August 3, 2023)   590

IDR Solutions Ltd. v. Whois Privacy Corp, D2016-2156 (WIPO December 12, 2016)   471, 488

iFinex Inc. v. xu shuaiwei, FA1711001760249 (Forum January 1, 2018)   472

Impala Platinum Holdings Limited v. Domain Admin, Privacy Protect, LLC (PrivacyProtect.org) / Domain Admin, Domain Privacy Guard Sociedad Anónima Ltd., D2020-2268 (WIPO November 13, 2020)   592

Imperial College of Science, Technology and Medicine v. Zahid Khan (for Imperial College Management School Alumni Association - ICMSAA), D2000-1079 (WIPO November 16, 2000)   548

In Loco Tecnologia da Informação S.A. v. Perfect Privacy, LLC. / Dermot O'Halloran, ZZG Ltd., D2019-2738 (WIPO March 24, 2020)   265, 663

Inbay Limited v. Ronald Tse dba Neosparx International, D2014-0096 (WIPO March 21, 2014)   225, 394, 476

Incase Designs Corp. v. Rogenie LLC, Rogenie Cordero, D2012-1491 (WIPO September 12, 2012)   355

Informa Business Information, Inc. v. Privacydotlink Customer 640040 / Domain Manager, Web D.G. Ltd., D2017-1756 (WIPO December 11, 2017)   505, 725

infospace.com Inc. v. Infospace Technology Co. Ltd., D2000-0074 (March 28, 2000)   56, 261

Ingersoll-Rand Co. v. Frank Gully, d/b/a Advcomren, D2000-0021 (WIPO March 9, 2000)   462

Innotek, Inc. v. Sierra Innotek, D2002-0072 (WIPO April 22, 2002)   406

Innovative Marketing and Distribution, Inc d/b/a Engel Coolers v. Michael Harrington, FA1606001678152 (Forum July 5, 2016)   293

Innoviti Technologies Private Limited v. Richard Cardenas, INNOVITI S.A.S., DCO2023-0108 (WIPO January 30, 2024)   639

Insider, Inc. v. DNS Admin / Contact Privacy Service, FA1912001874834 (Forum February 3, 2020)   145, 501, 709

Instagram, LLC v. Brian Breiter, Law Offices of Brian Breiter, D2022-2149 (WIPO August 24, 2022)   142, 451

Institut de Radioprotection et de Sûreté Nucléaire v. Domain Admin, FindYourDomain, D2021-4361 (WIPO March14, 2022)   150

Instrumentation Northwest, Inc. v. INW.COM c/o Telepathy, Inc., D2012-0454 (WIPO June 1, 2012)   228, 576, 591

Int'l Raelian Religion & Raelian Religion of France v. Mailbank.com Inc., D2000-1210 (WIPO April 4, 2001)   200

Intellect Design Arena Limited v. Moniker Privacy Services/David Wieland, iEstates.com, LLC, D2016-1349 (WIPO August 29, 2016)   81, 264, 583, 681

Intellogy Solutions, LLC v. Craig Schmidt and IntelliGolf, Inc., D2009-1244 (WIPO November 24, 2009)   666

Inter IKEA Systems B.V. v. Jan Everno (The Management Group II), CAC Case No. CAC-UDRP-105061)   610

Intercontinental Exchange Holdings, Inc. (ICE) v. Withheld for Privacy Purposes, Privacy service provided by Withheld for Privacy ehf / You Are, Not, D2021-1332 (WIPO June 11, 2021)   368

International Business Machines Corporation (IBM) v. Chait, Mitch, IBMS. D2023-2911 (WIPO September 24, 2023)   148

International Data Group, Inc. v. K McGovern, D2005-0960 (WIPO October 31, 2005)   397

International E-Z UP, Inc. v. PNH Enterprises, Inc., FA0609000808341 (Forum November 15, 2006)   294, 392

Internationale Spar Centrale B.V. v. Scientific Process & Research, Inc., D2005-0603 (WIPO October 6, 2005)   245

Intersystems Corporation v. Contact Privacy Inc. / Maree F Turner, D2017-1383 (WIPO September 18, 2017)   527, 612

Intocable, Ltd. v. Paytotake LLC, D2016-1048 (WIPO July 29, 2016)   64, 169

Intocast AG v. Lee Daeyoon, D2000-1467 (WIPO January 17, 2001)   380

Inversiones MCN S.A.S. v. Domains By Proxy, LLC DomainsByProxy.com / Tamarak Marketing, Tamarak Capital, D2022-3219 (WIPO October 20, 2022)   174

Invesco Ltd. v. Premanshu Rana, FA1705001733167 (Forum July 10, 2017)   417, 478

Irving Materials, Inc. v. Black, Jeff / PartnerVision Ventures, FA171000 753342 (Forum November 7, 2017)   541, 624, 750, 784

IslandAir, Inc. v. Flanders, FA0011000096098 (Forum February 8, 2001)   531

Israel Harold Asper v. Communication X Inc., D2001-0540 (WIPO June 11, 2001)   370

ITF v. Anonymize, Inc. / Domain Admin, Sébastien Schmitt, D2022-2196 (WIPO September 2, 2022)   xvii, xxix, 77, 111, 266, 472, 522, 642, 674

ITMetrixx, Inc. v. Kuzma Productions, D2001-0668 (WIPO August 2, 2001)   291

Itron, Inc. v. Super Privacy Service LTD c/o Dynadot / Nanci Nette, Name Management Group, D2022-1920 (WIPO July 26, 2022)   558

Itron, Inc. v. Super Privacy Service LTD do Dynadot / Nanci Nette, NameManagement Group, D2022-1920 (WIPO July 26, 2022)   558

J

J. Crew International v. crew.com, D2000-0054 (WIPO April 20, 2000)   114, 696

J. Crew International, Inc. v. crew.com, D2000-0054 (WIPO April20, 2000)   696

Jaber Media Corporation Inc. v. Ahmad Mahameed, D2021-2971 (WIPO November 5, 2021)   156, 546

Jack Brabham Engines Limited v. Sixstroke Engine Developments Pty Limited, D2007-0292 (WIPO April 25, 2007)   178

Jacques Lafitte SA v. 21st Century Communications SCP, D2000-0443 (WIPO July 25, 2000)   182

Jake's Fireworks Inc. v. Whois Privacy Services Pty Ltd / Vertical Axis Inc., Domain Administrator, Customer ID: 47520518994762, D2011-0779 (WIPO August 9, 2011)   191

James Linlor v. Host Master / McAfee LLC, FA2202001985124 (Forum March 31, 2022)   9

James Squires v. John Zuccarini, AF-218 (eResolution May 29, 2000)   364

Japan Airlines Company Limited v. TransHost Associates, JAL Systems and John A
Lettelleir, D2000 - 0573 (WIPO August 21, 2000)   427

Jappy GmbH v. Satoshi Shimoshita, D2010-1001 (WIPO September 28, 2010)   122

Javier Narvaez Segura, Grupo Loading Systems S.L. v. Domain Admin, Mrs. Jello,
LLC.,D2016-1199 (WIPO August 31, 2016)   163, 419

Javier Zetter Casillas v. Domain Hostmaster/Vertical Axis Inc., D2014-0400 (WIPO
June 6, 2014)   594

Jazeera Space Channel TV Station v. AJ Publishing aka Aljazeera Publishing, 2005-
0309 (WIPO July 19, 2005)   670

JDRF International v. Nguyen Benedicto, D2021-0267 (WIPO May 26, 2021)   30

Jeanette Winterson v. Mark Hogarth, D2000-0235 (WIPO May 22, 2000) (<jeanet-
tewinterson.com
)   75-76, 200

Jeffrey Dean Lindsay v. Lisa Katz / Domain Protection LLC, FA1805001787275
(Forum July 3, 2018)   563

JHO Intellectual Property Holdings, LLC, Elite IP Holdings LLC v. Mahad Taheri,
D2020-3504 (WIPOFebruary 16, 2021)   382, 517

Jireh Industries Ltd. v. DVLPMNT MARKETING, INC. / Domain Administrator,
FA1703001719671 (Forum April 14, 2017)   339

John McGinnis Halliday Gibson v. Domain Admin, D2022-4274 (WIPO December
23, 2022)   375

John Summers v. The Chronicle of Higher Education, D2019-0682 (WIPO May 26.
2019)   122

Johnson & Johnson v. Chad Wright, WebQuest.com, Inc., D2012-0010 (WIPO April
5, 2012)   382

Jonathan Ive v. Harry Jones, D2009-0301 (WIPO May 5, 2009)   371

Jones Apparel Group Inc. v. Jones Apparel Group.com., D2001-1041 (WIPO October
16, 2001) ("Jones Apparel 2")   555

Jones Apparel Group, Inc. v. jonesapparelgroup.com, D2001-0719 (WIPO July 19,
2001) ("Jones Apparel 1")   537

Jones Lang LaSalle IP, Inc. v. Virginia Wheeler, D2018-1269(WIPO July 18,
2018)   232

Jones v. Gregory, FA0209000125747 (Forum January 14, 2003)   42, 227, 232, 371,
537, 555, 560, 609, 695, 763

Jos Daniel v. Privacy Administrator, Anonymize, Inc. / Stanley Pace, D2020-1966
(WIPO September 11, 2020)   46

Joseph Leccese v. Crystal Cox, D2011-0679(WIPO June 30, 2011)   372

Julia Fiona Roberts v. Russell Boyd, D2000-0210 (WIPO May 29, 2000)   375

Julian Barnes v. Old Barn Studios Limited, D2001-0121 (WIPO March 26,
2001)   76, 381

Julie & Jason, Inc. d/b/a The Mah Jongg Maven v. Faye Scher d/b/a Where the Winds Blow, D2005-0073 (WIPO March 6, 2005)   588

JumpCloud, Inc. v. Peter Irion / SCS LLC   330, 393

Juraj Králik-ZAJO v. Deep Frontier, Jay Dove, D2015-1377 (WIPO October 20, 2015)   543

K

Kabbage, Inc. v. Oneandone Private Registration, 1&1 Internet Inc. - www.1and1.com / Robert Hanssen, Ridiculous File Sharing, D2015-1507 (WIPO November 20, 2015)   355

Kabushiki Kaisha Hitachi Seisakusho (Japan Corporation), d/b/a Hitachi, Ltd. v. Hilaire Shioura, DWS2004-0002 (WIPO July 23, 2004)   396

Kabushiki Kaisha Square ENX dba Square ENX Co. Ltd. v. NOLDC, Inc., D2006-0630 (WIPO July 14, 2006)   569

Kames Capital PLC v. Tom Harrison / Kames Capital Plc Limited, FA1604001671583 (Forum May 20, 2016)   362, 527

Karen Millen Fashions Limited v. Belle Kerry, D2012-0436 (WIPO May 7, 2012)   244, 617

Karma International, LLC v. David Malaxos,FA1812001822198 (Forum February 15, 2019)   211, 605, 698

Kathleen Kennedy Townsend v. B. G. Birt, D2002-0030 (WIPO April 2002)   235, 376

Kentech Group Limited v. Qtechweb,D2019-1609 (WIPO August 30, 2019)   337

Kevin Spacey v. Alberta Hot Rods, FA0205000114437 (Forum August 1, 2002)   375

Keystone Publishing, Inc. v. UtahBrides.com, D2004-0725 (WIPO November 17, 2004)   325

Khadi & Village Industries Commission v. Michael F Mann, Domain Asset Holdings, LLC., D2021-3242 (WIPO December 7, 2021)   59

Kimmel Center, Inc. v. Tech Support, Trade Out Investments Ltd., D2011-0293 (WIPO April 22, 2011)   319

Kimmel Scrap Iron & Metal Co. v. Michael Bader, P-1 Enterprises, D2016-1148 (WIPO August 8, 2016)   297

Kip Cashmore v. URLPro, D2004-1023 (WIPO March 14, 2005)   331

Kirkbi AG v. This Domain for Sale/Steve Morsa, D2003-0826 (WIPO December 12, 2003)   137

Kis v. Anything.com Ltd., D2000-0770 (WIPO November 30, 2000)   169, 227, 542-543, 566, 718

KitApps, Inc., dba Attendify v. Paddy Nay   220

Kitchens To Go, LLC v. KTG.COM, Whoisguard Protected / HUKU LLC, D2017-2241 (WIPO February 6, 2018)   56, 404

Klir Platform Europe Limited v. David Hendrix, UDRP-15008 (CIIDRC April 20, 2021)   174

Knud Jepsen A/S v. Rick Schwartz, Virtual Dates Inc., D2017-0679 (WIPO June 20, 2017)   345

Koninkljke KPN N.V. v. Telepathy Inc., D2001-0217 (WIPO May 7, 2001)   22, 207, 313

Kosmos Global Holding, S.L. v. Jewella Privacy - 00a3b, Jewella Privacy LLC Privacy ID# 924265 / Domain Manager, Orion Global Assets, D2022-2408 (WIPO September 8, 2022)   507

Kramer America, Inc. v. Eugeniy Alyamin, D2022-0340 (WIPO July 28, 2022)   424

Kubota Corporation v. Media Matrix LLC, D2022-3397 (WIPO November 23, 2022)   195

L

Labrada Bodybuilding Nutrition, Inc. v. Glisson, FA 250232 (Forum May 28, 2004)   675

Lacamas Shores Homeowners Association v. Catherine Arnold, D2017-0855 (WIPO June 20, 2017)   241

Lacoste Alligator S.A. v. Priscilla, Ranesha, Angel, Jane, Victor, Olivier, Carl, Darren, Angela, Jonathan, Michell, Oiu, Matthew, Pamela, Selima, Angela, John, Sally, Susanna, D2010-0988 (WIPO August 11, 2010)   353

Landmark Group v. DigiMedia.com, L.P., FA0406000285459 (Forum August 6, 2004)   418, 703

Lauren Singer v. Belsheba Nyabwa, D2020-0244 (WIPO March 16, 2020)   491

Law and Business Enterprises Worldwide S.L. v. Ann Labe, D2022-1040 (WIPO May 27, 2022)   427

Law Office of Graham C. Fisher, LLC v. Jack Toering / FindLocal, Inc, FA2212002023163 (Forum January 5, 2023)   431, 435

Law Offices of Jeffrey J. Antonelli, Ltd., Inc. dba Antonelli Law, Ltd. v. The Law Offices of Stephen C. Vondran, P.C., D2021-2428 (WIPO October 4, 2021)   585, 764

LAWCLOUD B.V. v. Wenjie Jiang, D2022-4908 (WIPO February 22, 2023) (<law-cloud.com
)   726

Lawrence Gurreri v. To Thai Ninh, FA1006001328554 (Forum July 12, 2010)   619

LDW Software, LLC v. Stella Chang, D2017-0430 (WIPO April 29, 2017)   619

Le Géant des Beaux-Arts, SARL v. BRUCE WONG, D2022-4632 (WIPO February 22,2023)   706

LE TIGRE 360 GLOBAL, LLC v. LeTigre, FA1606001681089 (Forum August 8, 2016)   407

Leap Real Estate Systems, LLC. v. BytePlay Limited   412

Legal & Gen. Group Plc v. Image Plus, D2002-1019 (WIPO Dec. 30, 2002)   443

Legally Co v. Domain Administrator, Name Find LLC, D2018-1958 (WIPO October 31, 2018)   65, 163, 525

LEGO Juris A/S v. DomainPark Ltd, David Smith, Above.com Domain Privacy, Transure Enterprise Ltd, Host master, D2010-0138 (WIPO March 10, 2010)   485, 510

LEGO Juris A/S v. Kamal Mahmoud, D2021-2354 (WIP0 October 4, 2021)   485, 510

Leidos, Inc. v. Gabriel Joseph / Clearer Technology, FA2207002005102 (Forum September 8, 2022)   444

Les Parfumeries Fragonard v. Sunny Elemba, D2020-1648 (WIPO August 12, 2020)   530

Lexon v. Registration Private, Domains By Proxy, LLC / Surety Management, D2019-2365 (WIPO December 12, 2019)   653

Leyton & Associés (SAS), Thésée (SAS), Leyton Consulting UK and Ireland Limited, Leyton Maroc, Leyton Belgium, Leyton UK Limited v. Drela Mateusz, Elephant Orchestra, D2009-1589 (WIPO January 20, 2010)   261

Liberty Puzzles, LLC v. Domain Manager / Data Point Limited, FA2204001994151 (Forum June 7, 2022)   332

LIBRO AG v. NA Global Link Limited, D2000-0186 (WIPO May 19, 2000)   251, 697

Lilly ICOS LLC v. Tudor Burden, Burden Marketing, D2004-0794 (WIPO December 20, 2004)   355

Limble Solutions, Inc. v. Domain Admin, Alter.com, Inc., D2022-4900 (WIPO March 8, 2023)   195, 726

Limble Solutions, Inc. v. Domain Admin, Alter.com, Inc., D2022-4900 (WIPO March 22, 2023)   195, 726

Limited Stores, LLC v. Infinite Wireless, D2013-1269 (WIPO August 29, 2013)   566

Line Publications, LLC v. Arjay Entertainment, LLC, D2006-1235 (WIPO December 22, 2006)   338

Link Clicks Inc. d/b/a Ad Here and TOTALLYFREESTUFF.COM v. John Zuccarini d/b/a Cupcake Patrol, D2000-1547 (WIPO January 22, 2001)   234, 537

Linklaters LLP v. WhoisGuard, Inc / David Balevic, edcc, D2021-0723 (WIPO May 4, 2021)   317

Liquid Nutrition Inc. v. liquidnutrition.com/Vertical Axis Inc., D2007-1598 (WIPO June 28, 2016)   638

Little Acorns Fostering Ltd. v. W P, The Cloud Corp / Al Perkins, D2017-1776 (WIPO October 18, 2017)   510

LittleThings, Inc. v. East Softwear, D2016-2254 (WIPO December 23, 2016)   356

Loblaws, Inc. v. Presidentchoice.inc/Presidentchoice.com, AF-0170a to 0170c (eResolution, June7, 2000)   660

Loco Tecnologia da Informação S.A. v. Perfect Privacy, LLC. / Dermot O'Halloran, ZZG Ltd., D2019-2738 (WIPO March 24, 2020)   265, 663

Lolo, LLC v. Domain Admin, Xedoc Holding SA,D2022-3621 (WIPO January 23, 2023)   168

Loris Azzaro BV, SARL v. Asterix & De Vasconcellos, D2000-0608 (WIPO September 4, 2000)   222

Lotto Sport Italia S.p.A. v. David Dent, D2016-2532 (WIPO February 13, 2017)   421, 482

Lowa Sportschuhe GmbH v. Domain Admin, Whois Privacy Corp., D2017-1131 (WIPO August 1, 2017)   592

Luma Institute, LLC v. Perfect Privacy, LLC / James Redfern/Luma   183, 260, 384

Lumena s-ka so.o. v. Express Ventures Ltd., FA00030000094375 (Forum May 11, 2000)   416

Luvilon Indus. NV v. Top Serve Tennis Pty Ltd., DAU2005-0004 (WIPO September 6, 2005)   253

Lyca Productions Private Limited v. Louis Caous, D2021-3544 (WIPO December 20, 2021)   386

M

Macado's Inc. v. C. B. Henderson, FA0804001180994 (Forum June 17, 2008)   296

Macmillan Publishers Limited, Macmillan Magazines Limited, and HM Publishers Holdings Limited v. Telepathy, Inc., D2002-0658 (WIPO September 27, 2002)   185, 621

Madonna Ciccone, p/k/a Madonna v. Dan Parisi and Madonna.com, D2000-0847 (WIPO October. 12, 2000)   312

Madrid 2012, A.A. v. Scott Martin-MadridMan Websites, D2003-0598 (WIPO October 8, 2003)   408

Magic Software Enterprises Ltd v. Evergreen Technology Corporation, D2000-0746 (WIPO October 4, 2000)   388

Magnum Piering, Inc. v. The Mudjackers and Garwood S. Wilson, Sr., D2000-1525 (WIPO January 21, 2001)   349, 509, 580

MAHA Maschinenbau Haldenwang GmbH & Co. KG v. Deepak Rajani, D2000-1816 (WIPO March 2, 2001)   341

Majid Al Futtaim Properties LLC v. Ayman Bajnaid, D2022-4129 (WIPO December 22, 2022)   241, 511, 595, 632

Majid Al Futtaim Properties Llc v. Domain-It Hostmaster, Domain-it!, Inc., D2021-0591 (WIPOApril 30, 2021)   241, 511, 595, 632

Malayan Banking Berhad v. Beauty, Success & Truth International   382

Maple Mountain Group, Inc. v. Kendra Roman, Roman Creative, D2022-4112
  (WIPO March 9, 2023)   398
Marco Rafael Sanfilippo v. Estudio Indigo, D2012-1064 (WIPO July 25, 2012)   340
Mark C. Spicher v. Frogi Design, s.r.o. / The Artwork Factory, s.r.o., D2015-0606
  (WIPO June 3, 2015)   315
Mark Overbye v. Maurice Blank, Gekko.com B.V., D2016-0362 (WIPOApril 15,
  2016)   505
MARLINK SAS v. Stephen Okonkwo, D2017-1356 (WIPO September 7,
  2017)   529
Marquette Golf Club v. Al Perkins, FA1706001738263 (Forum July 27, 2017)   324,
  351
Marriott International Inc. and Marriott Worldwide Corporation v. Avalon Resorts
  Pvt. Ltd., D2010-0172 (WIPO March 22, 2010)   473
Mars, Incorporated v. Ben Chen, FA1109001405770 (Forum October 17, 2011)   591
Massachusetts Port Authority ("Massport") v. Jay Taylor, Travel411.com, Inc. D2023-
  0859 (WIPO April 27, 2023)   330
MasterCraft Boat Company, LLC v. Debbie Hayes, FA1610001696484 (Forum
  November 23, 2016)   293
Match.com, LP v. Bill Zag and NWLAWS.ORG., D2004-0230 (WIPO June 2,
  2004)   35, 468
Matthew James Spratt v. Stephen Dainty, HHB Holidays & Travel Ltd., D2016-0306
  (WIPO April 20 2016)   326, 331
Maurice Mizrahi / Mizco International, Inc. v. Chi Hyon, FA1710001754962 (Forum
  November 20, 2017)   479
Maven Esthetics, LLC v. Diana Roth, The Browtique, D2021-3499 (WIPO
  December18, 2021)   9
MB Financial Bank, N.A. v. MBBANK, FA0602000644517 (Forum April 4,
  2006)   531
McLane Company, Inc. v. Fred Craig, D2000-1455 (WIPO January 11, 2001)   495
McMullan Bros Limited, Maxol Limited and Maxol Direct Limited Maxol Lubricants
  Limited, Maxol Oil Limited Maxol Direct (NI) Limited v. Web Names Ltd., D2004-
  0078 (WIPO April 16, 2004)   105
McMullan Bros. Limited, et al. v. Web Names Ltd., D2004-0078 (WIPO April 16,
  2004)   271, 582
McMullen Argus Publ'g Inc. v. Moniker Privacy Servs., D2007-0676 (WIPO July 24,
  2007)   420
MCP Holding Ltd. v. Linh Wang, D2010-1999 (WIPO February 4, 2011)   328
MD On-line, Inc. v. Yenta Marketing, Inc.,D2014-1468(WIPO November 8,
  2014)   466

Meat and Livestock Commission v. David Pearce aka OTC / The Recipe for BSE, D2003-0645 (WIPO October 27, 2003)   341, 594

Mechoshade Systems, LLC v. DNS Admin / Mecho Investments, FA1805001784649 (Forum June 18, 2018)   388, 407, 663

Media General Communications, Inc. v. Rarenames, WebReg., D2006-0964 (WIPO September 23, 2006)   62, 397, 631

Mediacom Communications Corporation v. ORM LTD / ORM Ltd., FA1509001640219 (Forum October 31, 2015)   353

Medtronic, Inc. v. Aytekin Yilmaz of Medo Tekstil Elektronik Al. Sat. Tic. Ltd., D2021-1758 (WIPO September 28, 2021)   382, 426

Melanie Martinez v. Michael Casasnovas, D2017-0905 (WIPO June 23, 2017)   409

Melinda French Gates v. John Clendenon, FA2207002003541 (Forum October 3, 2022)   137, 322

Melinda Gates v. Bruce B, FA1706001738284 (Forum August 17, 2017)   323

Mentor ADI Recruitment Ltd (trading as Mentor Group) v. Teaching Driving Ltd., 2003- 0654 (WIPO September 29, 2003) (LETS DRIVE and <letsdrive.com)   515

Mercado Libre, Inc.; Mercado Libre SRL; Mercado Libre Chile, Ltda.; Mercado Libre, S. de R. L. C.V.; Mercado Libre Venezuela, S.R.L.; Ebazar.com.br, Ltda.; Tech Fund, S.R.L. v. Alex Mariasov, D2021-1699 (WIPO August 9, 2021)   493

Mercer Human Resource Consulting, Ltd., Mercer Human Resource Consulting Inc. v. Konstantinos Zournas, D2007-1425 (WIPO November 23, 2007)   627, 706

Meredith Corp. v. CityHome, Inc., D2000-0223 (WIPO May 18, 2000)   167, 211, 576, 697, 714

Meta Platforms, Inc. v. 1 1, D2023-2634 (WIPO August 3, 2023)   131

Mi Cocina, Ltd. v. Melinda Garcia, D2023-4014 (WIPO December 9, 2023)   596

Micah Hargress v. PARAMOUNT INTERNET, FA1509001638609 (Forum November 13, 2015)   716

Michael Machat v. Jaden Thompson a/k/a Vaden Vampes, a/k/a Vampes Domains by Proxy   412

Microcell Solutions Inc. v. B-Seen Design Group Inc., AF-0131 (eResolution February 25, 2000)   323, 720

Micron Technology, Inc. v. Null International Research Center, D2001-0608 (WIPO June 20, 2001)   385, 560, 572

Microsoft Corporation v. MSNetworks, D2002-0647 (WIPO September 27, 2002)   141, 526

Microsoft Corporation v. Terrence Green / Whois Agent / Whois Privacy Protection Service, Inc., FA1602001661030 (Forum April 4, 2016)   141, 526

Miele, Inc. v. Absolute Air Cleaners and Purifiers, D2000-0756 (WIPO September 20, 2000)   316

Mile, Inc. V. Michael Burg, D2010-2011 (WIPO February 11, 2011)   120-121, 592

Miller Brewing Co. v. Hong, FA0309000192732 (Forum December 8, 2003)   374

Mimic Skateboards Inc. v. Domains By Proxy, LLC / Travis McGlothin, Point Distribution, D2019-0722 (WIPO May 23, 2019)   413

Mind Gym plc v. Intuition Publishing Limited, D2022-3598 (WIPO November 23, 2022)   544

Minibar North America Inc. v. Ian Musk & GEMS Global Electronic Minibar Systems AS, D2005-0035 (WIPO March 2, 2005)   344

Minka Lighting, Inc. v. Jon Hall, D2005-0684 (WIPO September 21,2005)   704

Minnow IT Ltd v. Domains By Proxy, LLC / David Hanley, D2022-0600 (May 4, 2022)   64

Mirama Enterprises Inc, d/b/a Aroma Housewares Company v. NJDomains, Abuse Contact: abuse@mail.com c/o Gerald Gorman, FA0510000588486 (Forum January 16, 2006)   727

Mississippi Lottery Corp. v. Jonathan Carr, FA1905001842961 (Forum July 15, 2019)   781

Missouri Lottery Commission v. SED Domain Services / Common Law, D2014-0118 (WIPO March 7, 2014)   315

Mister Auto SAS v. Wharton Lyon & Lyon, D2018-1330 (WIPO August3, 2018)   673

Mobile Communication Service, Inc. v. WebReg, RN, D2005-1304 (WIPO February 24, 2006)   628

Mobisy Technologies Private Limited v. Ibrahim Kazanci, D2019-0273 (WIPO March 6, 2019)   336

Modefine S.A. v. A.R. Mani, D2001-0537 (WIPO July 20, 2001)   427

Mogavero Investments, LLC v. James C. Clements, D2018-0728 (WIPO June 15, 2018)   164

Molson Canada v. %2d%2d, FA0204000112451 (Forum June 11, 2002)   210

Montane Ltd. v. Domain Hostmaster / Domain manager, Orion Global Assets, D2017-0309 (WIPO April 26, 2017)   171

Morgan Stanley v. Marcelo Augusto Dibbern / MS SERVICOS FINANCEIRO, FA2110001968545 (Forum November 19, 2021)   269, 528

Morgan Stanley v. robert, FA2201001980641 (Forum February 9, 2022)   269, 528

Motorola Inc. v. NewGate Internet, Inc.,D2000-0079 (WIPO April 27, 2000)   446

Mountain Top (Denmark) ApS v. Contact Privacy Inc. Customer 0133416460 / Name Redacted, Mountaintop Idea Studio, D2020-1577 (WIPO September 1, 2020)   180, 475, 682

Mr. Daniel Imhof, v. Name Redacted, D2023-1209 (WIPO May 16, 2023)   440

Mr. Gildo Pallanca-Pastor v. Tech Admin, Virtual Point Inc., D2020-1698 (WIPO August 20, 2020)   568, 664

Mrs. Eva Padberg v. Eurobox Ltd., D2007-1886 (WIPO March 10, 2008)   20, 303

Mutineer Restaurant v. Ultimate Search, Inc., FA0205000114434 (Forum August 23, 2002)   704

mVisible Technologies Inc v. Navigation Catalyst Systems Inc., D2007-1141 (WIPO November 30, 2007)   13, 62, 282, 510, 629

My Green Lab, Corp. v. Domain Administrator, See PrivacyGuardian.org / Green Your Lab, D2022-1262 (WIPO May 18, 2000)   344

My Health, Inc. v. Top Tier Consulting, Inc., FA1006001332064 (FORUM Aug. 26, 2010)   416, 684

My Passion Media Inc. v. Constantina Anagnostopoulos, Mytrueearth, D2021-0415 (WIPO June 18, 2021)   65, 121

Myriel Aviation SA v. Olli Jokinen, D2018-0828 (WIPO May 28, 2018)   190

N

[Name Redacted] v. ludashi us / jack zhang, FA2208002009845 (Forum October 1, 2022)   ii, iv-v, vii-xxiii, xxv-xxxii, 3-791, 793

N.V. Nutricia v. Rob Monster, FA2106001952511 (Forum August 2, 2021)   728-729

N.V. Organon and Schering Plough Corporation v. Fields Law Firm and Stephen Fields, FA0904001259266 (Forum June 16, 2009)   448

Nalli Chinnasami Chetty v. Anthony Nalli, FourPoints Multimedia Corp., D2019-2642 (WIPODecember 18, 2019)   558, 645

Nalli Chinnasami Chetty v. Brian Nally, IT Smart (ABN 51 225 934 240), D2022-4768 (WIPO February 2, 2023)   558, 645

Namecheap, Inc. v. KY SONG, FA1401001537272 (Forum March 12, 2014)   191, 776

Nat'l Ass'n of Prof'l Baseball League, Inc. v. Zuccarini, D2002-1011 (WIPO January 21, 2003) (<minorleaugebaseball.com   608

National Association for Stock Car Auto Racing, Inc. v. Racing Connection/The Racin' Connection, Inc., D2007-1524 (WIPO January 28, 2008)   448

National Cable Satellite Corporation, d/b/a C-SPAN v. Michael Mann / Omar Rivero, FA1707001741966 (Forum September 20, 2017)   58

National Dial A Word Registry Pty Ltd and others v. 1300 Directory Pty Ltd, DAU2008 -0021 (WIPO March 6, 2009)   278

National Football League v. Online Marketing International also known as International Marketing Group, D2008-2006 (WIPO March 2, 2009)   460

National Football League v. Thomas Trainer, D2006-1440 (WIPO December 29, 2006) (<nflnetwork.com
)   460

National Grid Electricity Transmission Plc, NGrid Intellectual Property Limited v. Re-Tron Technologies, D2013-0925 (WIPO July 11, 2013)   214, 359

National Securities Corporation v. Registration Private, Domains By Proxy, LLC / Ridgeway Support, Richard (Rick) Garber, D2018-0290 (WIPO March 23, 2018)   296

National Trust for Historic Preservation v. Barry Preston, D2005-0424 (WIPO August 10, 2006)   182

Natixis Wealth Management v. Viljami Ylönen, D2021-1719 (WIPO July 23, 2021)   461

NaturaLawn of America, Inc. v. Jeff Edwards, FA1102001372111 (Forum March 16, 2011)   192, 358

NCRAS Mgmt., LP v. Cupcake City, D2000-1803 (WIPO February 26, 2001)   354

Neal & Massy Holdings Limited v. Gregory Ricks, FA1403001549327 (Forum April 12, 2014)   339

Neiman Marcus Group, Inc. v. Neiman-Marcus, FA0212000135048 (Forum January 13, 2003)   425

Neometals Ltd v. Domain Admin, Domain Privacy Service, FBO Registrant / lisa deere, D2022-2360 (WIPO August 22, 2022)   174, 259

NETtime Solutions LLC v. NetTime Inc. c/o Chad Wagner, FA081000 1230152 (Forum December 19, 2008)   176

Neuberger Berman, Inc., v. Jacobsen, D2000-0323 (WIPO June 12, 2000)   155

Neusiedler Aktiengesellschaft v. Kulkarni, D2000-1769 (WIPO February 5, 2001)   178, 556

Newport News, Inc. v. Vcv Internet, AF-0238 (eResolution July 18, 2000)   464, 770

News Group Newspapers Limited v. Privacydotlink Customer 2383026 / Blue Nova Inc., D2019-0084 (WIPO April 10, 2019)   217, 395, 672

Newsday Printers and Publishers (P) Ltd. v. InetU, Inc., D2001-0085 (WIPO May 23, 2001)   698, 718, 720

Nextbite Brands, LLC v. Nextbite LLC, Nextbite General Trading Company, D2021-3114 (WIPO December 10, 2021)   174

Nicolas Karl Reep v. Ali Bazzi, FA2004001891242 (Forum May 19,2020)   339

Nicole Kidman v. John Zuccarini, d/b/a Cupcake Party, D2000-1415 (WIPO January 23, 2001)   347, 375, 435, 608

Nike Innovate C.V. v. Contact Privacy, Inc. Customer 1243971962 / Ladinu   144, 193

Nike Innovate C.V. v. Domains By Proxy, LLC / Jonathan Benloulou, D2022-0578 (WIPO April 27, 2022)   144, 193

NIKE, Inc. and Nike Innovate, C.V. v. Mattia Lumini and Yykk Snc. FA160600 1679233 (Forum July 15, 2016)   355

Nike, Inc. v. Azumano Travel, D2000-1598 (WIPO February 17, 2001)   355, 585

Nikon, Inc. v. Technilab. Inc., D2000-1774 (WIPO February 26,2001)   79, 97

Nintendo of America Inc. v. Sebastian Pozzi, FA2302002030700 (Forum March 27, 2023)   532

Nishan Systems, Inc. v. Nishan Ltd., D2003-0204 (WIPO May 1, 2003)   178

Nishimura & Asahi v. Super Privacy Service LTD c/o Dynadot, D2019-2070 (WIPO October 18, 2019)   30

Nokia Corp. v. Eagle, FA0801001125685 (Forum February 7, 2008)   617

Notar Eiendom AS v. LIPnet, D2000-1070 (WIPO December 8, 2000)   181

Nova Banka v. Iris, D2003-0366 (WIPO June 30, 2003)   297

Novartis AG v. Chris Taitague, FA1708001744264 (Forum September 11, 2017)   527, 557, 582, 613-614

Novartis AG v. Contact Privacy Inc. Customer 1246111874 / Andrew C. Sikula, Negotiation Matters Inc., D2020-1738 (WIPO August 27, 2020)   527, 557, 582, 613-614

NovAtel Inc. v. Registration Private, Domains By Proxy, LLC / Domain Admin, FindYourDomain.com   652

Novomatic AG v. DomainClip Domains Inc., D2022-4590 (WIPO March 6, 2023)   417

Nu Mark LLC v. Bui, Long, D2013-1785 (WIPO December 22, 2013)   373

NYBEST Services, LLC v. Jun Zhu, FA1603001667008 (Forum April 29,2016)   326

NZ Manufacturing, Inc. v. Eric Snell, FA1604001670641 (ForumJune 3, 2016)   299

O

Oakley, Inc. v. H intel, FA1207001454892 (Forum August 21, 2012)   617-618

OANDA Corporation v. Da Peng Wang, D2022-0339 (WIPO March 18, 2022)   609

Octogen Pharmacal Company, Inc. v. Domains By Proxy, Inc. / Rich Sanders and Octogen e-Solutions, D2009-0786 (WIPO August19, 2009)   117-118

Oerlikon Surface Solutions AG v. Bonded Labs, Bonded Labs, D2022 -3934 (WIPO January 5, 2023)   22

Oki Data Americas, Inc. v. ASD, Inc., D2001-0903 (WIPO November6, 2001)   92, 445

On AG, On Clouds GmbH v. Nguyen Luu, Withheld for Privacy Purposes, Privacy service provided by Withheld for Privacy ehf, Vuong Hoang, AN NGUYEN, NEO CORP., and Ngoc Tam Nguyen, D2021-1714 (WIPO July 28, 2021)   363

OnAirlines, Inc. v. buydmains, FA0404000250746 (Forum June 7, 2004)   252

One Freelance Limited v. TrafficTerminal, CAC 102537 (ADR.eu November 28, 2019)   360

One.com Group AB v. Stan N, CAC 103567 (ADR.eu April 31, 2021)   610

OnePhone Holding AB v. IndiGO Networks, D2007-1576 (WIPO December 22, 2007)   676

Oney Bank v. jalta ofi, D2023-4325 (WIPO December 22, 2023)   530

ONU S.R.L. Online Sale, LLC v. Online Sales, LLC, AF-0672 (Eresolution January 12, 2001)   673

Option One Mortgage Corporation v. Option One Lending, D2004-1052 (WIPO February 27, 2005)   394

optionsXpress Holdings, Inc. v. David A., FA1701001711999 (Forum February 15, 2017)   527

Oracle International Corporation v. Above.com Domain Privacy / Protection Domain, D2017-1987 (WIPO December 26, 2017)   526, 614

Orchard Supply Hardware LLC v. RareNames, Web Reg, FA0804001178941(Forum June 27, 2008)   705

OVB Vermögensberatung AG v. Michele Dinoia and SZK.com, D2009-0307 (WIPOMay 6, 2009)   474

Oxygen Media, LLC v. Primary Source, D2000-1167 (WIPO October 16, 2000)   608

Oystershell Consumer Health, Inc. v. Titan Networks, CAC 103658 (ADR.eu May 19, 2021)   421

P

PAA Laboratories GmbH v. Printing Arts America, D2004-0338 (WIPO July 13, 2004)   80

PACIFIC PLACE HOLDINGS LTD. v. RICHARD GREENWOOD, D2000-0089 (WIPO April 3, 2000)   500

PacketVideo Corporation v. PacketVideo Corporation, D2023-2702 (WIPO August 24, 2023)   620

Pade Publishing, LLC, a Colorado limited liability company v. Desert Resorts Inc., FA1411001588977 (Forum January 15, 2015)   405

Pandora Jewelry, LLC v. Debbie Sanford, D2010-0641 (WIPO June 10, 2010)   451, 524

Pangaea Laboratories Ltd, Pacific Direct Intertrading Pty Ltd v. Astrix Pty Ltd, DAU2015-0013 (WIPO June 3, 2015)   445

Pantaloon Retail India Limited v. RareNames, WebReg., D2010-0587 (WIPO 2010)   80, 161

Paper Denim & Cloth, LLC v. Pete Helvey, FA1201001425020 (Forum March 5, 2012)   489

Paragon Micro, Inc. v. Julian Pretto, D2010-0721 (WIPO July 1, 2010)   469

Paramount Stations Group of Fort Worth/Dallas, Inc. v. Netico, Inc., D2001-0715 (WIPO July 18, 2001)   490

Parfums Christian Dior v. 1 Netpower, Inc., D2000-0022 (WIPO March 3, 2000)   346, 387, 484

Pfizer Inc. v. Michael Chucks / Whoisguard Protected, Whoisguard Inc, D2014-0887 (WIPO July 28, 2014)   444, 611, 616

Pfizer Inc. v. Van Robichaux, D2003-0399 (WIPO July 16, 2003)   444, 611, 616

Phantom Fireworks Showrooms, LLC / Phantom I.P., LLC v. Frank Elliott / Jurassic Fireworks, Seasonal Sales Inc., D2021-4104 (WIPO January 31, 2022)   436

Pharmactive Biotech Products, S.L. v. HugeDomains.com, D2020-3529 (WIPO March 23, 2021)   632

Philip Berber v. Karl Flanagan and KP Enterprises, D2000-0661 (WIPO August 8, 2000)   370

Philip Colavito v. Domain Management, Oceanside Capital Corp.,D2020-2295 (WIPO November 30, 2020)   685

Philippe Pierre Dauman v. Dinner Business, D2013-1255 (WIPO September 6, 2013)   88, 371

Photographic Solutions, Inc. v. Fariborz R-Dehghan, D2008-0333 (WIPO April 29, 2008)   409

Photomaton v. Ehren Scheiberger, D2022-0593 (WIPO April 15, 2022)   66, 334

Pick Enterprises, Inc. v. Domains by Proxy, LLC, DomainsByProxy.com / Woman to Woman Healthcare / Just Us Women Health Center f/k/a Woman to Woman Health Center, D2012-1555 (WIPO September 22, 2012)   81, 644, 663

Picture Organic Clothing v. Privacydotlink Customer 4032039 / James Booth, Booth. com, Ltd.,D2020-2016 (WIPOOctober 5, 2020)   193, 394, 716

Pilot Fitness, LLC v. Max Wettstein / Max Wettstein Fitness, FA1808001799942 (Forum August 30, 2018)   647

Pivotal Corporation v. Discovery Street Trading Co. Ltd., Case No. D2000-0648 (WIPO August 17, 2000)   472

Pizza Hut, Inc. v. RJ, Inc., D2000-0939 (WIPO December 6, 2000)   456

PLAINWELL OVERSEAS CORP. v. NameTrust, LLC., CAC 102207(ADReu February 22, 2019)   702

Platterz v. Andrew Melcher, FA1705001729887 (FORUM June 19, 2017)   466

Playboy Enterprises International, Inc. v. Alano Fernandez, E-Magine, D2018-1457 (WIPO August 21,2018)   580

Plaza Operating Partners, Ltd. V. Pop Data Technologies, Inc. and Joseph Pillus, D2000-0166 (WIPO June 6, 2000)   42

Pleasure Cake SL v. TechTools, D2009-0580 (WIPO July 14, 2009)   237, 536

Pleasure Cake SL v. TechTools, D2009-0580 (WIPO July 14, 2009)   237, 536

Pocatello Idaho Auditorium Dist. v. CES Marketing Group, Inc., FA0112000103186 (Forum February 21, 2002)   504, 720

Ponthier S.A.S. v. Domains By Proxy, LLC / Shannon Ponthier, D2022-1787 (WIPO July 28, 2022)   667

Porto Chico Stores, Inc. v. Otavio Jambon, D2000-1270 (WIPO November 15, 2000)   573

Post.Com Limited v. Peter Neilson, D2002-0690 (WIPO September 17, 2002)   310, 336, 345

Powrachute Incorporated v. Buckeye Industries, AF-0076 (eResolution January 21, 2000)   321

Precyse Corporation v. Punta Barajas, SA, D2002-0753 (WIPO October 2, 2002)   244

Preston Gates & Ellis, LLP v. defaultdata.com and Brian Wick, D2001-1381 (WIPO February 13, 2002)   204, 433, 516

PRGRS, Inc. v. Pak, D2002-0077(WIPO April 24, 2002)   338

Primal Quest, LLC v. Gabriel Salas, D2005-1083 (WIPO December 15, 2005)   728

Printwerx International LLC v. LARRY ORGAN / EXACTDATA LLC., FA2010001916470(Forum November 16, 2020)   126

Private Media Group v. Anton Enterprises Inc. d/b/a Private USA, D2002-0692 (WIPO September 10, 2002)   293

Privity Pty. Ltd. v. Whois Agent, Domain Protection Services, Inc. / Rightside Group, Ltd., D2020-2742 (WIPO December 23, 2020)   699

Pro Confort SRL v. P-IER56, Ion Robu, D2008-0801 (WIPO August 8, 2008)   409

Proeza, S.A. de C.V. v. Domain Admin, D2018-0535 (WIPO June 12, 2018)   639

Progressive Specialty Glass Company, Inc. v. Progressive Specialty Co Inc., FA1507001629046 (Forum August 25, 2015)   679

ProjectPay Pty Ltd. v. Rohit Sur, D2022-2900 (WIPO October 17, 2022)   545

PROM Software, Inc. v. Reflex Publishing, Inc., D2001-1154 (WIPO March 4, 2001)   649, 720

Protanium B.V. v. Lars Munksoe, D2022-0030 (WIPO March 20, 2022)   254

Proto Software, Inc. v. Vertical Axis, Inc./PROTO.COM, D2006-0905 (WIPO October 10, 2006)   662

Prudential Insurance Company of America v. PRU.International, FA0111000101800 (Forum January 18, 2002)   138, 241, 263, 544, 692, 743-744, 754

Public Service Electric & Gas Company v. Definitive Sports Management LLC, D2012-0617 (WIPO May 4, 2012)   259

Pueblo International, Inc. v. xtra-Net Internet Service GmbH, FA0006000094975 (Forum July 17, 2000)   460

Puls Elektronische Stromversorgungen GmbH v. NetIdentity, D2002-0205 (WIPO May 31, 2002)   499

Pulse Sports LLC v. Wasea Qubadi, CAC 101777 (ADR.eu February 22, 2018) ("Sanabul 2")   557

Puma SE v. Client Care, Web Commerce Communications Limited, D2022-0015 (WIPO February 17, 2022)   284

Puretalk Holdings, LLC v. Domain Administrator / Fundacion Privacy Services LTD., FA1906001848525 (Forum August 5, 2019)   646

Q

QAS Systems Limited v. Hopewiser Limited, D2001-0273 (WIPO April 29, 2001)   149, 457

QlikTech International AB v. shenzhen kejianuoyouxiangongsi / liang wu, FA121200 1478158 (Forum February 7, 2013)   569

QNX Software Systems Limited v. Jing Rung, D2012-1597 (WIPO October 23, 2012)   219, 365

QTrade Canada Inc. v. Bank of Hydro, AF-0169 (eResolution June 19, 2000)   92, 659

Quadrific Media Private Limited v. Rajat Agarwal, D2017-1050 (WIPO August 31, 2017)   300

Quality Nonsense Limited v. Jerry Sandusky, FA1604001668646(Forum May 5, 2016)   334

Quicken Loans Inc. v. Laura Yun / Offshore Hosting Solutions Ltd., FA1510001644564 (Forum December 11, 2015)   347

Quikr India Private Limited v. Ujjwal, Green Apple Info, D2016-2631 (WIPO February 10, 2017)   373

R

R.E. 'Ted' Turner and Ted Turner Film Properties, LLC. v. Mazen Fahmi, D2002-0251 (WIPO July 4, 2002)   370

R.T. Quaife Engineering, Ltd. and Autotech Sport Tuning Corporation d/b/a Quaife America v. Bill Luton, D2000-1201 (WIPO November 23, 2000)   446

Rada Mfg.Co. v. J.Mark Press a/k/a/ J. Mark Cutlery, D2004-1060 (WIPO)   353

Raidofinance OU v. Domain Admin / Whois Privacy Corp., FA2111001972094 (Forum December 16, 2002)   251

Raincat Online Services v. fluder, CAC 101125 (ADReu February 1, 2016)   368

Ramsey Mankarious v. Stanley Pace, D2015-1100 (WIPO August 11, 2015)   201, 375

Randgold Resources Limited and Randgold & Exploration Co.Ltd. v. Pico Capital Corp., D2001-1108 (WIPO October 24, 2001)   536

Rapido TV Limited v. Jan Duffy-King, D2000-0449 (WIPO August 17, 2000)   252

RapidShare AG, Christian Schmid v. N/A Maxim Tvortsov, D2010-0696 (WIPO June 22, 2010)   320, 350

Realmark Cape Harbour L.L.C. v. Lawrence S. Lewis, D2000-1435 (WIPO December 11, 2000)   313, 424

Reboxed Limited v. Adesoji Adeyemi, D2021-0886 (WIPO June 2, 2021) 125, 675, 680

Red Nacional De Los Ferrocarriles Espanoles v. Ox90, D2001-0981 (WIPO November 21, 2001) 24, 154, 489

Redgrass SA v. Domain Admin, HugeDomains.(com, D2022-2433 (WIPO September 5, 2022) 642

Reed Elsevier Properties Inc. v. David Allen, FA0102000096667 (Forum March 21, 2001) 417

Reflex Marketing, LLC v. Mars Nic / Fei Guo / Ming Guo, D2019-2621 (WIPO January 6, 2020) 726

Rejuve Clinics LLC v. Merlin Kauffman, Rejuve Inc., D2019-2607 (WIPO February 6, 2020) 290, 597

Reliance Telecom Limited v. Domains ByProxy.com and Sukhraj Randhawa, D2013-1470 (WIPO October 8, 2013) 149, 568

Religare Health Insurance Company Limited v. Name Administration Inc. / Domain Administrator. D2019-2073 (WIPO November 29, 2019) 638, 700

Research In Motion Limited v. Privacy Locked LLC/Nat Collicot, D2009-0320 (WIPO May 8, 2009) 61, 267

Reuters Ltd. v. Teletrust IPR Ltd., D2000-0471 (WIPO September 28, 2000) 86

Reverend Dr. Jerry L. Falwell and The Liberty Alliance v. Lamparello International., FA0310000198936 (Forum November 20, 2003) 88, 102, 432

Reza IP Holdings LLC v. Taha Alireza, Velvet, D2022-0945 (WIPO June 28, 2022) 195

Richard L. Kane v. Nick Devine, D2001-1028 (WIPO October 2, 2001) 329

Richard Starkey v. Mr. Bradley, FA0612000874575 (ForumFebruary 12, 2007) 105

Ripple Labs Inc. v. Jessie McKoy / Ripple Reserve Fund, FA1806001790949 (Forum July 8, 2018) 231

Rising Star AG v. Moniker Privacy Services / Domain Administrator, D2012-1246 (WIPO August 16, 2012) 702

Riveron Consulting, L.P. v. Stanley Pace, FA1002001309793 (Forum April 12, 2010) 329, 336, 400, 465

RivNay, LLC v. STW Services LLP, FA1812001821756 (Forum January 31, 2019) 297

Robert Ellenbogen v. Mike Pearson, D2000-0001 (WIPO February 21, 2000) 99

Roberto Industria Alimentare S.r.l. v. Internet Administrator, Reflex Publishing, Inc., D2023-4528 (WIPO December 22, 2023) 66, 207, 660

Roberts v. Boyd, D2000-0210 (WIPO May 29, 2000) 328, 375, 502, 519-520, 523, 637

Robin Food B.V. v. Bogdan Mykhaylets,D2016-264 (WIPO April 1, 2016) 722

Rocket Mortgage, LLC v. RegistrationPrivate, Domains By Proxy, LLC / Michael Scheumack, Identity IntelligenceGroup (IDIQ), D2022-1840 (WIPO July 7, 2022)   159, 351

Rockhard Tools, Inc. v. jeff mcclure, FA2205001998526 (Forum July 8, 2022)   288, 504

Rodale, Inc. v. Cambridge, DBIZ2002-00153 (WIPO June 28, 2002)   686

Roland Mouret v. Domains by Proxy, Inc. and Sonia Long   326

Rollerblade, Inc. v. CBNO and Ray Redican Jr., D2000-0427 (WIPO August 24, 2000)   216, 243

Rollerblade, Inc. v. CBNO and Redican, D2000-0427 (WIPO August 24, 2000)   216, 243

Roman Polanski v. Matan Uziel, D2022-4360 (WIPO January 26, 2023)   435

Romantic Tours, Inc. v. Whois Protection Service, Inc., FA1003001316557 (Forum April 28, 2010)   600

Rovio Entertainment Corporation v. baobin chi, D2021-0888 (WIPO May 26, 2021)   31

Royal Bank of Canada v. RBC Bank, D2002-0672 (WIPO November 20, 2002)   425, 522, 572

Royal Caribbean Cruises, Ltd. v. James Booth, BQDN.com, D2019-1042 (WIPO July 17, 2019)   199, 506, 656

Royal Institution of Chartered Surveyors v. Martin Rushton, D2016-0951 (WIPO August 16, 2016)   103

Ruby's Diner, Inc. v. Joseph W. Popow, D2001-0868 (WIPO August 29, 2001)   294

Ryan Kavanaugh v. Proxy Protection LLC, Proxy Protection LLC / Love Ostlund cunow, web10media AB, D2022-0056 (WIPO April 15, 2022)   434

Ryan P. Boggs v. Name Administration Inc. (BVI), D2013-0583 (Forum June 4, 2013).   677

S

Sadig Alakbarov v. Yuxue Wang, D2019-2253 (WIPO November 18, 2019)   403

Safari Casino A.G. v. Global Interactive Ltd, AF-0288 (eResolution October 4, 2000)   309

Sage Global Services Limited v. Narendra Ghimire, Deep Vision Architects, DAI2023-0010 (WIPO September 1, 2023)   53, 151, 410, 413, 688

Sahil Gupta v. Michal Lichtman / Domain Admin, Mrs Jello, LLC., D2020-1786 (WIPO September15, 2020)   336, 716

Sai Machine Tools Pvt. Ltd. v. Mr. Sudhir Jaiswal, Shree Sai Extrusion Technik Pvt. Ltd, D2018-2560 (WIPO January 19, 2019)   364

Salem Five Cents Savings Bank v. Direct Fed. Credit Union, FA 103058 (Forum February 15, 2002)   189, 343

Salem Five Cents Savings Bank v. Direct Federal Credit Union, FA 103058 (Forum February 15, 2002)   189, 343

Sallie Mae, Inc. v. Michele Dinoia, D2004-0648 (WIPO October 18, 2004)   200

Sally Holdings, Inc. v. Pagelifter.com, D2006-0266 (WIPO May 17,2006)   397

Saltworks, Inc. v. Gary Pedersen, Salt Works, D2013-0984 (WIPO July 15, 2013)   378

Sampo Oyj v. Alexander Alekseev, Sampo, CAC 104559 (ADR.eu June 13, 2022)   553

San Diego Hydroponics & Organics v. Innovative Growing Solutions, Inc., D2009-1545 (March 3, 2010)   324

Sanabul v. Wasea Qubadi, FA1709001748693 (Forum October 18, 2017 ("Sanabul 1")   556-557

Sanofi-Aventis Aventis Pharma SA, Aventis Pharma Deutchland GmbH v. IN4 Web Services, D2005-0938 (WIPO November 24, 2005)   479

SAP AG v. SAP User List, D2009-1285 (WIPO November 8, 2009)   448

SAP AG v. UniSAP, Inc., D2009-0297 (WIPO April 28, 2009) (<unisap.com)   448

SAP SE v. Domains by Proxy, LLC / Kamal Karmakar, D2016-2497 (WIPO January 31, 2017)   148, 166, 232, 480

SAP SE v. Moritz Honig, VCSB Ltd., D2018-1346 (WIPO July 13, 2018)   148, 166, 232, 480

Sarah Lonsdale & Stuart Clark t/a RocknCrystals v. Domain Admin / This Domain is For Sale, HugeDomains.com   678

Saudi Arabian Oil Co. v. Orizon Multimedia Inc., D2020-2035 (WIPO September 15, 2020)   173

SBC Knowledge Ventures LP v. John Huberdeau aka J. Johnston, D2003-0642 (WIPO October 8, 2003)   408

Scalpers Fashion, S.L. v. Dreamissary Hostmaster, D2019-2937 (WIPO January 30, 2020)   662-663, 702

Scandinavian Leadership AB, Mindo AB v. Internet Masters, D2012-1273 (WIPO November 5, 2004)   153, 596

Schiavello (Vic) Pty Ltd. v. Gaynor Wedley, D2000-1634 (WIPO April 5, 2001)   224

Schoffstall Farm, LLC v. Privacy.co.com - 80580, Savvy Investments, LLC Privacy ID# 1048451 / Ashantiplc Limited, D2020-0591 (WIPO May 14, 2020)   120

Schweizerische Bundesbahnen SBB v. Gerrie Villon, D2009-1426 (WIPO January 11, 2010)   401

Scientific Specialties Service, Inc. v. Marc Grebow / PrivacyProtect.org, FA2005001896015 (Forum June 24, 2020)   295, 522

Scoop Soldiers Service Company, LLC v. Carl Gregory, FA2307002053790 (Forum August 29, 2023)   513

Scott Dylan v. K-Ventures FZE LLC, D2021-2977 (WIPO December 6, 2021)   507

Scottish Provident Limited v. Scottish Provident Ministry, D2002-1059 (WIPO January 9, 2003)   561-562

Screen-It Graphics of Lawrence, Inc. d/b/a Grandstand v. Registration Private, Domains By Proxy, LLC / Dorinda Brews, Spadion Corporation, D2017-1709 (WIPO October 16, 2017)   674

Scribd, Inc. v. Robert Brink, Host Master, 1337 Services LLC, Ly Tran, Oscar Enriquez, and Minh Le, Home, D2022-3887 (WIPO May 16, 2023)   276, 551

Scripps Networks, LLC v. Chief Architect, Inc., D2009-0633 (WIPO June 29, 2009).   320, 377

Scrum Alliance, LLC v. Contact Privacy Inc. Customer 1247644697 / Matthew Barcomb, D2021-2932 (WIPO October 25, 2021)   109, 441

SD Wheel Corp. v. Dustin Hoon / TrailBuilt.com, FA2109001967151 (Forum November 24, 2021)   310, 336, 344

SDT International limited company v. Telepathy, Inc., D2014-1870 (WIPO January 13, 2015)   300

SDT International SA-NV v. Telepathy, Inc., D2014-1870 (WIPO January 13, 2015)   39

Sears Brands, LLC v. Domain Asset Holdings, FA091200 298052 (Forum January 22, 2010)   191

Secondary School Admission Test Board, Inc. v. Joanna Severino and Richard Hosko, FA0501000408094 (Forum March 24, 2005)   93, 447

SecretLab SG Pte Ltd v. Jason Bright, Secret Lab LLC   199

Securus Technologies, LLC v. Domain Administrator, D2021-3383 (WIPO December 16, 2021)   126, 476, 668

Sell House Fast, LLC v. Billie Funderburk, FA1603001667961(Forum May 5, 2016)   330

Sensis Pty Ltd, Telstra Corporation Limited v. Yellow Pages Marketing B.V., D2011-0057 (WIPO March 15, 2011)   238

Sentara Healthcare v. Katherine Cole, D2023-0811 (WIPO April 27, 2023)   481

Sermo, Inc. v. CatalystMD, LLC., D2008-0647 (WIPO July 2, 2008)   106

Serta Inc. v. Charles Dawson, D2008-1474 (WIPO November 20, 2008)   479

Service Spring Corp. v. hao wang, D2018-2422 (WIPO December 17,2019)   653

Shakespeare Company LLC v. Bob Pflueger, D2010-1126 (WIPO Aug. 19, 2010)   427

Share Our Gifts Foundation, Inc. v. Freedom Bands Inc., Fan Bandz Inc a/k/a fanbanz, D2004-1070 (WIPO March 18, 2005)   519

Shesafe Pty Ltd v. DomainMarket.com, D2017-1330 (WIPOAugust 22, 2017)   716

Shirmax Retail Ltd. v. CES Marketing Group, Inc., AF-0104 (eResolution February 7, 2000)   117, 385, 416

Shirmax Retail Ltd./Detaillants Shirmax Lted v. CES Marketing Group, Inc., AF-0104 (eResolution February 7, 2000)   117

Shoe Mart Factory Outlet, Inc. v. DomainHouse.com, Inc. c/o Domain Administrator, FA0504000462916 (Forum June 10, 2005)   321, 715

Shopping.com v. Internet Action Consulting, D2000-0439 (WIPO July 28, 2000)   220, 271, 560

shopping24 Gesellschaft für multimediale Anwendungen SEPTEMBER 28mbH v. Christian Rommel, D2000-0508 (WIPO September 28, 2000)   81

Shotgun Software Inc. v. Domain Admin / Hulmiho Ukolen, Poste restante, D2017-1273(WIPO August 23, 2017)   615

Silvie Tomcalov a.k.a. Sylvia Saint v. Juan Campos, 2006-0379 (WIPO May 5, 2006)   534

Simon Property Group, L.P. v. Magno Torreja / Organization Name Redacted, D2023-2944 (WIPO August 28, 2023)   535

Simple Plan Inc. v. Michel Rog, FA2111001973743 (Forum January 4, 2022)   706

Sinclair Finance Company v. Nathaniel Young / SumValley   198

SiTV, Inc. d/b/a NUVO TV v. Javier F. Rodriguez, D2014-1143 (WIPO August 14, 2014)   173

Six Continents Hotels, Inc. v. Ahmed Marzooq, D2012-0757 (WIPO May 16, 2012)   605

Sixsigma Networks Mexico, S.A. DE C.V. v. DYNAMO.COM, AUTORENEWAL AND DNS, D2022-4534 (WIPO February 28, 2023)   665

SK Lubricants Americas v. Andrea Sabatini, Webservice Limited, D2015-1566 (WIPO December 15, 2015)   228, 500

Skattedirektoratet v. Eivind Nag, D2000-1314 (WIPO December 18, 2000)   432

Skillful Communications, Inc., v. Redacted for Privacy, Aquent / Aquent Aquent, Aquent, D2022-0910 (WIPO May 26, 2022)   163, 345, 403

SkillSoft Corporation v. R & S Mica Inc. and Julie Radhakrishnan, D2002-1065 (WIPO February 11, 2003)   639

Slingshot Transportation, Inc. v. InBok Lee, FA1904001841279 (Forum May 26, 2019)   186

Smart Design LLC v. Hughes, D2000-0993 (WIPO October 18, 2000)   113, 659

SmartContract Chainlink, Ltd. v. Zolmeister Zolmeister, FA2208002009185 (Forum September 27, 2022)   31, 588

Smokey Mountain Knife Works v. Deon Carpenter, AF-230 (a, b) (eResolution July 3, 2000)   508, 520

Snap Inc. v. Ali Alshumrani/Ali Aleryani, FA1805001788602 (Forum June 14, 2018)   152

Snap Inc. v. Domain Administrator / Domain Professionals, LLC / Domain Master / Global Personals, LLC / Domain Master / Worldwide Connect Partners, LLC., FA2102001933412 (Forum May 11, 2021)   126

Snap-on Incorporated v. Jeffrey Scotese, D2013-0577 (WIPO May 9, 2013)   578

SNCF Voyageurs v. Whois Agent, Domain Protection Services, Inc. / Antonio Vaz, D2021-2718 (WIPO December 15,2021)   150

So Bold Limited v. Daniel Lahoti, TechOps, VirtualPoint Inc., D2022-1100 (WIPO June 6, 2022)   472, 695

Sociedad Anonima de Capital Variable (CAMCO) v. Michael Mann, D2016-1709 (WIPO October 3, 2016)   475, 724

Sociedad Papiros Ltda v. Ivan Rico, FA 0003000094365 (Forum May 16, 2000).   516, 551

Societe des Hotels Meridien SA v. United States of Moronica, D2000-0405 (WIPO June 27, 2000)   238

Société des Produits Nestlé S.A. v. [Chinese characters] (guo li), D2022-1992 (WIPO August 26, 2022)   282, 369, 414, 550

Société des Produits Nestlé S.A. v. Boris Postolov, D2023-0212 (WIPO March 8, 2023)   282, 369, 414, 550

Société Librairie Fernand Nathan-Fernand Nathan & Cie v. Domain Administrator, DomainMarket.com, D2022-0016 (WIPO February 18, 2022)   156

Sodexo v. Daniela Ortiz, D2021-0628 (WIPO May 3, 2021)   140, 480, 613

Sodexo v. WhoisGuard Protected, WhoisGuard, Inc. / Gabriella Garlo, D2020-2706 (WIPO January 4, 2021)   140, 480, 613

Soft Trust Inc. v. Todd Hinton, Ikebana America LLC, D2020-2640 (WIPO December 4, 2020)   393, 460

SoftLayer Technologies, Inc. v. UltimatumHost.com / Rodrigo Martins, FA1202001429575 (Forum March 22, 2012)   214

Solidium Oy v. Privacy Service Provided by Withheld for Privacy ehf / EstormH Etormhosting, Estorm Programming, D2022-3139 (WIPO October 10 2022)   528

Solon AG v. eXpensive Domains.com Project, D2008-0881 (WIPO August 1, 2008)   497, 689, 697

Sonic-Crest Cadillac, LLC v. Hayes, FA0311000212652 (Forum January 14, 2002)   295

Sony Kabushiki Ka v. Sin, Eonmok, D2000-1007 (WIPO November 16, 2000)   350, 426

Sothys Auriac v. Nonie Crème, D2022-3862 (WIPO December 8, 2022)   672

Souq.com FZ LLC v. Ruiling Wang, Comcom Communications LLC, D2016-2085 (WIPO December 12, 2016)   585

SOUTHBank v. Media Street, D2001-0294 (WIPO April 11, 2001)   503

Southern Exposure v. Southern Exposure, Inc. FA0005000094864 (Forum July 18, 2000)   512

Spanish Original Brands, S.L. v. Anri Emmanuel Palomique Altea, Industex, Limited, D2023-5153 (WIPO January 31, 2024)   640

Speedo Holdings B.V. v. Programmer, Miss Kathy Beckerson, John Smitt, Matthew Simmons, D2010-0281 (WIPO May 18, 2010)   273

Sports Holdings, Inc. v. MB, D2006-1262 (WIPO November 28, 2006)   271

SportSoft Golf, Inc. v. Sites to Behold Ltd., FA0006000094976 (Forum July 27, 2000)   357

Square Peg Interactive Inc. v. Naim Interactive Inc., FA0311000209572 (Forum December 29, 2003)   590

St. Louis University d/b/a Saint Louis University v. SLUCOMPLIANCE PROJECT.ORG c/o Privacy Protect, LLC / Domain Admin, Privacy Protect, LLC (PrivacyProtect.org) / Micheal Todd Rice, D2017-1759 (WIPO November 15, 2017)   300

State Farm Mutual Automobile Insurance Company v. Robert Goldman / A4M, FA2207002003300 (Forum September 13, 2022)   360, 483

Stateside Merchants, LLC v. rong liu, FA2305002043263 (Forum June 7, 2023)   357

Steelcase Inc. v. Cimpress Schweiz GmbH, FA1706001737556 (Forum July 25, 2017)   612, 615

Stella D'oro Biscuit Co., Inc. v. The Patron Group, Inc. D2000-0012 (WIPO February 18, 2000)   206, 502

Steven Rattner v. BuyThisDomanName (John Pepin), D2000-0402 (WIPO July 3, 2000)   370

Steven Samblis v. Domains By Proxy, LLC / Friends Of PNCH, D2016-0579 (WIPO May 23, 2016)   288

Stichting BDO v. Yuci Ma, D2023-4371 (WIPO December 14,2023)   596

Substance Abuse Mgmt., Inc. v. Screen Actors Modesl [sic] Int'l, Inc. (SAMI), D2001-0782 (WIPO August 14, 2001)   117, 464

Success Bank v. ZootGraphics c/o Ira Zoot, FA0904001259918 (Forum June 29, 2009)   91, 161, 173, 226, 671, 675

Sullivan & Cromwell LLP v. Whitney Chatterjee / Sullivan&Cromwell / Sullivan & Cromwell / Gareth Rothweiler / ROSE CASTELLANOS, FA2212002022604 (Forum January 3, 2022)   277

SummerTech Inc. v. Jimmy Hill / iD Tech Camps, FA1512001652542 (Forum February 2, 2016)   389

Summit Group, LLC v. LSO, Ltd., FA0607000758981 (Forum Sept. 14, 2006)   417

Sumner p/k/a Sting v. Urvan, D2000-0596 (WIPO July 24, 2000)   76

Sun Ray Chinese School, Inc. v. Hui Chiu / Mei Hsu, FA1604001668860(Forum May 16, 2016)   299

Superiority, Inc. d/b/a Just Bulbs v. none/Mother boards.com, D2003-0491 (WIPO October 9, 2003)   770

Supermac's (Holdings) Limited v. Domain Administrator, DomainMarket.com, D-2018-0540 (WIPO May 17, 2018)   220, 490

Sustainable Forestry Management Limited v. SFM.com and James M. van Johns "Infa dot Net" Web Services, D2002-0535 (WIPO September 13, 2002)   675

Süta Süt Ürünleri Anonim Sirketi v. Privacy Administrator, Anonymize, Inc. / Independent Digital Artists, D2022-0615 (WIPO April 24, 2022)   630

Sutherland Institute v. Continuative LLC, D2009-0693 (WIPO July 10, 2009),   441

Swarovski Aktiengesellschaft v. Registration Private, Domains By Proxy, LLC, DomainsByProxy.com / Steve Hosie, CJ, LLC., D2015-2351 (WIPO March 7, 2016)   450

T

T.M. Lewin Shirtmaker Ltd. v. Hello Giller, D2023-1695 (WIPO July 6, 2023   350, 366

T.M. Lewin Shirtmaker Ltd. v. Hello Giller, D2023-1695 (WIPO July 6, 2023)   350, 366

Taeho Kim v. Skelton Logic, FA1002001305934 (Forum March 22, 2010)   619, 718

Taffo SRL v. Contact Privacy Inc. Customer 0141464573 / Agenzia Funebre Taffo di Taffo G. & C. SAS Societa/Ditta, D2019-2266 (WIPO November 19, 2019)   648

Take-Two Interactive Software Inc. v. Name Administration Inc., D2010-0845 (WIPO August 6, 2010)   339

Target Brands, Inc. v. Eastwind Group, FA0405000267475 (Forum July 9, 2004)   356, 374, 394

Tarmac Trading Limited v. Maureen Twist / Michael & Paul Wilson trading as Abbey Tarmac & Asphalt, D2021-3768 (WIPODecember 30, 2021)   475

Tata Communications International Pte Ltd (f/k/a VSNL International Pte Ltd) v. Portmedia Inc. / TRUEROOTS.COM c/o Nameview Inc. Whois, D2010-0217 (WIPO June 1, 2010)   116

Tatian Botton v. Mozur contactor: OlegMozur, FA2006001900809(Forum August 4, 2020)   430

Teaching Company, LLC, d/b/a The Great Courses v. Brendhan Hight, Marchex Sales, LLC, D2014-0448 (WIPO June 4, 2014)   235

Tecme S.A. v. Stephen Bougourd, D2020-2597 (WIPO November 24, 2020)   399, 687

Tecnologia Bancaria S.A. v. Marchex Sales Inc., D2014-0834 (WIPO September 24, 2014)   768, 786

Ted Britt Ford Sales, Inc. v. Contact Privacy Inc. Customer 0155442277 / Guy Emerson, D2020-0732 (WIPO April 28, 2020)   439, 463

Telaxis Communications Corp. v. William E. Minkle, D2000-0005 (WIPO March 5, 2000)   91, 173, 597

Telect, Inc. v. Arvind Reddy, D2017-1270 (WIPO August 15, 2017)   419

Télévision Française 1 (TF1) v. Khaled Bitat, D2007-0137 (WIPO March 20, 2007)   416

Telhio Credit Union, Inc. v. Braden McParlin, D2007-1224 (WIPO October 27, 2007)   295

Telstra Corporation Limited v. Nuclear Marshmallows, D2000-0003 (WIPO February 18, 2000)   53, 90, 232, 238, 458, 543, 572

Terana, S.A. v. RareNames, WebReg, D2007-0489 (WIPO June 6, 2007)   468-469

Teranet Land Information Services Inc. v. Verio, Inc., D2000-1123 (WIPO January 25, 2001)   661

Teresa Christie, d/b/a The Mackinac Island Florist v. James Porcaro, d/b/a Weber's Mackinac Island Florist, D2001-0653 (WIPO September 17, 2001)   314

Ternio, LLC v. Domains by Proxy, LLC / Sedo GmbH, D2020-2215 (WIPO November 16, 2020)   164, 395, 599

Ternio, LLC v. Domains by Proxy, LLC / Sedo GmbH, D2020-2215(WIPO November 16, 2020)   164, 395, 599

Tesco Stores Limited v. Mat Feakins, DCO2013-0017 (WIPO October 4, 2013)   366

Tesla Industries, Inc. v. Stu Grossman d/b/a SG Consulting, FA0508000547889 (Forum December 5, 2005)   210

Texans For Lawsuit Reform, Inc. v. Kelly Fero, D2004-0778 (WIPO October 31, 2004)   540, 636

Texas Capital Bank N.A. v. WhoisGuard, Inc. / Aleksandr Osipov, Private, D2018-1040 (WIPO June 19, 2018)   189

Texas Wind Power Company v. Wind Works c/o Savvy Dog Design, LLC., FA0903001252746(Forum May 12, 2009)   563

The American Automobile Association, Inc. v. 555 Metro Airport Transportation Service LLC., D2011-0588 (WIPO May 17, 2011)   700

The Atlantic Paranormal Society and Pilgrim Films and Television, Inc. v. Domain Admin, FA0901001242901 (Forum March 5, 2009)   460

The Chemours Company LLC v. WhoIs Agent, Domain Protection Services, Inc. / Gabriel Joseph, Clearer Technology, D2022-3013 (WIPO October 31, 2022)   272

The Coca-Cola Co. v. Svensson, FA0201000103933(Forum February 27, 2002)   719

The Curators of the University of Missouri v. Pamela Holley, MU Healthcare Victims, D2020-2693 (WIP0 December 3,2020)   108

The Forward Association, Inc. v. Enterprises Unlimited, FA0008000095491 (Forum October 3, 2000)   366

The Hartman Media Company, LLC v. Host Master, 1337 ServicesLLC, D2018-1722 (WIPO September 24, 2018)   33, 285

The Hebrew University of Jerusalem v. Alberta Hot Rods, D2002-0616 (WIPO October 7, 2002)   589

The Hype Company, S.L. v. Ehren Schaiberger, D2021-1850(WIPO September 13 2021)   708

The Indian Hotels Company Limited v. Roger Price, D2018-2325 (WIPO December 28, 2018)   398, 596

The Knot, Inc. v. In Knot We Trust LTD, D2006-0340 (WIPO June 26, 2006)   68

The Landmark Group v. DigiMedia.com, L.P., FA0406000285459 (Forum August 6, 2004)   418

The Law Society v. S.H. INC   626

The Medicis Pharmaceutical Corporation v. MRX Technologies, Inc., and Neil Gerardo, D2002-0462 (WIPO August 22, 2002)   307, 328

The New England Vein & Laser Center, P.C. v. Vein Centers for Excellence, Inc., D2005-1318 (WIPO February 22, 2006)   396

The New York Times Company v. Name Administration Inc. (BVI), FA1009001349045 (Forum November 17, 2010)   589-590

The New York Times Company v. New York Internet Services, D2000-1072(WIPO December 5, 2000)   589-590

The Perfect Potion v. Domain Administrator, D2004-0743(WIPO November 6, 2004)   198, 307

The Planetary Society v. Salvador Rosillo Domainsforlife.com, D2001-1228 (WIPO February 12, 2002)   574

The Posture Lab Pte Ltd. v. Privacy Administrator, Anonymize, Inc., D2022-4181 (WIPO December 19, 2022)   559

The Procter & Gamble Company v. Marchex Sales, Inc   645, 674

The Professional Golfers' Association of America (PGA) v. Provisions, LLC., D2004-0576 (WIPO September 13, 2004)   519

The Prudential Insurance Company of America v. PRU International, FA0111000101800 (Forum January 18, 2002)   138, 241, 263, 544, 744

The Prudential Insurance Company of America v. REDACTED PRIVACY, FA1809001806523 (Forum October 11, 2018)   138, 241, 263, 544, 744

The Prudential Insurance Company of America v. Terrance McQuilkin et al., FA150500 1618256 (Forum May 29, 2015)   138, 241, 263, 544, 744

The Resource Center for Pregnancy and Personal Health v. Abigail Hutchings, FA200200 1885848 (Forum March 30, 2020)   79, 441

The Reverend Dr. Jerry Falwell and The Liberty Alliance v. Gary Cohn, Prolife.net, and God.info, D2002-0184 (WIPO June 3, 2002)   101, 432

The Reverend Dr. Jerry L. Falwell and The Liberty Alliance v. Lamparello International., FA0310000198936 (Forum November 20, 2003)   88, 432

The Reverend Dr. Jerry L. Falwell and The Liberty Alliance v. Lamparello International., FA0310000198936 (Forum November 20, 2003)T 88, 432

The Royal Bank of Scotland Group plc v. Reserved Bench of Strategic Geographers / Domain ID Shield Service, D2012-1733 (WIPO November 8, 2012) 248

The Royal Edinburgh Military Tattoo Limited v. Identity Protection Service, Identity Protect Limited / Martin Clegg, WM Holdings, D2016-2290 (WIPO January 5, 2017) 450

The Travelers Indemnity Company v. jack Halua / Google Inc., FA1707001739643 (Forum August 21,2017) 612

The Trustees of Columbia University in the City of New York v. George Billis, FA160400 1671587 (Forum May 25, 2016) 527

The Vanguard Group, Inc. v. AD-X Network, Inc., D2000-0942 (WIPO October 18, 2000) 22, 533, 565

The Vanguard Group, Inc. v. Emilio Sa D2001-1453 (WIPO APRIL 7, 2002) 22, 533, 565

The Way International, Inc. v. Diamond Peters, D2003-0264 (WIPO May 29, 2003) 458, 575

Thermo Electron Corp. and Fisher Scientific Co., LLC and Fisher Scientific Intl v. Charlie Xu, FA 0605000713851 (Forum July 12, 2006) 409

Thirty & Co. v. Jake Marcum, D2016-1212 (WIPO August 16, 2016) 424

Thomas Pritzker, The Pritzker Organization, LLC v. Richard Brown, D2009-0911 (WIPO October 12, 2009) 371

Thomas Wang v. Privacydotlink Customer 546843 / Blue Nova Inc., D2018-1316 (WIPO August 27, 2028) 263

Thorpe Technologies, Inc. v. Domains By Proxy, LLC / Gregory Kudasz, Irukandji-USA, D2022-1456 (WIPO June 26, 2022) 400

Thread.com, LLC v. Poploff, D2000-1470 (WIPO January 5, 2001) 291

Thrive Networks, Inc. v. Thrive Ventures, Inc., D2003-0534 (WIPO August 26, 2003) 406

Thule Sweden AB v. Cameron David Jackson,D2016-0414 (WIPO April 12,2016) 523

Thursday Boot Company v. Domain Admin, WHOISprotection.cc, Cynthia Wagner, Michelle Gordon, Rita Gilbert, Rudy Fry, Rose Turner, Alice Murray, Gary Dillon, Lisbeth Rose, Gilbert Frasier, Gladys Sipes, Chauncey Thomas, Mark Copeland, Embla Gottfrid, Web Co., D2021-4291 (WIPO February 28, 2022) 287, 392

Tiara Hotels & Resorts LLC v. John Pepin, D2009-0041 (WIPO March 10, 2009) 162

Tiffany Chhuom, PLLC d/b/a Ethtech, Tiffany Chhuom, Peter Chhuom v. J S, D2023-2930 (WIPO September 15, 2023) 429

Time Inc. v. Chip Cooper, D2000-1342 (WIPO February 13, 2001)   78, 87, 176, 485

Time Inc. v. Max Martel, D2004-0122 (WIPO May 4, 2004)   78, 87, 176, 485

Timec Oil and Gas, Inc. v. Domain Admin, Privacy Protect, LLC (PrivacyProtect.org) / Guy Ngassa, The Solution Engineering Group, D2022-0064 (WIPO February 23, 2022)   322, 329

Tiny Prints, Inc. v. Oceanside Capital Corp. c/o Web Admin., FA1007001337650 (Forum October 8, 2010)   671

Tip Vy Spots LLC Vy v. Super Privacy Service c/o Dynadot, D2016-0872(WIPO June 29, 2016)   684

Tire Discounters, Inc. v. TireDiscounter.com, FA0604000 679485 (Forum June 14, 2006)   191

Titmouse, Inc. v. Paul Blank, D2022-2208 (WIPO August 9, 2022)   665

Toast, Inc. v. Jared Isaacman / Harbortouch, FA2208002007428 (Forum September 6, 2022)   127

TOBAM v. M. Thestrup / Best Identity, D2016-1990 (WIPO November 21, 2016)   121, 571, 638, 673

Tom Cruise v. Network Operations Center / Alberta Hot Rods, D2006-0560 (WIPO July 5, 2006)   427

Toner Connect, L.L.C. v. Privacy Protect, LLC / Realogue Corporation, D2018-2829 (WIPO February 21, 2019)   515, 563

Toronto-Dominion Bank v. Karpachev, D2000-1571 (WIPO January 15, 2001)   417, 522

Torus Insurance Holdings Limited v. Torus Computer Resources, D2009-1455 (WIPO January10, 2010)   120

Total S.A. v. Gustavo Cerda, D2011-2073 (WIPOFebruary 8, 2011)   275, 539, 629

Total Temperature Instrumentation, Inc. d/b/a Instrumart v. Laura Dunn, Virtual Office, D2018-0441 (WIPO April 14, 2018)   192

TotalEnergies SE v. Domain Administrator, Registrant of purchase-totalenergies.com / Albert Clement, Purchase Total Energies; Privacy service provided by Withheld for Privacy ehf / Harry Moore, Total; Junior Stephane, Total Energies Procurements; David Ha, D2022-3069 (WIPO October 14, 2022)   526

Tough Traveler, Ltd. v. Kelty Pack, Inc., Mike Scherer, and Inkling Pen Co., D2000-0783 (WIPO September 29, 2000)   237

Tourism and Corporate Automation Ltd. v. TSI Ltd., AF-0096 (eResolution February 7, 2000)   77, 349, 413

Town of Easton Connecticut v. Lightning PC Inc., FA0808001220202 (Forum October 12, 2008)   314

Toyota Jidosha Kabushiki Kaisha d/b/a Toyota Motor Corporation v. S&S Enterprises Ltd., D2000-0802 (WIPO September 9, 2000)   353

Toyota Motor Sales U.S.A. Inc. v. J. Alexis Productions, D2003-0624 (WIPO October 16, 2003)   318

TPI Holdings Inc. v. JB Designs, D2000-0216 (WIPO May 22, 2000)   252

TR v. Synopsys Inc., D2010-1264 (WIPO October 7, 2010)   ii, iv, vii-xxii, xxv-xxxii, 3-544, 546-790, 793

Trader Joe's Company v. Contact Privacy Inc. Customer 7151571251 (Unknown) / Michelle Cheung, D2022-3235 (WIPO October 20, 2022)   451

TranScrip Partners LLP, TranScrip Limited v. Abstract Holdings International Ltd, Domain Admin, D2021-2220 (WIPOSeptember 27, 2021)   150

Traxys North America LLC v. Joao Mota / Joao MotaInc, 14373-URDP (CIIDRC January 16, 2021) (TRAXYS and <tarxys.com
)   609, 611, 616

Tribeca Film Center, Inc. v. Lorenzo Brusasco-Mackenzie, D2000-1772 (WIPO April 1, 2001)   584

True North Media, LLC and Good Universe Media, LLC v. 1soft Corporation, Greg Thorne, D2012-1457 (WIPO September 28, 2012)   692

Tumblr, Inc. v. Above.com Domain Privacy/Transure Enterprise Ltd., Host Master, D2013-0213 (WIPO March 29, 2013)   366

Türkiye'nin Otomobili Giri'im Grubu Sanayi Ve Ticaret Anonim Sirketi v. The Office of George Gould, D2021-1949 (WIPO September 1, 2021)   265

Tuxedos By Rose v. Nunez, FA0007000095248 (Forum August 17, 2000)   327

Twitter, Inc. v. Geigo, Inc., D2011-1210 (WIPO November 2, 2011)   404

Two Way NV/SA v. Moniker Privacy Services, LLC / [4079779]: Domain Administrator, D2012-2413 (WIPO June 7, 2013)   235-236

Ty Inc. v. Joseph Parvin d/b/a Domains For Sale, D2000-0688 (WIPO November 9, 2000)   21, 105, 129, 274, 785

Ty Inc. v. Joseph Parvin d/b/a Domains For Sale, D2000-0688 (WIPO November 11, 2000)   21, 105, 129, 274, 785

U

U.S. Office of Pers. Mgmt. v. MS Tech. Inc., FA 198898 (Forum December 9, 2003)   312

UAB "BIOK laboratorija" v. Jinsoo Yoon, CAC 101743 (ADR.eu October 26, 2017)   171

Ubiquiti Inc. v. Reilly Chase / Locklin Networks, LLC, FA2110001970506 (Forum December 9, 2021)   494, 634, 705

UK Betting PLC v. Pam Oldfield, D2005-0637 (WIPO August 31, 2005)   358

Uline, Inc. v. Hulmiho Ukolen, D2016-0065 (WIPO March 13, 2016)   505

Union Square Partnership, Inc., Union Square Partnership District Management Association, Inc. v. unionsquarepartnership.com Private Registrant and

unionsquarepartnership.org Private Registrant, D2008-1234 (WIPO October 22, 2008)   289

United Computer Products, Co Inc. v. Domain Name Proxy, Inc Domain Name Proxy, Inc Domain Name Proxy, Inc Domain Name Proxy, Inc, D2008-0017 (WIPO February 22, 2008)   619

United Industries Corporation v. James Katz, FA2103001936864 (Forum April 28, 2021)   582

Universa Investments L.P. v. c/o WHOIStrustee.com Limited, Registrant of universablockchain.com / Alexander Borodich, Universa Corporation Ltd. / Alexander Borodich, D2020-1567 (WIPO August 20, 2020)   566

Universal City Studios, Inc. v. G.A.B. Enterprises, D2000-0416 (WIPO June 29, 2000)   422, 552

Uovo Art LLC v. Mira Hold, Mira Holdings, Inc., D2016-0214 (WIPO April 18, 2016)   184

UpsideOut, Inc. v. Lin Han, D2009-0388 (WIPO July 7, 2009)   561

US Publishers, Inc. v. US Immigration Organization, D2011-1214 (WIPO September 23, 2011)   605

Ustream.TV, Inc. v. Vertical Axis, Inc., D2008-0598 (WIPO July 29, 2008)   420

V

Vacation Pig, LLC d.b.a OOVO v. elmer rubio, FA2201001981434 (Forum February 14, 2022)   14, 179

Valeant Pharmaceuticals International, Inc. / iNova Pharmaceuticals (Australia) Pty Limited v. Luca Radu / Fundacion Private WhoIs / Maxim Conovalov / Vasju Pere, D2013-1918 (WIPO February 3, 2014)   277

Valero Energy Corporation and Valero Marketing and Supply Company v. Registration Private, Domains By Proxy LLC / Valero Energy Corporation, D2017-0087 (WIPO March 15, 2017)   612

Valero Energy Corporation, Valero Marketing and Supply Company v. Mike Farnworth, D2022-2768 (WIPO October 4, 2022   528

Validas, LLC v. SMVS Consultancy Private Limited, D2009-1413 (WIPO June 1, 2010)   465

Valio Ltd. v. Telepathy, Inc., CAC 100558 (ADR.eu May 30, 2013)   229

Vancouver Org. Comm. for the 2010 Olympic and Paralymic Games & Int'l Olympic Comm. v. Malik, FA0603000666119 (Forum May 12, 2006)   316

Vanguard Trademark Holdings USA LLC v. Nett Corp., FA0905001262162 (Forum July 26, 2009)   312, 591, 729

Vanguard Trademark Holdings USA LLC v. Wang Liqun, FA1506001625332 (Forum July 17, 2015)   312, 591, 729

Vantage Mobility International, LLC v. Michael Bilde / Embrand, FA1806001790831 (Forum July 29, 2018)   505

Vericheck, Inc. v. Admin Manager, Vericheck, Inc. v.Admin Manager, FA0606000734799 (Forum August 2, 2006)   750, 782

Verint Systems Inc. v. CRYSTALSTEVENS, D2002-0896(WIPO November 21, 2002)   113

VeriSign Inc. v. VeneSign C.A., D2000-0303 (WIPO June 28, 2000)   165, 775

Verner Panton Design v. Fontana di Luce Corp, D2012-1909) (WIPO November 19, 2012)   255, 257

Vernons Pools Limited v. Vertical Axis, Inc., D2003-0041 (WIPO March 12, 2003)   200

Verridian Plc v. Nadine Leech, D2008-1539 (WIPO November 20, 2008).   347

Vestel Elektronik Sanayi ve Ticaret AS v. Kahveci, D2000-1244 (WIPO November 11, 2000)   425

Veuve Clicquot Ponsardin, Maison Fondée en 1772 v. The Polygenix Group Co., D2000-0163 (WIPO May 1, 2000).   484

VFS Global Services PLC v. David Killam, D2022-3969 (WIPO December 22, 2022)   601-602

Via Varejo S/A, v. Domain Admin, D2015-1304 (WIPO October 17,2015)   25, 155, 768

Viacom International Inc. and MTV Networks Europe v. Rattan Singh Mahon, D2000-1440 (WIPO December 22, 2000)   243, 246

Victor Bekhet v. Kirk Uhler / Brian Jagger, D2021-0039 (WIPO March 22, 2021)   111, 376

Victron Energy B.V. v. Privacy Administrator, Anonymize Inc. / SARVIX, INC., D2022-1186 (WIPO June 2, 2022)   124, 197, 705

Video Only, Inc. v. Domain Name Systems, D2007-0607 (WIPO June 16, 2007)   286

Viking Office Products, Inc. v. Natasha Flaherty a/k/a ARS-N6YBV, FA1104001383534 (Forum May 31, 2011)   407, 679

Ville de Paris v. Jeff Walter, D2009-1278 (WIPO November 19, 2009)   120, 340, 769, 783

Ville de Paris v. Salient Properties LLC, D2009-1279 (WIPO December 3, 2009)   120, 340, 769, 783

Villeroy & Boch AG v. Mario Pingerna, D2007-1912 (WIPO February 14, 2008)   481

Virgin Enterprises Limited v. Derek Kagimoto, Virginiorbit, D2021-1828 (WIPO August 12, 2021)   71, 197, 632, 726

Virgin Enterprises Limited v. Domain Admin/This Domain is for Sale, Hugedomains. com, D2017-1961 (WIPO December 11, 2017)   71, 197, 632, 726

Virgin Enterprises Limited v. Domain Administrator, D2013-1678 (WIPO December 2, 2013)   71, 197, 632, 726

Virgin Enterprises Limited v. Internet Domains, D2001-1008 (WIPO October 16, 2001)   71, 197, 632, 726

Virutex Ilko S.A. v. Dynadot, LLC (Super Privacy Service LTD c/o Dynadot) / Embrand, Michael Bilde, D2020-3379 (WIPO April 9, 2021)   600

Visual Gis Engineering S.L. v. Nitin Tripathi, D2006-0079 (WIPO March 23, 2006)   247, 542, 636

Vitamin Well AB v. Privacy service provided by Withheld for Privacy ehf / Wen Batiz vegas, D2022-2148 (WIPO August 22, 2022)   522

Viz Communications, Inc., v. Redsun dba www.animerica.com and David Penava, D2000-0905 (WIPO December 29, 2000)   514

VOI Technology v. Domain Department, Arcanite Media Ltd., DSE2022-0002 (WIPO March 19, 2022)   718

Volkswagen AG v. Richard Roberts, HD Home Theater, D2016-0231 (WIPO April 21, 2016)   523

Voltas Limited v. Tim Treleaven, T2 PROJECTS, D2020-1485 (WIPO August 7, 2020)   188

Volvo Trademark Holding AB v. Auto Shivuk, D2005-0447 (WIPO October 14, 2014)   449, 734, 739

Volvo Trademark Holding AB v. Volvospares / Keith White, D2008-1860 (WIPO February 10, 2009)   449, 734, 739

Vorwerk International AG v. Jose Luis Martin, D2023-1419 (WIPO July 31, 2023)   294

VRL International Ltd. and International Lifestyles, Inc. v. Relevansanalys, D2009-0974 (WIPO September 3, 2009)   225

VS Media, Inc. v. Juan Chavarria, VGMedia, D2023-2124 (WIPO July 20, 2023)   605

Vudu, Inc. v. WhoisGuard, Inc. / K Blacklock, D2019-2247 (WIPO November 15, 2019)   682

W

W. Fla. Lighting v. Ramirez, D2008-1122 (WIPO October 2, 2008)   300

Wachovia Corporation v. American Consumers First, D2004-0150 (WIPO July 7, 2004)   192

Wal-Mart Stores, Inc. v. Richard MacLeod d/b/a For Sale, D2000-0662 (WIPO September 19, 2000)   136, 306, 352, 429, 448, 459, 585

Wal-Mart Stores, Inc. v. Sergio Cabrera, FA1008001344053 (Forum November 8, 2010)   136, 306, 352, 429, 448, 459, 585

Wal-Mart Stores, Inc. v. Walmarket Canada, D2000-0150 (WIPO May 5, 2000)   136, 306, 352, 429, 448, 459, 585

Wal-Mart Stores, Inc. v. Walsucks and Walmarket Puerto Rico, D2000-0477 (WIPO July 20, 2000)   136, 306, 352, 429, 448, 459, 585

WALA-Heilmittel GmbH v. Canada Jumeira / Contact Privacy Inc., D2013-0782 (WIPO July 13, 2013)   573

Wall Beds By Wilding, LLC, d/b/a Wilding Wall Beds v. Texas International Property Associates, Keyword Marketing, Inc., and Caribbean Online International Ltd., FA0712001124523 (Forum February 27, 2008)   245

Warner Bros. Entertainment Inc. v. Karl Allberg, FA2002001881913 (Forum February 19, 2020)   152, 193

Warner Bros. Entertainment Inc. v. Sharon Jerome / Michaelis Events, LLC, FA2309002064214 (Forum November 17, 2023)   152, 193

Wärtsilä Technology Oy Ab v. McKeith Powers, D2020-1525 (WIPO August 7, 2020)   616

Wasatch Shutter Design v. Duane Howell / The Blindman, FA1705001731056 (Forum June 23, 2017)   333, 374

Weatherall Green & Smith v. Everymedia.com, D2000-1528 (WIPO February 19, 2001)   113, 118

Web 3.0 Technologies Foundation v. Registration Private, Domains By Proxy LLC / Su Tingting, Hangzhou Midaizi Network Co., Ltd., D2021-3593(WIPO February 3, 2022)   153, 477, 729

WebSec Holdings, B.V. v. Marty Martin, Adapt Partners, D2023-0813 (WIPO May 1, 2023)   345

Weeds, Inc. v. Registration Private, Domains By Proxy, LLC / Innovation HQ, Inc   420, 598

Weider Publications, Inc. v. Nextlevel.com   216

Well-Link Industry Co. Ltd. v. Jeff Park, Nexpert, Inc., D2017-0036 (WIPO March 1, 2017)   178

Wellquest International, Inc. v. Nicholas Clark, D2005-0552 (WIPO July 10, 2005)   617

Westchester Media Company, L.P. v. Infa dot Net Web Services, FA0106000097759 (Forum August 3, 2001)   490

Westfield Corporation, Inc and Westfield Limited v. Graeme Michael Hobbs (Dynamic Marketing Consultants), D2000-0227 (WIPO May 18, 2000)   271

WEX Inc. v. Tom Soulanille, FA2204001991413 (Forum May 16, 2022)   345, 569

Whatsapp LLC v. elie galam, D2022-3684 (WIPO November 22, 2022)   529

Whispering Smith Limited v. Domain Administrator, Tfourh, LLC, D2016-1175 (WIPO September 27, 2016)   643, 722

White Ribbon Australia v. Whois Privacy Protection Service, Inc / Erin Pizzey   430

Wild PCS, Inc. and Tom Yang v. Perfect Privacy, LLC / Choi Lam, D2016-0017 (WIPO February 17, 2016)   240

William Grant & Sons Limited v. Dave Chandler, D2016-0476 (WIPO April 17, 2016)   524

Williams-Sonoma, Inc. v. EZ-Port, D2000-0207 (WIPO May 5, 2000)   267

Wilserve Corporation v. Willi Kusche, D2007-0004 (WIPO Feb. 26, 2007)   407

Wiluna Holdings, LLC v. Privacy.co.com, Inc Privacy ID# 1100134, FA1805001789612 (Forum July 16, 2018)   595

Wirecard AG v. Telepathy Inc., Development Services, D2015-0703 (WIPO June 22, 2015)   161, 504, 715

Wix.com v. Domain Admin, Privacy Protect, LLC (PrivacyProtect.org) / Luciana Gomes   567

World Wrestling Federation Entertainment, Inc. v. Ringside Collectibles, D2000-1306 (WIPO February 5, 2002)   82, 387, 501, 563

WorldClaim Global Claims Management v. Bishop, Atticus / Bishop   374

WorldClearing US LLC v. Oskar Duris a/k/a World Clearing US LLC. a/k/a WorldClearing Holding Inc.org zlozka a/k/a Matt, Johannes a/k/a Global Infoservice Establishment a/k/a WorldClearing Limited   556, 561

Worldcom Exchange, Inc v. Wei.com, Inc., D2004-0955 (WIPO January 5, 2005)   619

Wrestling Federation Entertainment, Inc. v. Michael Bosman, D99-0001 (WIPO January 14, 2000)   82, 387, 501, 563

X

X6D Limited v. Telepathy, Inc., D2010-1519 (WIPO November 16, 2010)   676, 721

Xiatech Consulting Ltd v. Privacy Administrator, Anonymize, Inc., D2022-1072 (WIPOMay 23, 2022)   322, 328

XNT LTD. v. Ekaterina Shelud'ko, ForexAW.com, D2022-4133 (WIPO January 23, 2023)   434

Xoft Inc. v. Name Administration Inc. (BVI), FA080200 1154179 (Forum April 25, 2008)   407, 584

Xtraplus Corporation v. Flawless Computers, D2007-0070 (WIPO March 9, 2007)   106

Y

Yahoo Holdings, Inc. v. Registration Private, Domains By Proxy, LLC / Technonics Solutions, D2017-1336 (WIPO August 11, 2017)   614

Yahoo! Inc. and GeoCities v. Data Art Corp., DataArt Enterprises, Inc., Stonybrook Investments, Global Net 2000, Inc., Powerclick, Inc., and Yahoo Search, Inc., D2000-0587 (WIPO August 10, 2000)   274

Yahoo! Inc. v. Bill Skipton d/b/a Cowboy Clothing, FA0510000575666 (Forum November 23, 2005)   357, 601

Yahoo! Inc. v. Syed Hussaini, FA0808001222425 (Forum October 30, 2008)   523

Yahoo! Inc. v. YAHOO.COM / YAHOO! INC., FA1311001532273 (Forum January10, 2014)   274, 601

Yakka Pty Ltd v. Carlton Handyman & Hardware Centre, D2002-0903 (WIPO November 11, 200)   237

Yapi Malzemeleri San. VE TiC. A.S v. Domain Administrator, Name Administration Inc. (BVI), D2015-1757 (WIPO December 15, 2015)   209, 682

Yell Limited v. Ultimate Search, D2005-0091 (WIPO April 6, 2005)   675

Yeshiva University University v. SS Media, Joy Dhivakar S Singh, D2010-1588 (WIPO November 24, 2010)   474

YETI Coolers, LLC v. Ryley Lyon / Ditec Solutions LLC, FA1605001675141 (Forum July 11, 2016)   93, 446

YMCA of Metropolitan Chicago v. Robert Milideo, FA1609001693986 (Forum October 19, 20016)   319

Z

Zero International Holding v. Beyonet Servs., D2000-0161 (WIPO May 12, 2000)   167, 224, 388, 406

Zoyo Capital Limited v. A. Zoyo, D2018-2234 (WIPO November 13, 2018)   625

ZydusLifesciences Ltd. (formerly known as Cadila Healthcare Ltd.) v. Jewella PrivacyLLC / DNS, Domain Privacy LTD., D2022-0880 (WIPO June 24, 2022)   536

TABLE OF US, EU, AND UK COURT DECISIONS

A

Abercrombie & Fitch Co. v. Hunting World, Inc., 537 F.2d 4, 9 (CA2 1976)   342

AIRFX.com v. AirFX LLC, No. CV 11-01064, 2011 WL 6846428, at *1 (D. Ariz. Dec. 29, 2011.   750-751, 757, 786-787

Alpha Recycling, Inc. v. Timothy Crosby, 14-cv-5015 (S.D.N.Y. March 23, 2016)   772

Alston v. Calculator.com, No. 20-cv-23013-BLOOM/Louis, at *1 (S.D. Fla. Aug. 3,2020).   206, 324, 776-777

American Girl, LLC v. Nameview, Inc., 381 F. Supp. 2d 876 (E.D. Wis. 2005)   743

Ar2, LLC d/b/a Liv Institute v. Rudnick, 14-80809-civ, 15 (S.D.FL, August 7, 2014)   761

Avery Dennison Corp. v. Sumpton, 189 F.3d 868, 875 and 877 (9th Cir. 1999)   4, 135, 732

Avery Dennison Corporation v. Jerry Sumpton, et al., No. CV 97-407 JSL (C.D. California, March 16, 1998)   135

B

Baklan v. All Answers Ltd, No. CV-20-00707-PHX-JZB, at *4 (D. Ariz. Oct. 14, 2020)   742

Barcelona.com, Inc. v. Excelentisimo Ayuntamiento De Barcelona, 330 F.3d 617, 624-25 (4th Cir. 2003)   48, 739

Black v. Irving Materials, Inc., 1 7-CV-06734-LHK (N.D. Cal 2019/2020)   xxviii, 145, 210, 220, 229, 340, 376, 378, 411, 453, 537, 541, 552, 624, 645, 682, 750, 778, 784-785, 787

Black v. Molson Canada (2002), 60 O.R. (3d) 457 (Ont. S.C.J.)   xxviii, 145, 210, 220, 229, 340, 376, 378, 411, 453, 537, 541, 552, 624, 645, 682, 750, 778, 784-785, 787

Blackshore Properties, Inc. v. EQN, an Internet domain name, et al., No. l:18-cv-1325, slip op. at 3 (E.D. Va., Jan. 28, 2019)   778

BMW v. Deenik, [Case c-63/97 1999 1 CMLR 1099]   148, 166, 227, 447

Bosley Medical Institute, Inc. v. Kremer, 403 F.3d 672, 680 (9th Cir. 2005)   747

Brookfield Communications, Inc. v. West Coast Entertainment Corp., 174 F.3d 1036 (9th Cir. 1999)   443, 514

Bulbs 4 E. Side, Inc. v. Ricks, 199 F. Supp. 3d 1151, 1165 (S.D.Tex. 2016)   771, 782

C

Cable News Network v. Cnnews.com, 162 F. Supp. 2d 484 (E.D. Va. 2001)   743, 745-746

Cable News Network v. Cnnews.com, 162 F. Supp. 2d 484 (E.D. Va. 2001) Aff'd, 56 F. App'x 599 (4th Cir. 2003)   743, 745-746

Calder v. Jones, 465 U.S. 783 (1984)   762-763

CloudCover IP LLC v. Buchanan, 2:21-cv-00237-DBB-JCB, at *1 (D. Utah Jan. 4, 2023)   759, 764

Coca-Cola Co. v. Purdy, 382 F.3d 774 (8th Cir. 2004)   437, 719

Continental Airlines, Inc. v. continentalairlines.com, 390 F. Supp. 501 (E.D. Va. 2005)   746

D

Debevoise & Plimpton LLP. v. DEBEVOISE-LAW.COM and DEBEVOISE-LAWS. COM, 1: 21 -cv-01386 (E. D .Va, Alexandria Div. 12/13/21)   745

Dent v. Lotto Sport Italia SpA, No. CV-17-00651-PHX-DMF, at *16 (D. Ariz. Mar. 10, 2020)   421, 483, 751, 787

Digital Telemedia Inc. v. C I Host, Inc., 04 Civ. 1734 (CSH) (S.D.N.Y. Feb. 8, 2006)   741

Direct Niche, LLC v. Via Varejo S/A, 15-cv-62344 (S.D. Fla., August 10, 2017), affd 898 F.3d 1144(11th Circuit August 3, 2018)   25, 155, 768

Dluhos v. Strasberg, 321 F.3d 365, 373 (3d Cir. 2003)   36, 737

Doe Lang v. Retirement Living Publishing Co., Inc., 949 F.2d 576 (2d Cir. 1991)   372

Dorer v. Arel, 60 F. Supp. 2d 558, 561 (E.D. Va. 1999)   13, 168, 206, 690-691

DSPT International v. Nahum, 624 F.3d 1213, 1219-20 (9th Cir. 2010)   769

Dynamis Inc. v. Dynamis.Com, 780 F. Supp. 2d 465 (E.D. Va. 2011)   767

E

E. & J. Gallo Winery v. Spider Webs Ltd., 286 F.3d 270 (5th Cir. 2002)   436, 738

Emerald City Mgmt., LLC v. Kahn, No. 4:14-CV-358, 2016 WL 98751, at *14 (E.D. Tex. Jan. 8, 2016)   769

Entrepreneur Media, Inc. v. Smith, 279 F.3d 1135, 1147 (9th Cir. 2002)   179

Eurotech, Inc. v. Cosmos European Travels Aktiengesellschaft, 213 F. Supp. 2d 612, 618 n. 10 (E.D. Va. 2002)   739

F

Fabick, Inc. v. Fabco Equip., Inc., 16-cv-172-wmc, at *6-7 (W.D. Wis. May 7, 2017)   736

Fuccillo v. Silver, No. 8:18-cv-1236-T-36AEP (M.D. Fla. Sep. 28, 2020)   748

G

Global Access Limited v. EducationDynamics, LLC., & Anor, QSC 373   49

Goforit Entertainment LLC v. Digimedia.com LP, 750 F. Supp.2d 712 (N.D. Tex. October 25, 2010)   601

Gong Zheng Jin v. 001HH.com, 1:14-cv-1120 (E.D. Va. Aug. 29, 2014)   779-780

GoPets Ltd. v. Hise, 657 F.3d1024 (9th Cir. 2011)   404, 751, 753

GoSecure Inc. v. Bhandari, Civil Action 1:21-CV-01222 (E.D. Va. Oct. 26, 2022)   668

Great-West Life & Annuity Insurance Company v. Empower Geographics, Inc., and Alex Machinis, Case No. 1:21-cv-04004 (District Court For The Northern District Of Illinois Eastern Division)   755

H

Harrods Ltd. v. Sixty Internet Domain Names, 302 F.3d 214, 228 (4th Cir. 2002)   20, 745-746

Hart v. Massanari, 266 F.3d 1155 (2001)   4, 33, 97, 103, 187, 220, 285, 287, 325, 360, 428, 439, 616, 673

Heron Dev. Corp. v. Vacation Tours, Inc., 2017 WL 5957743, *4 (S.D. Fla. 2017)   764

I

In re. West Point-Pepperell, Inc., 468 F.2d 200 (C.C.P.A. 1972)   520

J

J. Gallo Winery v. Gallo Cattle Co., 967 F.2d 1280, 1291 (9th Cir. 1992)   436, 738

JFXD TRX ACQ LLC v. Trx.Com, No. CV-23-02330-PHX-ROS (D. Ariz. Jan. 8, 2024)   760

Joshua Domond and Harold Hunter, Jr v. PeopleNetwork APS d/b/a Beautifulpeople. Com, Beautiful People, LLC, Greg Hodge, and Genevieve Maylam   649, 750

Joshua Domond and Harold Hunter, Jr v. PeopleNetwork APS d/b/a Beautifulpeople. Com, Beautiful People, LLC, Greg Hodge, and Genevieve Maylam, 16-24026-civ (S.D. FL. Miami Div. 11/9/17)   649, 750

K

Koorn v. Aveve NV Belgium et al., 3:20-cv-05946 (Washington W.D. 2020)   740

KP Permanent Make-Up, Inc. v. Lasting Impression I, Inc., 543 U.S. 111, 122 (2004)   262

Kremen v. Cohen, 337 F.3d 1024, 1030 (9th Cir. 2003)   753

L

Lahoti v. Vericheck, Inc., 586 F.3d 1190 (9th Cir. 2009)   750, 782

Lahoti v. Vericheck, Inc., 636 F.3d 501, 510-11 (9th Cir. 2011),   472, 637, 750, 782-784

Loo Tze Ming v. Fitness Anywhere LLC, No. CV-22-02042-PHX-SPL (D, Ariz. December 12, 2023)   760

Lucas Nursery and Landscaping, Inc. v. Grosse, 359 F.3d 806, 810 (6th Cir. 2004)   736

Lucent Technologies, Inc. v. Lucentsucks.com, 95 F. Supp 2d 528, 535 (E.D.Va., May 3, 2000)   495

M

Marchex Sales, Inc. V. Tecnologia Bancaria, S.A. 14cv1306 (E.D. Va. Alexandria Division May 21, 2015)   46, 645, 671, 673, 768

McGregor-Doniger Inc. v. Drizzle Inc., 599 F.2d 1126, 1131 (2d Cir. 1979)   135

McNeil v. Stanley Works, 33 F. App'x 322, 324 (9th Cir. 2002)   740

Mehdiyev v. Qatar National Tourism Counsel, 1:19-cv-03353 (D. Colorado 4/1/21)   759

Mira Holdings Inc. v. UHS of Del. (D. Arizona, 2023)   759

Mishawaka Rubber & Woolen Mfg., Co. v. S.S. Kresge Co   128

Mollan v. Torrance, 9 Wheat. 537, 539 (1824)   743-744

Mrs. Jello, LLC v. Camilla Australia Pty Ltd. 15-cv-08753 (D. NJ 8/1/2016)   163, 419

Mrs. U.S. Nat'l Pageant, Inc. v. Miss United States Org., LLC, 875 F.Supp.2d 211 (W.D. N.Y. 2012)   773

MTV Networks, Inc. v. Curry, 867 F. Supp. 202, 203-204 n. 2 (S.D.N.Y. 1994)   138

N

Name.Space, Inc. v. Network Solutions, Inc., 202 F.3d 573, 585-86 (2d Cir. 2000)   437

Natural and Tasty, LLC v. Moshe Parnes, 15-cv-4388 (D.N.J. August 10, 2015)   773

NBC Universal, Inc. v. NBC UNIVERSAL.COM, 378 F. Supp. 2d 715 (E.D. Va. 2005)   746

New Kids on the Block v. New America Pub., 971 F.2d. 302 (9th Cir. 1992)   93, 135, 445

New World Solutions, Inc. v. Namemedia Inc., 11-cv-2763 (SDNY December 15, 2015)   741

Newport News Holdings Corporation v. Virtual City Vision, Incorporated, d/b/a Van James Bond Tran, 650 F3d 423 (4th Cir. 2011), cert. denied, 132 S.Ct. 575, 181 L.Ed.2d 425 (2011)   464, 770

NextHome, Inc. v. Jenkins, No. 1:20-cv-01210-CCB, at *12 (D. Md. Apr. 12, 2021)   735

O

O'Toole v. Northrop Grumman Corp., 499 F.3d 1218 (10th Cir. 2007)   241

Octane Fitness, LLC v. Icon Health and Fitness, Inc., 572 U.S. 545, 555 (2014)   766

Office Cleaning Services Ltd. v. Westminster Window and General Cleaners Ltd. (1946) 63 RPC 39   187, 325

Office Space Solutions, Inc. V. Kneen, 15-cv-4941 (S.D.N.Y. July 14, 2015)   741, 772

P

Paccar, Inc. v. Telescan Technologies, L.L.C., 115 F. Supp. 2d 772, 780 (E.D. Mich. 2000)   738

Pace v. Daniel, No. C20-1455JLR (W.D. Wash. Feb. 19, 2021)   46, 740

Pace v. Lundh, No. C18-5965RBL, at *1(W.D. Wash. Mar. 4, 2020)   740

Panavision Int'l v. Toeppen, 141 F.3d 1316, 1319 (9th Cir. 1998)   731, 762

Panavision International v. Toeppen, 141 F.3d 1316, 1319 (9th Cir. 1998)   763

Park 'N Fly v. Dollar Park and Fly, 469 U.S. 189, 194 (1985)   342

Passport Health, LLC v. Avance Health System, Inc., 823 F. App'x 141, 150 (2020)   767

Pinterest, Inc. v. Qian Jin, C12-04586 (N.D. CA SF Div. 9/30/13)   508

Pirate Water Taxi, LLC, Yacht Starship Dining Cruises, LLC. and Dara Hindman v. Tampa Water Taxi Company, Case No: 8:22-cv-1878-KKM-MRM (MD Florida, Tampa Division 7/14/23)   782

Planned Parenthood Federation of America Inc. v. Bucci, No. 97 Civ. 0629, 1997 WL 133313 (S.D. N.Y. Mar. 24, 1997), aff'd, 152 F.3d 920 (2d Cir. 1998)   437

Pocketbook Int'l SA v. Domain Admin/SiteTools, Inc. and Philip Ancevski, No. CV 20-8708 (CD Cal. April 13, 2021)   742, 757, 759

Proulx v. Nrip LLC, CV-21-01211-PHX-DJH (D. Ariz. Oct. 20, 2021)   740

Prudential Ins. Co. of Am. v. PRU.COM, 546 F. Supp. 3d 476 (E.D. Va. 2021) aff'd No. 21-1823 (4th Cir. Jan. 23, 2023)   45-46, 263

Q

Quantum Fitness, Quantum Fitness Corp. v. Quantum Lifestyle Centers, 83 F. Supp. 2d 810 (S.D. Tex. 1999)   258

R

Ralston Purina Co. v. Thomas J. Lipton, Inc., 341 F. Supp. 129, 133 (SDNY 1972)   324

Rasmussen v. General Growth Properties, Inc., 2005 WL 3334752 (D. Utah, December 7, 2005)   408

Retail Services, Inc. v. Freebies Pub., 247 F. Supp. 2d 822, 827 (E.D. Va. 2003), aff'd 364 F.3d 535 (4th Cir. 2004)   784

Richard Blair v. Automobili Lamborghini S.p.A., CV-22-1439-PHX-ROS (D. Arizona Motion filed March 23, 2023)   757, 766

Ricks v. BMEzine.com, LLC, 727 F. Supp. 2d 936, 954 (D. Nev. 2010)   105, 205, 339, 403, 559, 645, 679, 722, 749, 771, 782, 786

S

S.H., INC. v. The Law Society, United Kingdom, CV10-0248 (W.D. Washington,at Seattle July 15, 2010)   626

Safeco Insurance Company of America v. Burr, 551 U.S. 47, 127 S. Ct. 2208-09 (2007)   484

Sallen v. Corinthians Licenciamentos LTDA, 273 F.3d 14, 28 (1st Cir. 2001)   45, 746-747

Schmidheiny v. Weber, 319 F.3d 581 (2003)   xxii, 404-406, 751-754, 756-757

Scholastic, Inc. v. Stouffer, 221 F. Supp. 2d 425, 444 (S.D.N.Y. 2002)   784

Schreiber v. Dunabin, 938 F. Supp. 2d 587, 598 (E.D. Va. 2013)   772

Sengoku Works Ltd. v. RMC Int'l, Ltd., 96 F.3d 1217, 1219 (9th Cir. 1996), as modified, 97 F.3d 1460 (9th Cir. 1996)   734

Shenzhen Big Mouth Techs. Co., et al.. v. Factory Direct Wholesale, LLC   774

Shields v. Zuccarini, 254 F.3d 476, 483 (3d Cir. 2001)   205, 608

Software, LLC v. Workforce.com, 20 C 7365 (N.D. Ill. Oct. 26, 2021)   619, 754

Solid Host, NL v. NameCheap, Inc., 652 F. Supp. 2d 1092,1101-02 (C.D. Cal. 2009)   776

Soter Techs. v. IP Video Corp., 20-cv-5007 (LJL), 19 (SDNY February 26, 2021)   771

Spacey v. Burgar, 207 F. Supp. 2d 1037 (C.D. Cal. 2002)   375, 743

Sporty's Farm L.L.C. v. Sportsman's Mar., Inc., 202 F.3d 489 (2d Cir. 2000)   135, 735

St. Luke's Cataract v. Sanderson, 573 F.3d 1186 (11th Cir. 2009)   783

Stenzel v. Pifer, No. C06-49Z (W.D. Wash. July 26, 2006)   741

Stephens v. Trump Org. LLC, 205 F. Supp. 3d 305, 313 (E.D.N.Y. 2016)   470, 773-774

Storey v. Cello Holdings, L.L.C., 347 F.3d 370, 381 (2nd Cir. 2003)   51, 733, 747

Strong Coll. Students Moving, Inc. v. CHHJ Franchising, LLC, CV-12-01156-PHX-DJH (D. Ariz., May 15, 2013)   48, 739

Symantec Corp. v. Johns Creek Software, Inc., No. C 11-03146 WHA, at *4 (N.D. Cal. Jan. 3, 2012)   770

T

Taiming Zhang v. Twitter Inc., 23-cv-00980-JSC (N.D. Cal. Aug. 23, 2023) 241

Taubman v. Webfeats, 319 F.3d 770 (6th Cir. 2003) 436

Telepathy, Inc. v. SDT International SA-NV, 14-cv-01912 (D. Columbia July 9, 2015) 39, 185, 228-229, 300, 418, 421, 504, 576, 591, 597, 621, 676, 714, 717, 721

The Prudential Ins. Co. of Am. v. Shenzhen Stone Network Info., 58 F.4th 785 (4th Cir. 2023) 45-46

Thompson v. Does 1-5, 376 F. Supp. 3d 1322, 1324 (N.D. Ga. 2019) 412, 773

Tireboots by Universal Canvas, Inc. v. Tiresocks, Inc., 20-cv-7404 (N.D. Ill. Nov. 28, 2023) 764

Toyota Motor Sales, U.S.A., Inc .v. Tabari, 610 F.3d. 1171 (9th Cir. 2010) 445

U

United Fed'n of Churches v. Johnson, No. 23-35060, at *3 (9th Cir. Nov. 30, 2023) 601, 764

United Fed'n of Churches, LLC v. Johnson, No. 2:20-cv-00509-RAJ, at *13 (W.D. Wash. Feb. 26, 2021) 601

US v. Nam Ping Hon, 904 F.2d 803, 806 (2d Cir. 1990) vii-x, xii-xxii, xxv-xxxii, 3-791, 793

Utah Lighthouse v. Foundation, 527 F.3d 1045, 1058 (10th Cir. 2008) 603

V

Verisign, Inc. v. Xyz.com LLC, 848 F.3d 292 (4th Cir. 2017) 7, 10, 13, 713, 733, 746

Verizon Cal. Inc. v. Navigation Catalyst Sys., Inc., 568 F. Supp. 2d 1088, 1097 (C.D. Cal. 2008) 738

Virtual Works, Inc. v. Network Solutions, Inc., 106 F. Supp. 2d 845 (E.D. Va. 2000) 767

Virtual Works, Inc. v. Volkswagen of America, 238 F.3d 264 (4th Cir. 2001) 767

Volvo Trademark Holding AB v. VOLVOSPARES.COM, No. 1:09cv1247 (AJT/IDD), at *5 (E.D. Va. Apr. 1, 2010) 449, 734, 739

Vondran v. Antonelli, No. CV-22-00790-PHX-DJH, at *1 (D. Ariz. Dec. 23, 2022) 585, 764-765

W

Walden v. Fiore, 134 S. Ct. 1115 (2014) 763

Walter v. Ville de Paris, 4:2009cv03939 (S.D. Texas Houston Div. July 5, 2012) 120, 126, 769, 783

Web-Adviso v. Trump, 927 F. Supp. 2d 32, 40 (E.D.N.Y. 2013) 774

www.ingramcontent.com/pod-product-compliance
Lightning Source LLC
Chambersburg PA
CBHW051319020426
42333CB00031B/3405